PURPLE MOUNTAINS & WILDERNESS

PURPLE MOUNTAINS & WILDERNESS

True Stories of the Great American West

GEORGE U. HUBBARD

Copyright © 2021 by George Hubbard

All rights reserved.

No part of this book may be reproduced in any form or by any electronic or mechanical means, including information storage and retrieval systems, without written permission from the author, except for the use of brief quotations in a book review.

ISBN (print): 978-1-7358338-4-2

Cover, Section Illustrations, and Story Maps by Kyson A. Barlow

Map of Western Territories, 1848:
National Archives and Records Administration
https://history.house.gov/HouseRecord/Detail/15032436115

Unless otherwise noted at the end of each story, photographs were taken and are owned by the author.

*In Loving Memory
Of
Billie S. Hubbard*

My traveling companion, researcher, promoter, and wife for 66 years. She enjoyed finding these stories as much as I enjoyed writing and sharing them. The following is one of her fabric art note cards entitled, "Colorado Memories" created in 2009.

CONTENTS

Foreword   xv
Preface   xxiii

HISPANIC BEGINNINGS

Introduction   5

SPANISH

The First Thanksgiving?   11
~ El Paso, TX ~

Knotted Cords Coordinated the Pueblo Revolt of 1680   13
~ Santa Fe, NM ~

The Miracle of San Miguel   17
~ Socorro, TX ~

A Supreme Act of Charity   19
~ Estancia Plains, NM ~

The Lady in Blue   23
~ Santa Fe, NM ~

MEXICAN

Early Mexican Culture Had Charm and Romance   29
~ Los Angeles, CA ~

Did the Flag of 1824 Fly Over the Alamo?   31
~ San Antonio, TX ~

Drawing a Black Bean Meant Death   35
~ La Grange, TX ~

A Boy Soldier for Pancho Villa   39
~ Baytown, TX ~

Two Friends Save Each Other's Lives   41
~ Columbus, NM ~

Pancho Villa Was a True Gentleman   45
~ Weslaco, TX ~

WESTWARD EXPANSION

Introduction   51

MOUNTAIN MEN

Uncle Dick Wootton Earns His Nickname   55
~ Denver, CO ~

Kit Carson Takes a Wife   59
~ Green River, CO ~

American Trappers Challenge the British   63
~ Mountain Green, UT ~

Conquering the Black Canyon of the Gunnison   67
~ Gunnison, CO ~

The Martin Handcart Company Is Caught in the Snow   71
~ Martin's Cove, WY ~

MINERS

The Great Diamond Hoax   79
~ San Francisco, CA ~

The Naming of Virginia City, Nevada   83
~ Virginia City, NV ~

Water and Silver Don't Coexist Well   85
~ Tombstone, AZ ~

There Is No Night in Creede   89
~ Creede, CO ~

Running a Hotel Wasn't That Easy   93
~ Denver, CO ~

If You Hide It, You May Lose It   95
~ Tahlequah, OK ~

SETTLERS

Homesteading Sometimes Had Its Humorous Moments   99
~ Oak Creek, CO ~

The Oklahoma Land Run of 1889 Gives Rise to Sooners and Boomers   103
~ Guthrie, OK ~

If You Don't Have Snowshoes, Try Walking on Quilts   107
~ Panguitch, UT ~

The Donner Party Leaves a Vital Legacy   111
~ Henefer, UT ~

You Don't Mess With Thomas Grover   115
~ Centerville, UT ~

INDIANS

Introduction 121

WAY OF LIFE

Never Bet Against the Comanches in a Horse Race 125
~ Bronte, TX ~

Squaw Fights 129
~ Santa Clara, UT ~

It May Be Better for the Dead to Stay Dead 133
~ Pawhuska, OK ~

Mormons Avert a Paiute Massacre 135
~ Las Vegas, NV ~

Chief Kicking Bird Was No Coward 139
~ Jacksboro, TX ~

RELATIONSHIP WITH WHITE MEN

Billy Bowlegs, the Seminole Chief Who Could Not Be Conquered 143
~ Ft. Gibson, OK ~

The Medicine Lodge Peace Council 147
~ Jacksboro, TX ~

The Quakers Try to Civilize the Indians 151
~ Jacksboro, TX ~

Buffalo Bill Takes on Chief Yellow Hand 153
~ Warbonnet Creek, NE ~

Chief Washakie Was a Friend of the White Men 157
~ Fort Waskakie, WY ~

The Indians Help Peter Shirt Plow His Fields 161
~ Parowan, UT ~

Emma Lee Is Terrified by Some Navajo Indians 163
~ Marble Canyon, AZ ~

Saline Smithson Was a Special Pioneer 165
~ Woodruff, AZ ~

RELIGION AND CUSTOMS

The Last Man to Die by Creek Law 171
~ Okmulguee, OK ~

Are The Tonkawas a Forgotten People? 173
~ Bastrop, TX ~

The Ghost Dance Symbolized the Indians' Last Great Hope 175
~ Mason Valley, NV ~

COMMUNICATION LINKS

Introduction 185

MESSAGES

Mail Service Was Important to the Western Miners 189
~ Amargosa, NV ~

The Jackass Express Precedes the Pony Express 193
~ Sutter Creek, CA ~

Pony Express Riders Never Turned Back 195
~ Schellbourne, NV ~

Buffalo Bill Rode Hard for the Pony Express 199
Nebraska and Wyoming

TRANSPORTATION

That Was No Lady 203
~ Riverside, AZ ~

The Poetic Stagecoach Robber 205
~ San Francisco, CA ~

When the Rio Grande Railroad Built Into Rollinsville ... 209
~ Rollinsville, CO ~

The Harvey Houses Were an American Institution 211
~ Temple, TX ~

Minnie Isgreen Twice Escaped Death 215
~ Salt Lake City, UT ~

Ezekiel Saw the Wheel, and Reverend Cannon Saw the
Flying Machine 219
~ Pittsburg, TX ~

The Santa Fe Trail Had No Comforts 223
~ Bent's Fort, CO ~

Train Travel in the Late 1800s Had Its Interesting
Aspects 225
~ Grenada, CO ~

Who Stole My Depot? 227
~ Lamar, CO ~

LAW AND ORDER

Introduction ... 235

FRONTIER JUSTICE

Frontier Courts Got the Job Done ... 239
~ Nevada City, NV ~

Mary McCann Was Too Busy to Stand Trial ... 243
~ Bodie, CA ~

We Need More Jails ... 245
~ Bishop, CA ~

Justice, Even If Informal, Was Sure ... 249
~ Mount Pleasant, TX ~

"My Name is Bat Masterson" ... 253
~ Lamar, CO ~

WEAPONS

The Colt Revolver Revolutionized Frontier Warfare ... 257
~ Washington, TX ~

The Winchester Rifle Took Its Toll in More Than One Way ... 259
~ San Jose, CA ~

Did Al Packer Eat His Companions? ... 263
~ Gunnison, CO ~

Reynolds Got There Just in Time ... 265
~ Denver, CO ~

The Original Sons of Katie Elder ... 267
~ Ridgway, CO ~

GUN SLINGERS

Elfego Baca Had More Lives Than a Cat ... 271
~ Reserve, NM ~

Sam Dittenhoefer Outwits Billy the Kid ... 275
~ Santa Fe, NM ~

The Third Time Was Not a Charm for Black Jack Ketchum ... 277
~ Clayton, NM ~

It Took Two Hangings to End Bill Longley's Life ... 281
~ Evergreen, TX ~

Ned Christie Held Off the Lawmen for Seven Years ... 283
~ Tahlequah, OK ~

"Doc" Holliday: If You Can Find Him, You Can Have Him ~ Glenwood Springs, CO ~	287
"Big Nose" George Couldn't Win For Losing ~ Rawlins, WY ~	291

PEOPLE

Introduction	301

PIONEERS

A Remittance Woman Succeeds at Homesteading ~ Weed, NM ~	305
Eilley Orrum: The Washoe Seeress ~ Gold Hill, NV ~	309
Henry Flipper is Dismissed From the Military ~ Fort Sill, OK ~	313
Buffalo Bill: May He Rest in Peace ~ Denver, CO ~	317

ENTREPRENEURS

Ferry Carpenter Brings the Cattlemen and Sheepmen Together ~ Rifle, CO ~	325
No One is Going to Rob this Bank ~ Denver, CO ~	329
Emperor Norton ~ San Francisco, CA ~	333

POLITICIANS

Harry Tammen Adjourns the Colorado Legislature ~ Denver, CO ~	339
Governor Gilpin Gets His Reward ~ Glorieta Pass, NM ~	343
Sunday School is Dismissed ~ Austin, TX ~	345
Quanah Becomes the County Seat of Hardeman County ~ Quanah, TX ~	349

CHARACTERS

Russian Bill: A Make-Believe Bad Man ... 353
~ Tombstone, AZ ~

A Memorable Lesson in Humility ... 357
~ Temple, TX ~

Carry Nation Attempts to Purify Denver ... 361
~ Denver, CO ~

ANIMALS

Introduction ... 369

LARGE ANIMALS

Old Blue Was King of the Longhorns ... 373
~ Dodge City, KS ~

The Indians Were Resourceful Hunters of Buffalo ... 377
~ Colorado ~

Cleo Hubbard Made the Buffalo Behave ... 379
~ Claude, TX ~

The Cowboys Challenge the Cavalry to a Horse Race ... 381
~ Dallas, Fort Worth, and San Antonio, TX ~

Old Bill's Horse Stayed With Him ... 385
~ Alamosa, CO ~

Mules, Though Essential Beasts of Burden, Had Minds of Their Own ... 389
~ Santa Fe, NM ~

"Jeff Davis' Folly" Was a Unique Experiment ... 391
~ Camp Verde, TX ~

Old Ephraim Was a Bear to Remember ... 395
~ Cache National Forest, UT ~

Sea Monsters? In Utah? ... 399
~ Bear Lake, UT ~

SMALL ANIMALS

The Saga of Bummer and Lazarus ... 405
~ San Francisco, CA ~

Spike Was Born to Fight ... 409
~ Clarendon, TX ~

A Dog Named Thornburg? ... 413
~ Meeker, CO ~

The Lacey Dogs Brought in the Hogs ... 417
~ Llano, TX ~

The Lobos Were Mean but Noble Animals   421
~ San Marcos, TX ~

Those Majestic Rocky Mountain Bighorn Sheep   425
~ Colorado ~

SOCIAL, ACTIVITIES, AND CULTURE

Introduction   431

CULTURE

Culture? In Death Valley?   437
~ Death Valley, CA ~

Ina Coolbrith Helps Launch Several Western Writing Centers   441
~ San Francisco and Oakland, CA ~

Reading, 'Riting, and 'Rithmetic   445
~ Elk Springs, CO ~

The Christmas Star of Palmer Lake   451
~ Palmer Lake, CO ~

AMUSEMENT

Never Underestimate the Power of Women   457
~ Temple, TX ~

E Clampus Vitus   459
~ Sierra City, CA ~

When a Dance is Held in Your Honor, You Should Attend   463
~ No Man's Land, OK ~

From Bloomer Girls to the Major Leagues   467
~ Ouray, CO ~

HOME LIFE

Flour Sacks Make Excellent Frontier Underwear   473
~ Texas ~

Home Remedies on the Frontier   475
~ Lee's Ferry, AZ ~

CITY LIFE

Temple, Texas Goes to War Against Its Rats 479
~ Temple, TX ~

Saints Roost: Utopia in the Texas Panhandle 481
~ Clarendon, TX ~

"Water Works" Wiley Saves the Day for Muskogee 485
~ Muskogee, OK ~

CULTURES

The Fredericksburg Easter Fires Commemorate a Treaty 489
~ Fredericksburg, TX ~

How Do You Move a Wagon Without a Team? 491
~ Norse, TX ~

"You Had a Better Pig Sty at Home" 495
~ La Grange, TX ~

If We Can't Fight Someone Else, We'll Fight Among Ourselves 497
~ San Antonio, TX ~

The Chinese Tong War at Weaversville 501
~ Weaverville, CA ~

Chinese Coolie Labor Gets the Central Pacific Over the Mountains 505
~ Sacramento, CA ~

Other Books By George U. Hubbard 509

FOREWORD

There have always been men (and possibly women) who have yearned to know what lay beyond the horizon. Norse explorer Erik Thorvaldsson and Spanish and Portuguese explorers Christopher Columbus, Ferdinand Magellan, and Hernán Cortés were among the earliest to have a major impact on the land that would become known as the "Americas." They were quickly followed by French explorers Jacques Cartier, Samuel De Champlain, Jacques Marquette, and Louis Joliet. Over time, the peoples, animals, and geography "discovered" by these and other explorers led to legends that piqued imaginations for centuries.

The indigenous people of the Americas had populated the lands since before the birth of Christ. One of the unifying aspects of all of the various tribes was their belief in the "Great White God" or "Great Spirit" who would one day return. When the European explorers arrived, many of the indigenous peoples' initial reactions were that the explorers were from the "Great White God" who had come to save them. Sadly, the opposite was true. These Native Americans, given the name Indians by Christopher Columbus, who thought he had landed in India, were viewed by the Europeans with vile contempt. The

Indians were considered to be only slightly more evolved than animals.

Thomas Jefferson wrote a letter to Marquis de Chastellux dated June 7, 1785, in which he offered a glimpse into his struggle to make sense of racial differences and similarities. As part of his reply to the charges of French scientists that plant and animal life, including humans, degenerated in America, Thomas Jefferson asserted:

> And I am safe in affirming that the proofs of genius given by the Indians of N. America, place them on a level with Whites in the same uncultivated state . . . . I believe the Indian then to be in body & mind equal to the whiteman. I have supposed the black man, in his present state, might not be so; but it would be hazardous to affirm, that, equally cultivated for a few generations, he would not become so.

History has proven that genius knows no ethnic, racial, language, gender, or age barriers.

In 1803, President Jefferson consulted experts before writing detailed instructions to Meriwether Lewis (1774–1809) instructing him to "explore the Missouri River basin, conduct scientific and ethnographic studies, and find a route to the Pacific Ocean. Lewis, his private secretary and a U.S. army captain, spent months in scientific studies to prepare for the mission." These instructions were written before Jefferson knew of the finalization of the Louisiana Purchase. Jefferson was particularly concerned that the "expedition establish an American presence among the Native American tribes and secure their trading and diplomatic loyalties for the United States."

The westward migration was "officially" sanctioned—as long as it was for the benefit of the United States of America. In spite of the enormous human costs, the overwhelming majority of white Americans saw western expansion as an opportunity. To them, access to western land offered the promise of independence and prosperity to anyone willing to meet the hardships of frontier life.

FOREWORD

On December 5, 1848, President James K. Polk transmitted his annual message to Congress. He used this map as an exhibit to illustrate his desired plan for the land acquired through the Treaty of Guadalupe Hidalgo that ended the Mexican-American War earlier in the year. The land included the present-day states of California, Nevada, and Utah, as well as parts of Arizona, Colorado, New Mexico, and Wyoming. The map shows the latitude of 36°30' established in the Missouri Compromise of 1820: Slavery was prohibited in the Louisiana Territory in areas north of this latitude, and Polk advocated extending the prohibition to the Pacific Ocean to cover the newly acquired acreage. The table on the left-hand side describes the territories and their boundaries and lists the square mileage of land that fell north and that fell south of 36°30'. The table on the right-hand side tallies the total square mileage of free states (454,340 square miles) and slave states in the Union (610,798 square miles). The Compromise of 1850, actually a series of different bills, resolved the status of the new territory and diffused sectional tension over slavery for a time.

-- National Archives and Records Administration

FOREWORD

According to University of Wisconsin History professor Frederick Jackson Turner, it was the frontier that shaped American institutions, society, and culture. The experience of the frontier, the westward march of pioneers from the Atlantic to the Pacific Coast, distinguishes Americans from Europeans, and gives the American nation its exceptional character.

Many painters and writers cited the American West as their inspiration. The West began to symbolize the American identity: rough and rugged individualism willing to face new challenges. Mark Twain is credited with deliberately manipulating contemporary conceptions of the American West by creating and then modifying a public image that eventually won worldwide fame. He established the central role of the western region in the development of a persona that helped redefine American manhood.

So when did it become the *Wild West*?

The 1860s through the 1890s gave birth to the period known as the *Wild West* and laid a foundation to its ensuing mythology. It was an era of cowboys, Indians, pioneers, outlaws, and gunslingers brought together by the purposes of expansion, defense, greed, and reinvention.

The *Wild West* was so named for the lawlessness of the untamed territories west of the Mississippi River from 1865-1895. While the *Old West* was famous for cowboys, native Indians, trailblazers, pioneers, and prospectors, the *Wild West* was infamous for the outlaws, gangs and gunfighters such as Wyatt Earp, "Wild Bill" Hickok, "Billy the Kid", Butch Cassidy, the Sundance Kid, Frank and Jesse James, and the Clanton gang. The most notorious event was the gunfight at the O.K. Corral in Tombstone, Arizona.

Contributing to the international intrigue and mystic of the lands west of the Appalachians were the outright wars fought to control the territories and their vast natural resources/wealth. The War of 1812 (which really started in 1810 in Florida with Tecumseh before moving west and lasting until 1815); the Texas Revolution with its infamous Battle of the Alamo in 1835, followed by the Battle of San Jacinto in

1836; the Mexican-American War from 1846-1848; and the Utah War of 1857-1858 are the better known wars that are still mentioned in U.S. history classes. Lesser known turf wars were included in the Sheep War from 1870-1900 between the sheepherders and the cattlemen that were fought over grazing rights (and between homesteaders and cattle barons). The longest and fiercest of all of the wars across the frontier were the almost continuous wars between the United States government and the various Native American tribes, which lasted until 1924. The government was determined to own all of the land from the Atlantic Ocean to the Pacific Ocean.

Around 1893 as she embraced the panoramic view from the top of Pikes Peak (Colorado), English professor Katherine Lee Bates penned the poem *America: A Poem for July 4th.*

> *O great for halcyon skies,*
> *For amber waves of grain,*
> *For purple mountain majesties*
> *Above the enameled plain!*
> *America! America!*
> *God shed His grace on thee,*
> *Till souls wax fair as earth and air*
> *And music-hearted sea!*
>
> *O great for pilgrim feet*
> *Whose stern, impassioned stress*
> *A thoroughfare for freedom beat*
> *Across the wilderness!*
> *America! America!*
> *God shed His grace on thee*
> *Till paths be wrought through wilds of thought*
> *By pilgrim foot and knee!*
>
> *O great for glory-tale*
> *Of liberating strife,*

FOREWORD

When once or twice, for man's avail,
Men lavished precious life!
America! America!
God shed His grace on thee
Till selfish gain no longer stain,
The banner of the free!

O great for patriot dream
That sees beyond the years
Thine alabaster cities gleam
Undimmed by human tears!
America! America!
God shed His grace on thee
Till nobler men keep once again
Thy whiter jubilee!

Though modified twice to the words we now sing in our patriotic song, *America the Beautiful,* Bates' original poem captured the awe-inspiring beauty and majesty of the *Frontier,* the *Old West,* and the *Wild West.* The lure that captivated all who fought for, journeyed across, and created the renowned Great American West continues to this day.

— Elizabeth Hubbard

References:
https://www.loc.gov/exhibits/jefferson/jeffwest.html

https://www2.palomar.edu/users/scrouthamel/ams105/american_west.htm

http://www.american-historama.org/1881-1913-maturation-era/wild-west.htm

FOREWORD

https://www.biography.com/news/wild-west-figures

https://www.history.com/topics/westward-expansion/wilderness-road

https://en.wikipedia.org/wiki/List_of_wars:_1800%E2%80%931899

https://americanliterature.com/author/katharine-lee-bates

PREFACE

America's westward expansion, justified in the minds of many by the concept of Manifest Destiny, was an epic movement. Conquering and settling the West was especially challenging because of the arid climate, the formidable mountain ranges, and the resistance of the Indians who were there first. It is an incredible story of hardship, courage, and inventiveness. The overall accomplishments of those who settled the West should make us proud as we reflect on their achievements against overwhelming odds. And when we view them as people with desires, determination, and feelings, rather than just as impersonal names, their accomplishments become our heritage and our enjoyment as we learn about them.

This book is not an attempt to tell the complete story of the American West. That is the historians' job. Rather, this book is an attempt to capture the flavor and essence of those times.

This book is both a serious work and a light-hearted work.

This is a light-hearted book in the sense that it is a collection of short vignettes depicting the humor and drama of people, places, and events in the settlement of the great American West. The stories are true, and they provide lively and interesting reading. Because the

PREFACE

stories are also short, this book could be described as a "bedroom book" or a "bathroom book."

This is also a serious book in the sense that it attempts to portray the human-interest aspects of life on the frontier. From these stories, the reader should gain an added appreciation for the adventure, laughter, and challenges of those times. The stories are organized into meaningful categories, and each category begins with an introduction that places its stories into their correct historical context. Therefore, this book should provide mortar to cement the historian's bricks into a more meaningful whole.

INTRODUCTION

AFTER COMPLETING THEIR CONQUEST OF MEXICO AND ITS AZTEC rulers, the newly arrived Spaniards began to spread southward into Central America and northward into what is now the southwestern portion of the United States. From Texas to California, the Spanish established missions, and they created villages. They engaged in agriculture, and they nurtured vast herds of livestock.

The Spaniards had a twofold interest in this northern territory: (1) the search for more gold and (2) the Christianizing of the native population. Spanish sponsors and entrepreneurs sent exploring parties to search for expected wealth, and the Church sent its priesthood to tame and convert the Indians. Armed Conquistadors supported both endeavors. Although the hoped-for wealth never materialized in any substantial measure in the north, the subjugation and Christianization of the southwest Indians bore remarkable results. Sometimes with love, but often with ruthlessness, the Fathers imposed their religion upon the Indians. They achieved some noteworthy successes, but for the most part, they succeeded merely in covering the Indian's internal religion with an outward veneer of Christianity. The Spaniards' continued efforts of subjugating the

Indians eventually brought pockets of revolt, culminating in the great Pueblo Revolt of 1680 in New Mexico.

When Mexico gained its independence from Spain in 1821, a general withdrawal of Spaniards occurred as their former holdings came under Mexican authority. The departing Spaniards left large numbers of cattle and horses in Texas, and although left to themselves, this livestock thrived and multiplied. It was the expectation of free livestock as well as free fertile land that lured so many Americans to fill the void left by the Spanish in Texas.

Under its assumed doctrine of Manifest Destiny, the United States was not to be denied possessing the lands lying between its early western borders and the Pacific Ocean. Texas declared its independence from Mexico following Sam Houston's victory over General Santa Anna at San Jacinto in 1836. The war between the United States and Mexico, which began in 1846 and terminated with the Treaty of Guadalupe Hidalgo in 1848, transferred most of California and the Territory of New Mexico from Mexico to the United States. In 1854, when Mexican President Santa Anna sold 19,000,000 acres of land in southern New Mexico and southern Arizona to the United States in a transaction known as the Gadsen Purchase, the border between the two nations finally became permanently fixed.

Although American authority replaced Mexican authority in these ceded lands, the Hispanic culture remained. Much of the Mexican population remained in their towns and villages. Family land grants dating from the Spanish period remained in force, although severely challenged and usurped in some cases because of lack of legal documentation.

As Americans poured into these areas, the remaining Hispanics clung to their language, religion, and social customs. In many cases, the mixing of Anglo and Hispanic cultures produced a charming and romantic era as the Americans learned to enjoy the more carefree and relaxed lifestyle of the Hispanics.

It wasn't all peace and harmony, however. Although the border was now fixed, both sides perpetrated occasional illegal incursions into the other side's territory. The most noteworthy of these incursions occurred in 1916 when the Mexican revolutionary, Pancho Villa, led his army across the border to plunder Columbus, New Mexico, in retaliation for his recent defeat by a Mexican federal army that the United States had aided.

The stories that follow are intended to present human interest glimpses into these Spanish and Mexican periods. The stories tell of a variety of situations that typify the adventures, drama, and humor of those times.

SPANISH

THE FIRST THANKSGIVING?
- EL PASO, TX -

THE PILGRIMS ARRIVED AT PLYMOUTH Colony is 1620, and after a nearly disastrous winter, they planted and reaped a bounteous harvest the following year. As a gesture to their God in thanking Him for their deliverance from near starvation, and to solidify their friendly relationship with the neighboring Indians,  Governor William Bradford appointed a day in the autumn of 1621 as a day of "feasting and thanksgiving." This feast has become known to later generations as America's first Thanksgiving. But far away from Massachusetts, and long before the year 1621, another Thanksgiving was celebrated on what is now American soil.

In January 1598, Don Juan de Onate, a wealthy mine owner from Zacatecas, Mexico, set out from southern Chihuahua with 500 settlers, including ten Franciscan priests and several lay brothers, to colonize the province of New Mexico. The group consisted of Spaniards, Mexican Indians, and a few Africans. After traveling three months across hot, parched, and desolate lands, the group arrived at a spot on the Rio Grande River where they could pass over to the other side. Onate gave the name of El Paso del Rio del Norte (the Pass of the River of the North) to the area, and the city of El Paso was later established at that spot.

After crossing the river, the tired settlers paused for a few days at a spot now occupied by present-day San Elizario, about 15 miles southeast of El Paso, where they refreshed themselves and gave thanks to their God. In their celebration, held on April 30, 1598 (23 years before the Pilgrims), they expressed their thanks with a solemn Mass followed by a sumptuous feast.

After several days of rest and revitalization, Onate and his party moved onward into New Mexico. Anglo settlement of the El Paso area was yet to come. But with regard to the Thanksgiving observance, modern-day Texans who like to brag about their state can claim another "first."

Reference:

Display cases at the El Paso International Airport.

KNOTTED CORDS COORDINATED THE PUEBLO REVOLT OF 1680
- SANTA FE, NM -

IN 1680, THE PUEBLO INDIANS revolted and drove the Spanish out of central New Mexico and back into Mexico. Considering that Pizarro subdued the entire Inca empire with a relatively small force and Cortes did the same with the Aztecs, it seems strange that the inhabitants of a handful of squalid Pueblo villages could accomplish such a feat against the heavily armed Spanish conquistadors and missionaries.

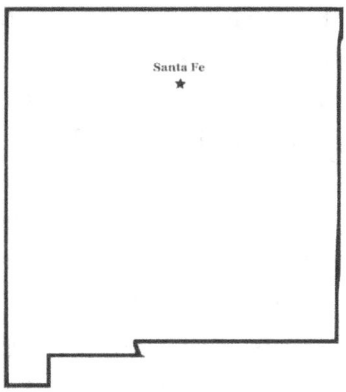

The Pueblos were not a united people. They were divided into three different linguistic groups, and their villages were independent entities with frequent squabbling among them. But they had one thing in common—they hated the Spanish.

Both the conquistadors and missionaries were guilty of brutality and enslavement of the Indians. The Pueblos were especially resentful of the Spaniard's thrusting their religion on them. This white man's religion became essentially a veneer that the majority of Pueblos adopted outwardly but which did not replace their tribal traditions and beliefs. As their resentment of their Spanish overlords increased over the years, it became clear that a rebellion was likely.

So how was the uprising accomplished among such a downtrodden and loosely related people? It was done through organization. Most historians give credit to a Pueblo Indian named Po'pay for providing that organization. Rising to the occasion in 1680, Po'pay led the Pueblos, along with the Zunis and Hopis to the west, in throwing off their Spanish shackles.

In 1675, Po'pay had been arrested, along with 46 others, and accused of practicing witchery and sorcery. Three were hanged, and the rest were physically punished and then released. Publicly humiliated, Po'pay became determined to rid the area of the hated Spanish.

In 1680, Po'pay began meeting with the elders of the various Pueblo villages, and they set the date of August 13 as the day when they would simultaneously rise up and overthrow their Spanish masters. The whole scheme had to be kept very secret. Po'pay even had his son-in-law killed to thwart a suspected leak.

Po'pay introduced the notion of knotted cords, which runners took to the various Pueblo villages. Each day, a knot would be untied, and when the last knot was undone, the uprising would occur. Thus, despite language differences and communication problems caused by distances, a secret and well-coordinated plan was in place. The last of the knots would be untied on August 13.

There were information leaks, however, so Po'pay changed the date to August 11. Even though word got to the Spanish authorities in Santa Fe that the attack was coming, they were expecting the revolt to occur on August 13 as originally planned. Another advantage for the Pueblos was that the Spanish were incredulous that the Indians could mount any effective threat.

One small Pueblo village jumped the gun, and on August 10, they murdered Father Juan Pio, who had ridden there from Santa Fe to say Mass for the inhabitants. Then on August 11, as the knots indicated, the Indians in village after village turned on their Spanish masters and began slaughtering them. Those who escaped made their way to Santa

Fe seeking protection from Governor Antonio de Otermin. But as the slaughter continued, the Spanish en masse retreated out of New Mexico to the El Paso area. A month later, Otermin led 150 soldiers and more than 100 Indian allies back to Santa Fe, but they were once again defeated and driven back to Mexico. Twelve years later, the Spanish did return to New Mexico, where they stayed until early in the 19th century, but they never managed to assimilate the Pueblos into the Spanish culture. In 1980, the tricentennial of the uprising, Pueblo Indians throughout New Mexico held festivals commemorating the rebellion. With fairs, dances, and feasts, they proudly remembered their successful rebellion, and runners with knotted cords ceremoniously traversed the roads from village to village.

When asked what they had accomplished three hundred years ago, Herman Agoyo, an administrator in the All Indian Pueblo Council Tricentennial, replied, "Because of the Pueblo revolt, we survived. We preserved our culture."

Then Agoyo added, "If it hadn't been for the rebellion, we would all be like them."

Reference:

James K. Page, "Rebellious Pueblos Outwitted Spain Three Centuries Ago," Indian Pueblo Cultural Center, Albuquerque, NM

THE MIRACLE OF SAN MIGUEL
- SOCORRO, TX -

THEY SAY THAT GOD SOMETIMES works in mysterious ways. This was certainly true in the minds of the villagers of Socorro, Texas, who witnessed what they considered to be a miracle back in 1845.

Socorro, a sleepy Mexican settlement 18 miles southeast of present-day El Paso, was settled in 1680 by Spanish refugees and Piros Indians fleeing from the Pueblo Revolt in New Mexico. The settlers gave the new community the same name as the New Mexico community from which they had come. Under the leadership of Governor Don Antonio de Otermin and Father Francisco de Ayeta, the residents founded a mission, and in 1691 they built a permanent adobe church which they dedicated to Nuestra Senora de la Limpia Concepcion de los Piros del Socorro (Our Lady of the Immaculate Conception of the Piros of Socorro). In 1829, a flood destroyed the church, but they rebuilt it, completing the task in 1840.

The "miracle" occurred in 1845, when an oxcart carrying a statue of San Miguel (St. Michael) entered Socorro bound from Mexico City to Santa Fe. There had been recent heavy rains in the area, and the streets of Socorro were quagmires of mud. The wheels of the cart sank into the mud, and it was stuck. Although oxen were tugging in front and Indians were pushing in back, the cart refused to move. Despite the best efforts of animals and people, the cart was hopelessly stuck. To the villagers, this was a sign from God that He wanted the statue to stay in Socorro to serve as a special blessing to the mission there. They uncrated the statue and carried it to the local mission. Thus San Miguel became the unofficial patron saint of Socorro, Texas, one of the oldest continuously occupied settlements in the Southwest. Visitors to the Mission church (now known as Socorro Mission la Purisima) can see the statue prominently located to the left of the altar.

An interesting sidelight about Socorro is that it was originally located to the south of the Rio Grande, but during the flood of 1829, the river changed its course, and Socorro is now north of the river. When the Rio Grande became the official dividing line between Texas and Mexico, the residents of Socorro found themselves to be new citizens of the United States rather than of Mexico.

Reference:

Historical markers at the Socorro Mission and at the El Paso Airport.

A SUPREME ACT OF CHARITY
~ ESTANCIA PLAINS, NM ~

WHAT HAPPENS WHEN TWO governments bestow land grants to the same piece of property to two different families? It can lead to problems, as it did in the case of the Estancia Plains southeast of Albuquerque, New Mexico.

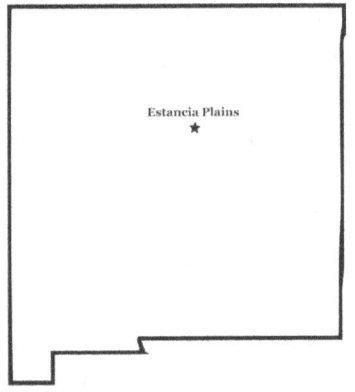

In 1811 the Spanish Alcalde, acting for the Governor of New Mexico and the King of Spain, granted the Estancia Plains to Bartolomé Baca. Believing they had legal title to the land, the Bacas later sold it to the prominent and highly respected Otero family. In 1845, Governor Manuel Armijo of New Mexico granted 300,000 acres of land that happened to be in the middle of the Baca Grant to Antonio Sandoval. Sandoval deeded the land to his nephew, and it was eventually sold to Joel P. Whitney, a Boston millionaire.

As initial possessors of the land, the Oteros established a ranch, and all was well until August 1883, when the ranch foreman sent a scribbled note to Don Manuel Otero saying, "They have run me off. Come!"

Rushing to the ranch, Don Manuel found that Joel's son, James Whitney, along with seven men, had taken possession of the ranch house. "This is my house," Otero said to Whitney. "By what authority are you here?"

"I've got a writ of possession from up at Antelope Springs," Whitney responded.

"I'll not leave until I see your authority."

The impetuous Whitney then whipped out his pistol. "This is my authority."

Both men shot at the same time. Whitney fell, wounded in the jaw, and Otero stumbled out the door with blood spurting from his neck. Additional shots were fired by others in the room until Dr. Henriquez, who had accompanied Otero to the ranch, took charge, stopping further hostilities and administering first aid to both Whitney and Otero. James Whitney eventually recovered from his wound, but Manuel Otero died shortly after the shooting.

Public opinion was very much against the Whitneys in the affair, and while James Whitney lay in St. Vincent's hospital in Santa Fe, officials served him with a warrant for murder. It was here at the hospital that a singular act of mercy and charity occurred.

Sister Blandina Segale, director of nursing at the hospital, knew of the circumstances of the shooting, and she was well acquainted with certain members of Manuel Otero's family. Calling one of the nurses, Sister Maria Teresa, into her office, Segale asked if Sister Maria was ready to make an unusual sacrifice.

"Yes, I am ready," Sister Maria responded. It would be difficult, but she had to do it. Going to Whitney's bedside, Sister Maria looked down upon the wounded man. She hesitated momentarily, and then summoned her resolve so she could speak from the heart.

"I forgive you as 1 hope to be forgiven," she said to James Whitney. "I am Manuel Otero's sister."

Sister Maria's charity came just in time. That night, members of Whitney's family sneaked him out of the hospital. He was later apprehended, brought to trial, and allowed to leave New Mexico for California. And in the end, neither family was able to obtain clear title to the disputed land grant.

New Mexico had become a territory of the United States in 1850, and the question of the conflicting Estancia grants was finally decided in U.S. courts. Because Mexico had established its independence from Spain in 1811 and Mexican record keeping at that time was quite incomplete, no legal foundation could be verified for either of the two grants. Consequently, ownership was denied to both parties, and in 1898 the U.S. Supreme Court placed the disputed land into the public domain.

Both parties had shot at one another on that fateful day for nothing.

Reference:

Erna Fergusson, *Murder and Mystery in New Mexico* (Albuquerque: Merle Armitage Editions, 1948).

THE LADY IN BLUE
~ SANTA FE, NM ~

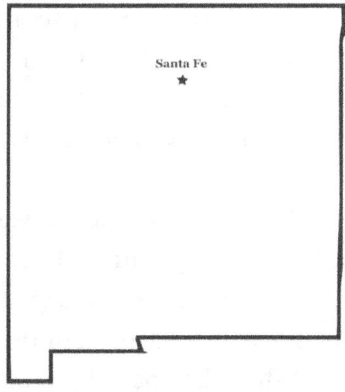

ABOUT THE YEAR 1629, FRAY ALONSO de Benavides responded to a request from the Jumano Indian tribe of New Mexico to send missionaries to teach and baptize the tribal members. The Indians, who had come to Benavides at the Ysleta Mission, explained that their request stemmed from visits by a lady in blue who had taught them in their own language and who had instructed them to seek baptism from the Spanish Fathers. Benavides, the most famous of the Franciscan friars in New Mexico, was quite touched by the Indians' tale.

Benavides was especially intrigued when this visiting group of Jumanos commented about a picture of the Mother Luisa de Carrion on display at the mission. They said that the lady in blue looked just like the lady in the picture, except that the lady who had visited them was young and very pretty. Indians from other tribes, upon visiting Benavides and looking at the picture of Mother Luisa, made similar observations.

The legend of the lady in blue is in the lore of many Indian tribes throughout the Southwest, especially in New Mexico and Texas. In a letter from Fray Damian Manzanet to Don Carlos de Siguenza, Manzanet reported the following from a visit to a group of Tejas Indians in Texas.

> While we were at the Tejas Hasinai village, after we had distributed clothing to the Indians and to the governor of the Tejas, that governor asked me for a piece of blue baize in which to bury his mother when she died; I told him that white cloth would be more suitable, and he answered that he did not want any other color than blue. I then asked him what mysterious reason he had for preferring the blue color, and in reply he said they were very fond of that color, particularly for burial clothes, because in times past they had been visited frequently by a beautiful woman, who used to come down from the hills, dressed in blue garments, and that they wished to do as that woman had done.

The governor acknowledged that he had never seen this lady, described as young and beautiful, but his mother and others had seen her. As a result of these visits, he and his people had an understanding of one true God, born of the Holy Virgin, and now in Heaven.

While the Spanish in this hemisphere were learning about the lady in blue, Spaniards in Spain were also learning about her. At the age of 15, Sor Maria de Jesus de Agreda was placed by her mother in a Franciscan convent in the small town of Agreda. Vowing to follow in the footsteps of the canonized Saint Teresa of Avila, Sor Maria began reporting miraculous visions to her confessor. These visions included trances in which Sor Maria was transported by angels to New Mexico where she preached to the Indians in their own language. In relating these visions, Sor Maria was very detailed and specific regarding geography and people. She claimed to have visited Gran Quivera in New Mexico several times, and she named other villages and missions in that area. She also claimed to have been present when Benavides baptized Indians at the Piro pueblos.

By 1627, Maria's claims of visions and transportings had become common knowledge throughout Spain. The story also made its way to the New World during that year. Many historians believe, however, that Benavides did not hear of these things until 1629. In 1631, Benavides made a trip to Spain seeking funds for expanded missionary work, and as part of that trip he spent two weeks with Sor Maria questioning her and listening as she detailed her experiences. Feeling that she could not possibly have known of some of the details she related without actually having been present in the New World, Benavides became fully convinced that she had actually done the things she was claiming.

The foregoing is a factual account of the legend of the lady in blue as far as it is currently understood. Analysis and conclusions are left to the reader. That there was such a legend among many of the Indian tribes in New Mexico and Texas is an indisputable fact.

References:

Charles H. Heimsath, "The Mysterious Woman in Blue," in 1. Frank Dobie, *Legends of Texas,* Vol. 2 (Gretna: Pelican Publishing Company, 1995).

Paul Kraemer, "Benavides Revisited: Franciscan Lobbyist of Medieval Visionary?" *La Cronica de Nuevo Mexico,* March 2003.

MEXICAN

EARLY MEXICAN CULTURE HAD CHARM AND ROMANCE
- LOS ANGELES, CA -

INA COOLBRITH, WHO LATER BECAME California's first poet laureate, grew up in Los Angeles in the 1850s. Los Angeles, at that time, was considered to be a sleepy Mexican village with all the charm and romance one might expect in such a culture. The pretty, young American girl became a favorite of the Hispanics living there. It was a romantic setting for Ina, one that she treasured throughout her life. She always loved to reminisce about those early years.

As a teenager, Ina attended a ball where she had the honor of leading the grand march on the arm of no less than Pío Pico, the former Mexican governor of California. Spying the attractive young Ina, Pico asked if the Muchachita Americana would do him the honor of opening the ball with him.

"He danced divinely," she later recalled, "although even then an old man."

Another of Ina's reminiscences adds to the charm of the setting.

Ella Sterling Cummins, having heard Ina tell of the experience, reports it as follows:

> She was standing by the road one day when some Mexican-Californians came riding by, with jingling spurs, and embroidered saddles, and arms full of flowers. "See the pretty little Americana," called out one of the gallant swarthy race, and as he spoke, he showered his flowers upon her. And thus she was properly christened by the spirit of the old times and dedicated to the service of the New California.

In our modem hustle and bustle, are there some qualities of life from earlier times that we would do well to retain?

References:

Jeanne E. Francoeur, "Ina Coolbrith, Our Poet – In Past and Present," *The Woman Citizen (1913).*

Ella Sterling Cummins, *The Story of the Files* (San Francisco, 1893).

DID THE FLAG OF 1824 FLY OVER THE ALAMO?
- SAN ANTONIO, TX -

ALTHOUGH SOME HISTORIANS DISAGREE, it is believed by many that the heroic defenders of the Alamo fought under a modified Mexican flag.

In the first conflicts that eventually led to the fight for independence, the thousands of settlers in Texas simply wanted just treatment and an end of cruel oppression by the Mexican government. This is not to say that thoughts of independence did not exist. But the earlier skirmishes were attempts to obtain the just and fair treatment guaranteed by Mexico.

The Mexican constitution of 1824 essentially organized Mexico into a republic of self-governing states. Although Texas was denied that political recognition and was attached to Coahuila, the Texas settlers were to have the same rights as the Mexican settlers. In addition, Mexico encouraged immigration and settlement in its outer reaches with the idea that the newcomers would be integrated into the Mexican culture. Immigrants by the thousands flocked into Texas, but it soon became apparent to the Mexicans that the expected integration would not occur. The continued influx of settlers into Texas caused the Mexican government to see this area slipping out from under Mexican control. Taking matters into his own hands, President Santa Anna stripped Texans of their political rights, and he became more and more oppressive and ruthless in dealing with the Texans, as they were then called. The guarantees of the constitution of 1824 were being almost completely ignored.

Although the majority of the gallant band of 158 Texans who defended the Alamo against some 1,500 Mexican soldiers were fighting with independence in mind, a few were still expressing themselves as Texans who merely wanted their promised rights.

As a symbol of their campaigns to win a more just treatment, it is believed by some historians that the Texans in the Alamo flew a modified version of the Mexican flag (among other flags) with its green, white, and red vertical stripes. The eagle had been removed from the center white portion of the flag, and the numerals "1824" had been sewn in its place. The flag, which probably pre-dated the battle of the Alamo, was intended to remind the Mexicans that what the Texans really wanted was a restoration of the constitutional guarantees of 1824.

Did such a flag really fly at the Alamo? The only Texan flag to survive the battle was that of the New Orleans Greys. Although some historians insist that the "1824 flag" never existed at the Alamo, replicas of the flag are on display in the visitors' center at the Texas State Capitol grounds, at the San Antonio public library, and at Baylor University's student union building, along with explanatory plaques describing its use at the Alamo. The truth of the matter may never be known.

Reference:

J. R. Edmondson, The Alamo Story: From Early History to Current Conflicts (Plano: Republic of Texas Press, 2000).

DRAWING A BLACK BEAN MEANT DEATH
- LA GRANGE, TX -

A FEW YEARS AFTER TEXAS GAINED ITS independence at San Jacinto and General Santa Anna was released, the Mexican general again became president of Mexico. Ignoring his promise to refrain from further hostilities, Santa Anna continuously threatened to retake Texas. In September 1842, a Mexican army unit commanded by General Adrian Woll captured San Antonio. Texans immediately rallied to the call, and after intensive combat forced the Mexican army to retreat below the Rio Grande River.

The Texans, under the command of General Alexander Somervell, gave chase, marched to the Rio Grande, and captured Laredo. Somervell, however, refused to let his relatively small force cross over into Mexico where a larger enemy force awaited. Three hundred of the pursuing force ignored Somervell's order to return to their homes, and this small band, under Colonel William S. Fisher, continued down the Rio Grande to the Mexican town of Mier. Crossing the river on Christmas Eve in a driving rain, they entered the town and gave battle to the Mexican contingent camped there. With losses on both sides, the fighting was heavy until the Mexican General Ampudia asked for a brief truce.

Ampudia told the Texans that 800 fresh Mexican troops were due to arrive. If the Texans would surrender now, he promised that they would soon be on their way home after prisoner exchanges. Colonel Fisher advised the Texans to submit. "Ampudia is a man of his word. He can be trusted." But Ampudia was not a man of his word, and soon the Texans found themselves embarking on a 1,000-mile march to Mexico City, flanked on either side by Mexican guards with fixed bayonets.

Arriving at the town of Salado on February 10, 1843, the Texans decided to make a break for freedom. The next morning at breakfast, they overpowered their guards, captured and mounted horses, and set out for freedom and home. Traveling in unfamiliar and desolate country, they lost their way and ran out of food. They were on the verge of starvation when they found themselves surrounded by a Mexican detachment commanded by General Mexia. The kindly general gave them a few days to recover their strength and then marched them back to Salado.

Word came from Santa Anna that all the prisoners should be put to death. By correspondence, General Mexia and others pled with Santa Anna to spare and release the Texans. Their efforts achieved partial results, as Santa Anna softened his orders to the effect that one tenth of the Texans be shot.

On the appointed day, one of the Mexican officers approached the Texans with an earthen pot containing 159 white beans and 17 black beans. Those Texans drawing the black beans would be the ones to die. The commissioned officers were ordered to draw first, followed by the enlisted men in alphabetical order by last name.

Captain Ewen Cameron, who was to make the initial draw, had noticed that the Mexicans had put the white beans into the pot first and then put the black beans on top without mixing them. Thus he whispered to his fellow officers, "Dig deep, boys." Cameron drew out a white bean as did every other officer except Captain Eastland.

William A. A. "Big Foot" Wallace was one of the last to draw a bean, and the remaining whites and blacks were well mixed by that time. Wallace, however, thought that he had observed that the black beans were slightly larger than the white. Acting on this assumption, he fingered the beans in the jar, and with two remaining in his hand, he drew out the smaller. It was white, and Wallace survived another of many ordeals in his colorful life.

At sundown the selected prisoners were tied, blindfolded, and made to sit down on a log. The fateful command was given, and the deed was done. Sixteen Texans died immediately, and one, James L. Shepherd, was merely wounded. Pretending death, Shepherd lay still until after dark, when he got up and escaped into the night. A few weeks later, he was captured and killed by the Mexicans. Captain Cameron, who had drawn the first white bean, was also executed by the Mexicans following a later escape attempt.

Five years after the Black Bean episode, the remains of the slaughtered were dug up and reburied at LaGrange, Texas, where a large monument erected by the State of Texas marks their last resting place.

References:

E. G. Littlejon, *Texas History Stories* (Richmond: B. F. Johnson Publishing Co., 1901).

John C. Duval, *Adventures of Big Foot Wallace* (Omaha: University of Nebraska Press, 1966).

Thomas J. Green, *Journal of the Texan Expedition Against Mier* (New York: Arno Press, 1973).

Sam W. Haynes, *Soldiers of Misfortune* (Austin: University of Texas Press, 1990).

A BOY SOLDIER FOR PANCHO VILLA

- BAYTOWN, TX -

THERE SEEMED TO BE NOTHING special about the slightly built Hispanic man who spent his latter years working the graveyard shift as a machine operator at the Baytown (Texas) Ice Company. But as a youth in Mexico, Jesus M. Gonzales had experiences that would dazzle Hollywood film makers.

When just a lad, Jesus learned to hate the Mexican federal army because some soldiers had tried to kill his father for no good reason. At the age of 11, wearing a sombrero and with ammunition belts draped on his body, Gonzales joined the revolutionary fighting forces of General Emiliano Zapata. Shortly thereafter, he found himself riding with Pancho Villa's forces, and Villa made the lad a captain at the age of 14. He was seeking retribution at an early age.

On one memorable occasion in 1915, Gonzales was leading his forces through a narrow street of a Mexican village when they suddenly found the street blocked by federal troops with a submachine gun. Charging on his horse with a lariat, Gonzales managed to rope the machine gunner just as the gunner shot at him.

"I used the rope to pull him and his gun to the ground, but his last two shots struck me in the chest," he later recalled.

Gonzales fell from his saddle, but his foot caught in the stirrup. The horse bolted and ran down the street, dragging both Gonzales and the lassoed machine gunner. One can easily imagine the spectacle that was presented.

Although the bullets missed Gonzales's heart by only a single centimeter, he survived the ordeal, and Pancho Villa, who paid Gonzales's hospital bills, gave the boy the choice of returning to active duty or becoming a civilian. Having had enough combat, Gonzales chose the latter. But his escapades were not quite over.

In a Mexican cantina in 1924, Gonzales had a run-in with a federal soldier who pointed his sword at Gonzales's stomach and threatened to kill him. Somehow, Gonzales gained the upper hand and killed the soldier. He then decided that life across the border in the United States would be more to his liking.

After living in various parts of the United States, Gonzales, at the age of 40, married a 25-year-old widow, and they settled in Baytown in 1942, where he fathered ten children. In 1975, he began a long but successful legal struggle to obtain a pension and a small land grant from the Mexican government, something due to all military veterans. He now had the pension, a 125-acre tract of land, and protection from the government. "It's not for me, but for my kids. If they go down to Mexico and have trouble, any government agency will help them because I am a veteran."

Reference:

The Houston Chronicle, Undated clipping on display at the Baytown (Texas) Historical Museum.

TWO FRIENDS SAVE EACH OTHER'S LIVES
~ COLUMBUS, NM ~

THINGS WERE TENSE ALONG THE Texas and New Mexico borders during Pancho Villa's forays in northern Mexico. In 1916, citizens of El Paso were especially fearful that Villa would cross the Rio Grande at Juarez and attempt to ravage their city.

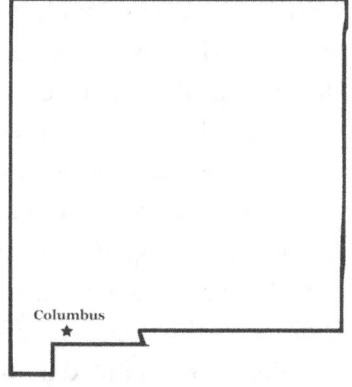

Villa, who had planned to subdue the Mexican state of Sonora, was furious that the United States had allowed armed Mexican nationals to enter Texas at Eagle Pass and then travel by train over United States soil through El Paso and on to Arizona to reinforce the Sonoran defenders below the border. After being mauled and defeated at Auga Prieta in Sonora, Villa decided to give vent to his rage by raiding Columbus, New Mexico, as a token of retaliation against the United States.

"We're going to kill gringos, boys," he told his decimated troops on the eve of the attack.

With loud shouting and shooting, Villa's forces galloped into

Columbus early on the morning of March 9, 1916, awakening the peacefully sleeping citizens. Guests at the Commercial Hotel fled in panic, as did the local citizenry. At least ten Americans were killed as the Mexicans thoroughly sacked and then burned the hotel, the grocery stores, and several other buildings.

Chaos and pandemonium reigned everywhere. The enigma of the situation is that Colonel Herbert J. Slocum, who commanded a U.S. Army detachment at Columbus, had been warned the night before that an attack was coming, but Slocum chose to ignore the warning.

At the time of the attack, Laura Ritchie, wife of the hotel's manager, was asleep with her three daughters in their hotel apartment. It's nice to have a friend when you need one, and on this occasion, Laura was very glad to have one. Laura had been friendly with a Yaqui Indian named Juan Favela, who was employed as a servant of the Ritchies. Considering Favela as more of a family member than a servant, she always made sure that he had plenty to eat, and she did other niceties for him whenever she could. A strong bond of friendship and loyalty existed between the two.

When the attack started, Favela proved to be a friend indeed. Dashing into the hotel through the back door, Favela broke down Mrs. Ritchie's door and managed to convince her and her daughters of what was happening outside. He led the four half-dressed women outside and concealed them where they would be safe, shooting two Villistas in the process. Unfortunately, Favela was unable to save Mr. Ritchie, who was killed in the attack.

An interesting postscript is that after the attack, American authorities arrested Favela and were going to hang him for complicity with the Mexicans. It was this same Favela who knew in advance of the coming attack and who had tried to warn the Americans. Opportune testimony by Mrs. Ritchie and her daughters saved his life.

They say that true friendship knows no bounds. In this case, each friend survived the ordeal because of the helpful intervention of the other.

References:

Elias L. Torres, *Twenty Episodes in the Life of Pancho Villa* (Austin: The Encino Press, 1973).

Joseph Raymond Monticone, *Revolutionary Mexico and the U S. Southwest: The Columbus Raid* (Master of Arts Thesis at California State University, Fullerton, 1981).

PANCHO VILLA WAS A TRUE GENTLEMAN
- WESLACO, TX -

PANCHO VILLA, THE MEXICAN REBEL who championed the cause of the poor and oppressed, was a true gentleman. At least that is how Arletta Crick and her family thought of him.

In the early 1900s, the Crick family lived on a farm in the Rio Grande Valley not far from Weslaco.

Occasional visitors would come, and Arletta was one of those persons who never turned away anyone in need. She made food and hospitality available to any stranger who knocked on her door.

One day while the family was sitting at the table enjoying a noon meal, they heard a knock at the door. Rising from the table as was her custom, Arletta opened the door and found herself face to face with Pancho Villa, the infamous Mexican revolutionary. True to form, Arletta invited him to come in. Ordering his men to remain outside, Villa stepped into the house as invited, sat down at the table with the family, and enjoyed the food that Arletta placed before him.

After partaking of what was available, Villa and his men left without disturbing anything. However, they returned at various times, and each time, Villa enjoyed Arletta's usual hospitality. But it was not a one-way street. One day, a wagon arrived at the Crick farm loaded with bags of beans, corn, and other foodstuffs. Driven by some of Villa's men, the wagon load was Villa's way of expressing his thanks to Arletta for her hospitality to him.

"Villa was always a gentleman," said Verle Crick, one of Arletta's sons who remembers the visits.

Reference:

Verle Crick, son of Arletta Crick.

INTRODUCTION

THE MORE DIFFICULT THE TASK, THE MORE CAPABLE ARE THE PEOPLE attracted to such endeavors. Conquering the great American west and its harsh climatic conditions involved a series of extremely difficult tasks, and it required a special breed of people. Trappers, explorers, prospectors, railroad builders, and homesteaders—they came, and they conquered. Heroic tales abound about their hardships and their accomplishments.

Spaniards from the south are the first known white men to enter the Southwest. It is believed that Coronado came in the 1500s in search of gold. Spanish military expeditions came in 1664 and 1706 in pursuit of runaway Indians from New Mexico.

Following explorations by Joliet in 1673 and La Salle in 1682, the French laid claim to Colorado. After making unsuccessful searches for gold and silver, they withdrew, leaving the area to the Spanish. Spanish padres, Fathers Dominguez and Escalante, are noted for their exploration of southwestern Colorado in 1776 while searching for a route from Santa Fe to California.

President Thomas Jefferson's Louisiana Purchase in 1803 opened the way for the Americans to come into the Colorado mountains, and come they did. Army explorations under Pike, Long, and Fremont, along with fur trapping by mountain men such as Kit Carson, Thomas "Broken Hand" Fitzpatrick, Dick Wootton, Bill Williams, Jim Bridger, and many others, constitute the beginnings. Fur trapping and possible routes to California were the initial lures.

From Alaska the Russians came for a short while, occupying Fort Ross in northern California, but they left seven years before the discovery of California's gold.

Religion was another factor, as evidenced by the Mormon migration into the Great Basin region in 1847, and into all the west from that nucleus. California's mild climate and fertile soil lured many to that land, but the discovery of gold on John Sutter's property at Coloma in 1848 provided the major attraction to California. Gold and silver discoveries in Nevada and Colorado brought prospectors and miners and entrepreneurs to those areas.

The promise of free lands and the vast ranges for livestock operations were major lures. But perhaps the greatest of the lures was the challenge of it all—the challenge of coping with and conquering the harsh mountain winters, the torrid desert summers, the mountainous terrain, and the arid environment. A special breed of people was required. Many came. Some died. Some went back to the east. But many stayed and conquered.

Whatever the cause, America's westward expansion was inevitable. The concept of Manifest Destiny decreed America's expansion from the Atlantic all the way to the Pacific.

The stories in this section treat a cross-section of the white man's penetration of the great American west. Although the selected stories certainly do not give a complete historical picture, they do illustrate human interest aspects of this penetration by presenting the humor of some situations and the drama of others. Other stories throughout the balance of this book add to the picture of conquering a very inhospitable region of this nation.

MOUNTAIN MEN

UNCLE DICK WOOTTON EARNS HIS NICKNAME

- DENVER, CO -

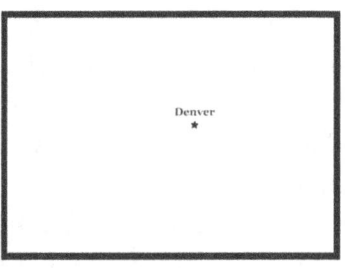

IT WAS GOING TO BE A DREARY AND lonely Christmas for the prospectors in Montana City and Auraria. The two prospector camps on the banks of Cherry Creek in what would later become the nucleus of Denver, Colorado, were in impoverished straits. True, gold had been found in Cherry Creek, but there wasn't very much of it. And so on Christmas Eve of 1858, the miners and their families had little to look forward to other than another cold day with barely enough provisions for a meager subsistence.

Toward the end of the day before Christmas, when their spirits were at their lowest, the people of Auraria were surprised to hear the crack of a whip. Looking up, they saw a wagon approaching through the frozen ruts of the icy road. The driver certainly didn't look like Santa Claus, but he was just as welcome.

"Any Indians camped near here?" the driver yelled out.

"Arapahos, about ten miles downstream," was the reply.

"I come up from Taos to trade with 'em," drawled Richens Lacey

Wootton, the driver. Then, noting the forlorn countenances among the people surrounding his wagon, he sympathetically added, "Unless you all'd be interested in a little swappin'." Wootton, wise to the mountains and their inhabitants, had sized up the situation correctly. He became Santa Claus.

In a rather disorderly manner, the people gathered around the wagon waving bags of gold dust to trade for the coffee, tobacco, apples, and other supplies Wootton had brought.

"Give Uncle Dick a tent, and he'll set you up a proper store," Wootton shouted.

"We'll do better than that," one miner shouted back. "You can use my cabin."

But the real coup de grâce was when Wootton unveiled three barrels of Taos Lightning. "Have a Christmas drink on me," he cried out.

Taos Lightning was powerful stuff, and according to legend, no man lived long enough after drinking it to become addicted to it. But that night they tried. Word of the liquid bonanza soon reached Montana City, and they came with their tin cups to share in the festivities.

Christmas day found the miners alive and well and full of enthusiasm. In Montana City they sang "The Star Spangled Banner" and "The Girl I Left Behind Me" between mouthfuls of succulent venison and gulps of Taos Lightning. In Auraria, there was singing and dancing around a great bonfire as German fiddles played boot-stomping tunes. And in both camps, Wootton was referred to familiarly as Uncle Dick by rejuvenated miners who now considered him as almost their patron saint.

The name, Uncle Dick, stuck, and from that time forward, Richens Lacey Wootton was known as "Uncle Dick" Wootton, a nickname he carried proudly the rest of his life.

Reference:

Howard Louis Conard, *Uncle Dick Wootton* (Lincoln: University of Nebraska Press, 1980).

KIT CARSON TAKES A WIFE
- GREEN RIVER, CO -

To those familiar with America's westward expansion, Kit Carson needs no introduction. Trapper, scout, Indian fighter, Indian agent, infantry officer—Carson was in every part of the West. This legendary hero was authentic, and it might easily be said that he *was* the west.

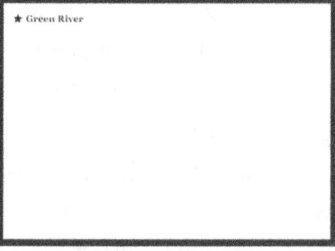

In the summer of 1835 and at the age of 26, Kit Carson attended a rendezvous of trappers, traders, and Indians on the Green River in what is now northwestern Colorado, and he quickly became fascinated by the Soup Dance, which had become one of the nightly rituals among the Arapahos encamped there. In dancing fashion, the Arapaho girls, each with a large spoon of soup in her hand, would approach the braves and trappers. The men and girls would alternately retreat and advance in time with the music. Amid the laughter and gibes of the onlookers, each girl would move from man to man until finding one to her special liking, and she would offer him the spoon of soup. If he accepted and drank the offering, they became dancing partners; if he refused, the offended girl would throw the soup into his face.

Fascinated not only by the Soup Dance, Carson set his eyes on one particular Arapaho girl whom he considered the most beautiful of them all. But Carson had a rival. A large Frenchman named Shunar, six foot three inches in height and strong as an ox, was the bully of the rendezvous. In his usually drunken state, Shunar ignored the rules of the dance and seized whatever girl he wished. "Enfant de race! I'm de beeg buck of dis lick, moi!" he bragged. He was always ready to fight, and none of the trappers had the heart to oppose him. None, that is, until Kit Carson came into the camp.

On Carson's first night at the rendezvous, Shunar appropriated the pretty Indian girl, made off into the woods with her, but came back alone after she escaped his drunken advances. The next day, as Kit Carson eyed the girl in the light of day, he was even more taken by her beauty. Night after night he joined in the Soup Dance with hopefulness in his heart while the girl, Waa-nibe, took delight in dancing with everyone else. There was nothing Carson could do, for it was girl's choice.

Finally the climax came. Waa-nibe eyed Carson and approached with her big yellow spoon full of soup. Shunar bullied his way to where Carson was standing, and the two of them stood shoulder to shoulder with neither giving an inch. As Waa-nibe came nearer, Shunar, full of expectation, lunged for the girl, only to have her soup thrown into his face. She then threw down her empty spoon and offered to dance with Kit Carson.

With matrimony in mind, Kit Carson visited Waa-nibe's father a few days after dancing with her and asked his permission for their union. Kit sat and talked in sign language with the father, Nickahochithinaahnie, who smoked and gave an occasional nod of understanding. But the father decided that the final approval should come from Detenin, Waa-nibe's brother. Upon being summoned, Detenin entered the tent, and it became instantly apparent that something was wrong. Detenin neither looked at Carson nor acknowledged his presence. As Detenin and his father talked, Carson was gradually able to decipher their conversation.

It seemed that Waa-nibe, only that morning, had confided to her brother that on the night she had thrown the soup into Shunar's face, he later found her and carried her again into the woods where he attempted to molest her. He would have revenge for her humiliating act against him. He held her tightly, and the more she struggled, the more the big Frenchman laughed. Like the other modest girls of her tribe, Waa-nibe was wearing her chastity belt made of hair rope that wound around her waist, passed between her thighs, and was knotted cunningly in front. Pausing to reach for his knife so he could cut the rope, Shunar allowed Waa-nibe to slip from his grasp. With her own knife, she wounded him and made her escape. As a result of this encounter, Detenin hated Shunar, and because Shunar was a white man, Detenin now hated all white men.

As soon as Kit Carson realized the situation, he stormed furiously out of the tepee, grabbed his revolver from his pack, and went after Shunar. "Hyar's an American, Shunar, and the meanest kind at that. Thar's plenty of men in camp can lick the hindsights offen you, only some of 'em are scairt of your brag. Wal you caint scare me. I'll rip your guts out! Savvy?"

Shunar turned, ran back to his lodge, mounted his best horse, and rode to the river in anticipation of the duel with Kit Carson. Shunar had armed himself with a rifle, while Carson had only his revolver. As they rode toward one another on their horses, Carson somehow closed in and shot Shunar before Shunar could get his rifle pointed. Although Shunar was not mortally wounded, Kit Carson had won both the duel and the girl.

That night, Carson again sat in the tepee with Detenin and his father, the Indians' animosity having abated. Waa-nibe was called in, and as she sat beside Carson, her father threw a blanket over the two of them. He then went outside and displayed the new gun, the three mules, and the five blue blankets Carson had given him as the dowry for the bride.

Kit Carson and Waa-nibe lived together happily, but only for a relatively short time. After giving birth to two sons, Waa-nibe died of an unspecified cause.

Reference:

Stanley Vestal, *Kit Carson: The Happy Warrior of the Old West* (Boston: Houghton Mifflin, 1928).

AMERICAN TRAPPERS CHALLENGE THE BRITISH
~ MOUNTAIN GREEN, UT ~

PETER SKENE OGDEN'S EXPLOITS AS A trapper and explorer in the early west are legendary. As a chief trapper for the Hudson Bay Company, Ogden led several beaver trapping expeditions and spent many years along the Snake River and in the Pacific Northwest. The degree to which Ogden was immersed in the frontier environment is indicated by noting that he was twice married to Indian women: 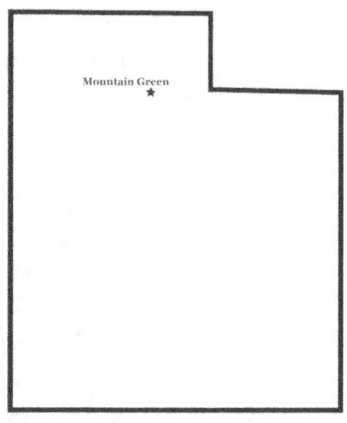 first to a Cree, and second to a Spokane woman known as Princes Julia. Julia was the daughter of a Flathead chief to whom Ogden paid 50 ponies. Because of his fame and influence as a mountain man, Ogden's name is attached to several northwestern sites such as Ogden, Utah, and Peter Skene Ogden State Park in Oregon.

In those formative years, the Oregon Territory was contested between Great Britain and the United States. America's claim to Oregon dates back to the Lewis and Clark expedition of 1805-06. The British entered the picture when they occupied Fort Astoria at the mouth of the Columbia River during the War of 1812. The British claims were further strengthened by the physical presence of trappers in the employ of the North West Company and the Hudson Bay Company. These trappers gave the British a virtual monopoly over the Oregon territory. In 1818 Great Britain and the United States formally agreed on a policy of "joint occupation." Although American trappers began in the 1820s to challenge the British monopoly, the "joint occupation" policy remained in force until the 1840s.

In the 1820s the British surmised that if they were to attain complete control over Oregon, they would have to find a way to stop American migration into that territory. In attempting to support the British cause, the officials of the Hudson Bay Company increased their trapping activities throughout the area. They felt that if they could remove all the beavers from the northwestern streams, they could discourage American encroachment into that area and thus help save Oregon for Great Britain. As one step in implementing this policy, they organized a trapping expedition into the Snake River area, and Ogden, a Canadian by birth, agreed to lead the expedition after several other trappers declined the opportunity.

Peter Skene Ogden Historical Marker

During this 1824-25 expedition, Ogden and his party ventured into what is now northern Utah. After trapping the Bear River and the Ogden Valley region, Ogden moved to the southeast and established a camp near present-day Mountain Green. Two groups of American trappers visited the Mountain Green area while Ogden was there, and the natural animosities between the Americans and the British erupted when the second group of Americans, led by a man named Gardner, arrived.

Gardner ordered Ogden to leave the area on the basis that he was trespassing on American soil. Ogden responded that it had not yet been determined as to which nation had jurisdiction, and he had no intention of leaving unless so ordered by his superiors in the Hudson Bay Company.

If they were truly on American soil, as Gardner claimed, several of Ogden's men saw the opportunity of freedom from their debts and obligations by joining the Americans. In addition, the Americans were offering a higher price for beaver pelts than the Hudson Bay trappers were getting. There had been a few defections before Gardner's arrival, and now there were more.

The controversy continued for five days, and on one occasion, one of Gardner's party threatened Ogden with a cocked pistol, but Ogden stood his ground and wisely refrained from initiating violence against the numerically superior Americans. But during the overall confrontation, Ogden saw 23 of his men defect to the Americans, taking 700 pelts with them. The promise of American freedom and wealth became irresistible. Still Ogden held his ground. But when the Americans threatened armed conflict, Ogden saw that he had no choice but to leave before further defections and possible bloodshed occurred.

One wonders how this conflict would have ended if both parties had realized that all arguments and promises regarding British or American jurisdiction were irrelevant. The two groups of trappers were camped south of the 42nd parallel, which meant that they were on Mexican soil instead of being on what they thought was their own territory.

References:

David E. Miller, Ed., "Peter Skene Odgen's Journal of His Expedition to Utah, 1825," *Utah Historical Quarterly*, Vol. 20.

David E. Miller, Ed., "William Kittson's Journal Covering Peter Skene Odgen's 1824-1825 Snake River Country Expedition," *Utah Historical Quarterly*, Vol. 22.

S. Matthew Despain and Fred R. Gowans, "Peter Skene Ogden," *Utah History Encyclopedia.*

CONQUERING THE BLACK CANYON OF THE GUNNISON
~ GUNNISON, CO ~

"IT IS IMPASSABLE," DECLARED THE Hayden surveying party when they encountered the Black Canyon of the Gunnison River in 1873. The Spanish explorers Escalante and Dominguez bypassed the area in 1776. Captain John Gunnison, for whom the river 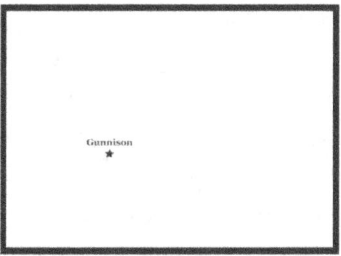 was later named, also bypassed the canyon in 1853. To the Hayden surveyors some twenty years later, traversing the canyon would be forever an impossible task.

The Black Canyon is not the deepest canyon in the world, nor is it the widest. In fact, it is its narrowness that makes it so formidable. Its black cliffs rise almost perpendicularly to a height of 1,800 feet above the river. It presents a spectacular sight to the visitor and an impossible journey to the traveler.

Horace Greeley must have had General William Jackson Palmer in mind when he said, "Bring me men to match my mountains." In the 1870s Palmer was building his Denver and Rio Grande Railroad westerly from Pueblo, Colorado, and tracks through the Black Canyon would save many miles of circumvention. "It can't be done," he was told by those who knew, but this simply meant a greater challenge to the headstrong Palmer.

Refusing to be deterred, Palmer succeeded in building the railroad fifteen miles into the previously impossible canyon, and he intended to push the tracks through the remainder of the canyon and on to the town of Delta. Just before Christmas of 1882, Palmer sent Byron Bryant and a surveying crew into the remaining depths of the canyon to chart the course and determine the cost. Each day, they entered the canyon, worked during the few hours of available sunlight, and climbed back out. In less than a month, half the men had quit, but Bryant and a core crew persisted, and after sixty-eight days, they reached the western end of the canyon. Upon hearing Bryant's estimate of over $100,000 a mile for railroad construction in the worst stretches of the canyon, Palmer changed his mind and brought the railroad out at Cimarron. The complete canyon was still unconquered.

A final engineering attempt to conquer the canyon occurred in 1900-01. Farmers and ranchers in the Uncompahgre Valley near Montrose needed more water for their crops and livestock. The Uncompahgre River could not satisfy their needs, but if some of the waters of the Gunnison could be diverted to their parched acres, the farmers and ranchers would be able to survive and prosper. A tunnel seemed to be the answer, but could it be done?

William Torrence, of the Montrose Power and Light Company, led a party of surveyors into the canyon to search for a feasible location for the mouth of the tunnel. The search, planned for a week, lasted a month. When they reached a constriction called The Narrows, they found themselves hemmed into a canyon forty feet wide and 1,700 feet deep. At this point they gave up and climbed out the nearest side canyon.

The following year, Torrence tried again. This time a government hydrographer named Abraham Lincoln Fellows accompanied him. After several days they came to The Narrows again, and again it appeared impassable. Torrence was ready to quit again, but Fellows would have none of that.

"I'm going forward," he proclaimed, and shouting "Good-bye," he jumped into the icy waters and disappeared.

Visually, Torrence searched in vain for Fellows. Then deciding that Fellows's body should be recovered, Torrence jumped in also. The raging waters swept him through the narrows and finally tumbled him onto a rock outcropping where he was able to pull himself to safety. As Torrence slowly regained his feet, there beside him was Fellows, grinning and laughing. After hearty laughter by both men, they realized that they had successfully passed "the point of no return."

Torrence and Fellows did more swimming before their task was completed. In nine days they traveled thirty-three miles, crossed the river seventy-six times, and lost fifteen pounds apiece. In so doing, they found the right spot for a tunnel.

In 1909, after four years of construction, a six-mile tunnel through the Vernal Mesa was sufficiently completed for water to start flowing. A celebration and a formal opening of the tunnel were in order, and President William Howard Taft came to participate in the ribbon-cutting ceremony. The upper portion of the Black Canyon had been conquered by the railroad and the irrigation project. The lower portion is still in its pristine condition and ever will be. In 1933, President Herbert Hoover assured its preservation by designating the Black Canyon of the Gunnison to be a National Monument.

References:

Tess Carmichael, "The Uncompahgre Project 1890-1909," *Journal of the Western Slope*, Vol. 8, No.4, Fall 1993.

Rose Houk, *Black Canyon of the Gunnison*, Southwest Parks and Monuments Association, 1991.

Displays at the Black Canyon National Monument Visitors' Center.

THE MARTIN HANDCART COMPANY IS CAUGHT IN THE SNOW
~ MARTIN'S COVE, WY ~

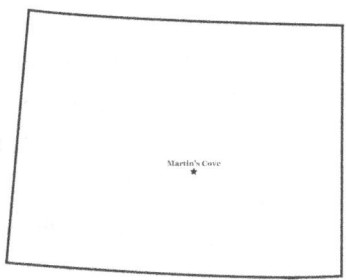

PROBABLY NO EPISODE IN THE WESTERN movement can compare in tragedy to the experiences of the Utah-bound Martin and Willie handcart companies who became trapped in the snow and freezing weather while crossing Wyoming. The plight of the snowbound Donner Party who missed getting over the summit of the Sierra Nevada Mountains by just one day is the only other weather-related tragedy that comes close to the experiences of the Martin and Willie companies.

Setting out from Florence, Kansas Territory (now Nebraska) toward the end of August in 1856, the members of the Martin Company knew they were getting a late start and that weather might be a problem. But they were determined to proceed rather than wait until the following spring. The Willie Company had left two weeks earlier after much discussion of the advisability of starting so late in the season. Despite having received advice to the contrary, the members of both companies voted to proceed.

Winter came earlier and with more severity than expected. In

October, both the Martin and Willie companies were stalled in Wyoming with freezing temperatures and four to five feet of snow. Their plight was desperate as hunger, illness, exposure, and death decimated their numbers. Of the 400 to 500 people who started with the Willie Company, seventy-seven perished. The toll for the Martin Company was more severe. Five hundred and seventy-six persons started the journey, and about 150 lost their lives before reaching their destination.

The Martin Company found itself snowbound in a ravine between the Platte and Sweetwater rivers, an area now known as Martin's Cove. Being unable to continue their journey, they suffered untold hardships and loss of life.

Ephraim Hanks, the first rescuer to reach the Martin Company, recounts some of his experiences. After reviving a man who was thought to be dead, Hanks tended to the others as best he could.

> Many I washed with warm water and castile soap until the frozen parts would fall off, after which I would sever the shreds of flesh from the remaining portions of their limbs with my scissors. Some lost toes, some fingers, and others whole hands and feet.

In addition to the tragedy of these experiences, there were also a few incidents of a human interest nature.

Tamar Loader dreamed one night that her sweetheart, still in England, and another man had arrived to rescue her. In the dream, the sweetheart faded away, but the other man remained clearly. When Tamar first saw Thomas E. Ricks, one of the rescuers, she told her mother, "That is the man." Some time later, Tamar became the wife of Thomas Ricks.

Sarah Franks and her fiancé George Padley were planning to be married when they reached Salt Lake City. When George died of pneumonia and exposure, Sarah could not bear the thought of wolves devouring the flesh of his body, and the ground was too frozen for a grave to be dug. Taking the long fringed shawl from her own shivering body, Sarah wrapped it around George's frozen body and had men suspend the body in a tree to be buried by those who would follow later.

One of the more tragic episodes is that of Ellen "Nellie" Purcell. At nine years of age, Nellie lost both her parents, who were laid to rest in snow banks. After being rescued and transported to Salt Lake City, Nellie received immediate medical attention. When the doctor removed the shoes and stockings from Nellie's feet, the skin and pieces of flesh came off also.

There was nothing to do except amputate her blackened lower limbs, and the doctor did the surgery without the use of anesthetics. But in completing the surgery, the doctor failed to pull the flesh down to provide a cushion for the severed bones. The legs healed with the bones exposed, which meant that she could never again walk uprightly on her legs. For the rest of her life, Nellie moved about painfully on her knees.

Nellie's life, however, was not over. She married William Unthank and raised a family. She helped her husband provide for the family by taking in washing, knitting stockings, carding wool, and crocheting table pieces. Nellie's local church leaders gave occasional assistance as needed, and Nellie repaid them by taking her children once a year to clean the chapel. The children carried water and cleaned the windows, and Nellie, on her knees, scrubbed the floor. It was observed by some that in Nellie's later years, patience and serenity, rather than bitterness, could be seen in her wrinkled face.

On one occasion in a Sunday School class, the experiences of the Martin and Willie Handcart Companies became the topic of discussion, and several class members criticized the Church leaders severely for permitting such a tragedy to occur. The following account has been written about how the discussion terminated.

> One old man (Francis Webster) in the corner sat silent and listened as long as he could stand it, then he arose and said things that no person who heard him will ever forget. His face was white with emotion, yet he spoke

calmly, deliberately, but with great earnestness and sincerity.

He said in substance, "I ask you to stop this criticism. You are discussing a matter you know nothing about. Cold historic facts mean nothing here, for they give no proper interpretation of the questions involved. Mistake to send the Handcart Company out so late in the season? Yes! But I was in that company and my wife was in it, and Sister Nellie Unthank whom you have cited here was there, too. We suffered beyond anything you can imagine and many died of exposure and starvation, but did you ever hear a survivor of that company utter a single word of criticism? Every one of us came through with the absolute knowledge that God lives for we became acquainted with Him in our extremities.

"I have pulled my handcart when I was so weak and weary from illness and lack of food that I could hardly put one foot ahead of the other. I have looked ahead and seen a patch of sand or a hill slope and I have said, I can go only that far and there I must give up for I cannot pull the load through it. I have gone to that sand and when I reached it, the cart began pushing me! I have looked back many times to see who was pushing my cart, but my eyes saw no one. I knew then that the Angels of God were there.

"Was I sorry that I chose to come by handcart? No! Neither then nor any minute of my life since. The price we paid to become acquainted with God was a privilege to pay and I am thankful that I was privileged to come in the Martin Handcart Company."

References:

Remember: The Willie and Martin Handcart Companies and their Rescuers -- Past and Present (Riverton Wyoming Stake, 1997).

LeRoy R. Hafen and Ann W. Hafen, *Handcarts to Zion: The Story of a Unique Western Migration, 1856-1860* (Glendale: The Arthur H. Clark Company, 1960).

Joseph Fielding Smith, *Essentials in Church History* (Salt Lake City: Deseret Book Company, 1950).

MINERS

THE GREAT DIAMOND HOAX
- SAN FRANCISCO, CA -

THE TWO RAGGED AND NONDESCRIPT miners looked uncomfortable and ill at ease when they walked into San Francisco's Bank of California in December of 1871 and asked for a safe deposit box for the two heavy bags they were carrying. When the teller explained that the bank could not accept such a deposit without knowing what was in the bags, they reluctantly opened them and showed a fortune in rough, uncut diamonds. Although the teller agreed to secrecy in the matter, news of the deposit soon reached the ears of Bill Ralston, treasurer of the bank.

After consulting with some of his mining friends, Ralston located the two prospectors, Philip Arnold and John Slack, and summoned them to his office. At first they were reluctant to talk, and they couldn't remember exactly where they had discovered the gems, although they agreed they could find the spot again. It was "somewhere out there." Finally, after much persuasion, they agreed to sell half interest to Ralston, conditional to his having the mine inspected. But Arnold and Slack insisted on blindfolding the inspector when they got within a few miles of the location so that if the deal should not be consummated, they would still be the only ones who knew of the exact location of the mine.

Ralston selected General David S. Colton of the Southern Pacific railroad as the inspector. Colton visited the mine, scooped up some of the gems himself, and returned to San Francisco trembling with excitement. He and Ralston showed their diamonds to a local jeweler who declared them to be real, and together they estimated that the mine must be worth well over $50,000,000. Next, Ralston sent a sampling of the diamonds to Mr. Tiffany in New York for another appraisal, and again their value was extolled. Tiffany, in the presence of Horace Greeley and other distinguished Easterners, estimated the small sample to be worth $150,000. News of the discovery reached England and Europe, and Baron Rothschild became interested. To a doubter, Rothschild proclaimed, "Do not be so sure. America is a very large country. It has furnished the world with many surprises already."

As a final precaution, Ralston hired Henry Janin, America's foremost mining expert, to inspect the mine site (now known to be in Wyoming), and again the report was positive. So the San Francisco and New York Mining and Commercial Company was organized with $10,000,000 of capital stock divided into 100,000 shares. A Mr. Gansl represented the House of Rothschild as one of the board members. Two million dollars was immediately raised from 25 nationally known financiers who paid $80,000 each. The new company made payments of over $600,000 in cash to Arnold and Slack.

The bubble burst a few months later when a diamond nugget was discovered bearing marks made by a lapidary saw. That discovery led to other findings which clearly showed that the mine had been salted with $35,000 worth of gems purchased in Europe, a modest investment for over $600,000 in returns. Slack was never heard of again. Arnold, who had retired to his home in Kentucky, repaid $100,000 in return for having all charges against him dropped. Ralston, with a $300,000 personal loss, returned all the money put up by the investors. The source of the original $35,000 remains a mystery.

Reference:

Asbury Harpending, *The Great Diamond Hoax* (Norman: University of Oklahoma Press, 1958).

THE NAMING OF VIRGINIA CITY, NEVADA
~ VIRGINIA CITY, NV ~

JAMES FENNIMORE, A NONDESCRIPT miner from Virginia, won fame rather than fortune in the Nevada gold fields. Fennimore may never have been aware of his claim to fame, for because of his addiction to whiskey, he was seldom aware of any thing that was really happening.

Believing he had killed a man in the Kern River country in California, Fennimore crossed the Sierra Nevada Mountains and arrived at the Gold Canyon mines in the Washoe area of what is now western Nevada in 1851. He changed his name to James Finney, but that didn't make much difference to anyone. Because Finney frequently raved about his home state of Virginia, hardly anyone in the Washoe knew any name for the elderly, drunken prospector other than "Old Virginia."

Old Virginia did his share of prospecting, and he is credited by some with having discovered the Comstock Lode. But he was not destined for wealth. He is said to have sold his interest in one claim for an old horse, a pair of blankets, and a bottle of whiskey.

At the time, there was only a single street laid out on Sun Mountain (now Mount Davidson), along which a few board shanties were clustered. Old Virginia was one of the residents. One night, making his way home from one of his sprees, Old Virginia stumbled and fell, breaking his whiskey bottle on the stone step of his cabin. Waving the neck of the bottle in the air, he uttered his now famous words: "I christen thee Virginia Town." Somehow, the name stuck even though there was a later movement to rename the town Winnemucca in honor of the respected Paiute Indian chief. Virginia Town became Virginia City, and it became the site of the famous Comstock Lode, the richest mining area the world has ever known.

Old Virginia departed this life in July 1861. On another drunken spree in nearby Dayton, Nevada, he tried to ride a horse that didn't want to be ridden. On being tossed off, he landed on his head, sustaining a fractured skull, and he died a few hours later.

References:

Dan De Quille, *The Big Bonanza* (New York: Alfred A. Knopf, 1967).

Robert West Howard, *This is the West* (Chicago: Rand McNally & Company, 1957).

Irving Stone, *Men to Match My Mountains* (New York: Doubleday & Company, Inc., 1956).

WATER AND SILVER DON'T COEXIST WELL
~ TOMBSTONE, AZ ~

TOMBSTONE, ARIZONA WAS BOOMING in 1881. Its silver mines produced over five million dollars' worth of ore that year. The three-year-old camp had six hundred houses and four thousand people. And there were constant reports of new strikes. Water, of course, was in short supply, just as it was throughout the West. So when miners in Tombstone's Sulphuret silver mine struck water in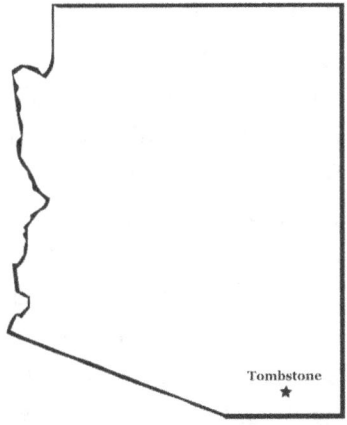
1881, they thought they had found the solution to the area's problems of dryness. Water, one of the essential elements for human existence, is a treasured resource in the West.

At first the miners and citizens of Tombstone were overjoyed. Instead of hauling their silver ore nine miles to the San Pedro River for processing, they could now do the work at home. And the water now gushing through the rocks in the mine would be a boon to the whole town of Tombstone.

Tombstone's local newspaper, the *Epitaph,* reported the find in optimistic terms.

> One well informed and very conservative mining man yesterday remarked to the Epitaph reporter that in his opinion the camp had been benefited 100 per cent by the encountering of water in the Sulphuret. It would inspire renewed confidence in the permanency of the veins, it would relieve the mines of the expense of hauling ore so many miles to the river; it would tend to bring more capital to Tombstone district than would a dozen "big strikes" in the upper levels of the mines themselves.

The water had come as a complete surprise. Although the mining men suspected the presence of water, they thought it would be at least 1,000 feet down. But the water now flowing was at the 500-foot level, and it was flowing into all the mines at that level. Nothing had been built into the mine workings to dispose of water at that level. The Sulphuret mine had to close. The mining companies installed huge pumps at the Contention and Grand Central mines, and these worked until May 12, 1886, when fire destroyed the Grand Central pump house and hoisting works. The Contention's pumps by themselves could not keep both mines dry, and both mines suspended operations. Six years later, fire also destroyed the idle pump house and hoisting works at the Contention mine. Because of the water, mining in Tombstone was dead.

Visitors to Tombstone frequently ask, "Why don't they just pump the water out of the mines?" This has been tried twice. But ore extraction below the water level must bring in a revenue commensurate with the cost of pumping, and with the subsequent declines in the price of silver, the profitability of continued mining ceased to exist. It is believed that vast deposits of silver still lie untouched in the hills around Tombstone, and the deposits are being guarded and preserved by the water just above.

Reference:

Douglas D. Martin, *Tombstone's Epitaph* (Albuquerque: University of New Mexico Press, 1951).

THERE IS NO NIGHT IN CREEDE
- CREEDE, CO -

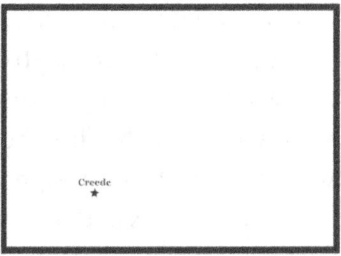

IN 1889 NICHOLAS CREEDE AND George L. Smith were down and out prospectors in southwestern Colorado. In discouragement, Creede flung his pick into the air, and when he saw what the pick landed upon, he cried out "Holy Moses." The pick had discovered a high grade vein of silver beside Willow Creek. Creede and Smith staked their claim, and another "silver rush" began. News of the Holy Moses Mine spread quickly, and a new mining boom town was born. By 1892, the new mining town of Creede, Colorado, boasted a population of 10,000 people.

The railroad built into Creede, and several trains arrived and departed each day. A contemporary account states that "the trains are jammed when they come in—men sit on each other and on the arms of seats and on the platforms. The depot is half buried with the supplies for tourists, prospectors, speculators, gamblers, bartenders, and dancehall girls."

As with most mining camps during boom times, Creede was very much alive and somewhat on the wild side. During its heyday, notorious characters such as Bob Ford, Soapy Smith, Calamity Jane, Bat Masterson, and Poker Alice roamed Creede's main street. For a while, law and order were handled very loosely.

In May 1892, Jack Pugh tried to move in on some property owned by Mayor Osgood. A few nights later while Pugh and his mistress, Lillian Shields, were having drinks in the local saloon, the mayor entered and had words with Pugh. Marshall Karg then arrived, and the mayor told Karg to stay there and keep a watch on Pugh until the mayor returned. While the mayor was away, Pugh shouted insults at Karg. Pugh fired a shot at Karg, and although wounded, Karg fired a fatal shot at Pugh. Three weeks later, Lillian was in the same saloon having drinks and playing cards with her new lover, William Rumidge. Under the influence of the liquor, Rumidge began taunting Lillian and making fun of her poor card playing. Infuriated, Lillian drew a pistol from her clothing and shot Rumidge, killing him. In the ensuing inquest, Lillian was set free.

In June 1892, fire destroyed the bridges across Willow Creek and nearly every building in town. The citizens rallied and quickly rebuilt the town. After the fire, the Vaughn Hotel included tents along with a wooden structure. A sign in front of one of the tents said, "Good accommodations and no danger of fire."

Despite such conditions, Creede was booming with wealth and liveliness, and optimism and gaiety were in the air. Cy Warman, editor of the *Creede Chronicle*, captured the flavor of the times in a poem published in the *Chronicle*.

> *Here's a land where all are equal-*
> *Of high or lowly birth-*
> *A land where men make millions,*
> *Dug from the dreary earth.*
> *Here meek and mild-eyed burros*
> *On mineral mountains feed.*
> *It's day all day in the daytime,*
> *And there is no night in Creede.*

The cliffs are solid silver,
With wond'rous wealth untold,
And the beds of the running rivers
Are lined with the purest gold.
While the world is filled with sorrow,
And the hearts must break and bleed-
It's day all day in the daytime,
And there is no night in Creede.

In the minds of many of the Creede faithful, two lines in the poem should be accorded immortality as one of the classic gems of English literature.

It's day all day in the daytime,
And there is no night in Creede.

For years, Warman's poem has been considered a commemoration of the prosperity and openness of life in Creede. Although it is quite likely that this was Warman's intent, it is only fair to point out that the poem was first published in March, 1892 during the same week that Creede became illuminated by electrical lighting.

References:

Displays in the Rocks and Mineral section of the Denver Museum of Nature and Science.

Pat Richmond, "The Silver Thread Scenic Byway." *San Luis Valley* (Official Guide of the San Luis Valley Information Center).

Ken Jessen, *Colorado Gunsmoke* (Loveland: J.V. Publications, 1986).

RUNNING A HOTEL WASN'T THAT EASY
~ DENVER, CO ~

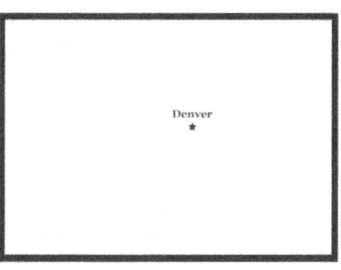

PEOPLE IN THE WESTWARD MOVEMENT needed places to sleep, and almost all sizeable mining camps and railroad towns had at least one hotel. These early hotels might be tents with cots, or they might be wooden structures, or they might be a combination of wood and canvas. The common element was that they had beds for rent and they offered a degree of protection from the elements.

The hotels were usually run by women—wives of prospectors or local residents, for example. Running a hotel involved cooking, cleaning, laundering, and other things considered to be woman's work in those days. Besides, if the men took time for those chores, they would not be out looking for precious metals or be conducting their business affairs.

Mary Jane Megquier was one such hotel manager. Her brief description of her daily life gives a typical view of the lives of those who owned and managed hotels for the western frontiersmen.

In the morning the boy gets up and makes a fire. By seven o'clock I get up and make coffee, make the biscuits, fry the potatoes, then broil three pounds of steak, and as much liver. At eight the bell rings, and they are eating until nine. After breakfast I bake six loaves of bread, then four pies, or a pudding. Then we have lamb, beef, and pork, bake turnips, beets, potatoes, radishes, salad, and that everlasting soup. For tea we have hash, cold meat, bread and butter, and some kind of cake. I make six beds every day and do the washing and ironing. Had I not the constitution of six horses, I should have been dead long ago.

It was not at all unusual that so-called "woman's work" could be more demanding and draining than "man's work."

Reference:

Displays at the Western Museum of Mining and Industry, Colorado Springs, CO

IF YOU HIDE IT, YOU MAY LOSE IT
- TAHLEQUAH, OK -

JOE PAYNE WAS A DEPUTY SHERIFF WHO didn't like wasting his time. So in 1881 when he lost the trail of some lawbreakers he had followed into the hills south of Tahlequah, Oklahoma, 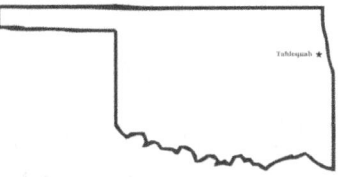 he chose to do some deer hunting rather than return home completely empty handed. After walking for some time and not finding any deer, Payne sat down on a creek bank to remove a pebble from his shoe. Glancing down into the water, he saw something glistening in the sunlight. Although Payne was a deputy sheriff and not a prospector, he nevertheless knew silver when he saw it. The gleam appeared to him to be a vein of pure silver at least three feet wide and stretching across the entire creek bed.

Several days later, Payne returned to the creek with a hand auger with which to test the thickness of his silver vein. After working for several hours, he determined that the vein was more than four feet thick, and that several tons of rich ore were there to be had. The creek, however, was on Indian territorial land, and mining on those lands was forbidden by law.

Believing that the law would be changed some day, Payne determined that the best course of action for now was to conceal the vein and then return to mine it when he could legally do so. Cutting down several large trees, he laid them across the stream in such a way as to conceal his find. If silt should build up against the trees or the creek change its course, the felled trees would still serve as the needed landmark.

The months turned into years, and before Payne could file a legal claim, he died. Before his death in 1904, he drew a map which he gave to a close friend hoping that the friend could profit from the discovery. But the map was too cryptic, and the unnamed friend could not make heads nor tails of it. It may be assumed that the silver vein, if it did exist at all, is still under the felled trees waiting for someone else to come along and look down.

Reference:

Steve Wilson, *Oklahoma Treasures and Treasure Tales* (Norman: University of Oklahoma Press, 1976).

SETTLERS

HOMESTEADING SOMETIMES HAD ITS HUMOROUS MOMENTS
- OAK CREEK, CO -

IN 1913, YOUNG GUY BATTON accompanied his parents and brothers to Moffatt County, Colorado where the family would homestead a 160-acre tract. Guy's father had gone ahead and had built a makeshift cabin for the family's first home.

Traveling on the Moffatt Railroad from Denver, the rest of the Battons arrived in Oak Creek, where Mr. Batton met them. They spent the night in a rented room above a saloon, but they did not sleep well because of the loud noises below. The next morning the family purchased a box of groceries and hitched a ride to their cabin nine miles out from Oak Creek.

Their experiences were typical of a homesteading family. Without horses or machinery, they had no way to plow the land for planting. Guy spaded some ground and planted a few seeds. He writes that "the gophers watched me and as soon as the things started to come up they ate them down to the roots."

The family gathered meat by shooting rabbits, chickens, and

grouse. One neighbor loaned them a cow for much-appreciated milk. From time to time, other neighbors loaned horses and machinery. Survival was a cooperative effort.

Despite the hardships of eking out an existence, the homesteaders did find time to socialize and to have fun. In addition to visits to neighbors, gatherings occurred twice a month at the school house following twice-monthly farmers' meetings. The women brought cakes and sandwiches, and a fiddler provided the music. The dances frequently lasted until daylight. Batton observed that "the pious ones who would not go to a dance, would go to the farmers meeting—and as long as they were there, they might as well stay and dance."

Women were in short supply in that area, and one of Guy's bachelor friends suggested they have some fun by writing to *The Denver Post* to advertise for girls. Guy wrote the letter in which he said the girls "would have the opportunity to become well off when they proved up on their land and accumulated a herd of cattle." He signed the letter "Twenty Mile Homesteader," as they lived twenty miles from the post office in Steamboat Springs. They mailed the letter without telling anyone what they were doing.

Shortly thereafter, one of the men returned from Steamboat Springs and reported that the postmaster wanted to know who the "Twenty Mile Homesteader" was. A bundle of letters for him had arrived in the post office.

One of Guy's brothers went to the post office the next day and brought back the letters. They were white, pink, blue, and perfumed— from girls wanting a western husband. There were about 40 letters, and some included pictures. Some wrote that they could cook the bacon if the boys could bring it in. A few wanted assurances that they would become wealthy. If they had to be poor, they could be poor alone.

Passing the word around, Guy made a big cake and a big pot of coffee. The boys then got together for an all-night party to read the letters and decide who would answer which ones. One old cowpuncher came asking for some of the letters. He wanted a girl also.

Batton concluded his account by saying, "We had a lot of fun writing and a lot of the girls seemed real nice, but none of us got married."

Reference:

Guy C. Batton, "Homesteadin' in the Rockies" (*True West*, September-October, 1964)

THE OKLAHOMA LAND RUN OF 1889 GIVES RISE TO SOONERS AND BOOMERS
~ GUTHRIE, OK ~

WHEN ONE THINKS OF OKLAHOMA'S role in the westward expansion, one normally thinks of Indians, railroads, and the great Land Run of 1889. As Indian Territory, Oklahoma was the 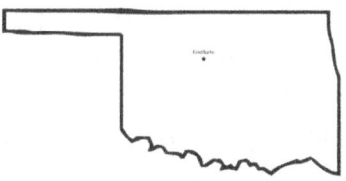 dumping ground for displaced Indian tribes from the east and southeast. Numerous tribes such as the Seminole, Choctaw, Creek, Cherokee, Osage, and many others were uprooted from their natural habitats and placed on reservations in Indian Territory where, for the most part, they still remain. The infamous Trail of Tears was one of the pathetic episodes of America's westward expansion.

Railroad expansion through Oklahoma became a major enterprise. Fierce and bitter rivalries marked the expansion of the railroads as the different lines competed with one another to be the first to build south into Texas or west to the lucrative Pacific coast.

White encroachment into Indian Territory had reached such an extent that in 1889 the Territory was formally opened to white settlement. Thus began a series of "Runs," in which various portions of the Territory became legally available to the white settlers.

The first of these Runs, which was into the "Unassigned Lands" of western Oklahoma, was to begin at high noon on April 22, 1889. The idea was that every person who wanted to be included would have an equal opportunity for land acquisition. On the appointed day, over 50,000 would-be settlers lined up at the northern border of the area, and at the sound of the cannons at high noon, they started into the territory to claim any portion of land not already occupied by someone ahead of them. These were the "Boomers."

By midnight, all the homesteads and every town lot in Guthrie, Kingfisher, Stillwater, Oklahoma City, El Reno, and Norman were taken. Willa Cather commented in one of her books that it took God six days to make the world, but it took only one day for the Boomers to make Oklahoma.

The Santa Fe railroad had previously built into Guthrie, and on the day of the first Run, a Santa Fe train was also at the starting line filled with settlers whose eyes were on Guthrie. Although the train's engineer had orders not to go any faster than the fastest horse, the train managed to reach Guthrie first.

The Boomers were a mixed blend of people from all climes and with all backgrounds, and there are many anecdotes about the characters involved. For example, one would-be settler was there with two mules and a wife, all of which he had stolen from a farmer in Caldwell, Kansas. After being arrested by the sheriff, the settler had to surrender the mules, but the farmer back in Kansas was content to let the settler keep the wife.

The Boomers who started at the boom of the cannons were long considered the honorable participants in the Run. Then there were the "Sooners," the more enterprising people who crossed the line early and who were already on the more choice pieces of land when the Boomers arrived. Many of the Sooners were rightfully evicted by the arriving Boomers, but many managed to hold on to their choice selections.

At first, the term "Sooner" was regarded as a term of reproach, but over the years it came to be synonymous with the concepts of enterprise, taking the initiative, leadership, etc. Oklahoma became proudly known as the Sooner State, and "Boomer, Sooner" is now the fight song of the University of Oklahoma.

Reference:

Edward Everett Hale, *Oklahoma, A Guide to the Sooner State* (Norman: University of Oklahoma Press, 1941).

IF YOU DON'T HAVE SNOWSHOES, TRY WALKING ON QUILTS
- PANGUITCH, UT -

THE GREAT QUILT WALK FROM Panguitch to Parowan in southern Utah is one of the more unique episodes of the settlement of the Great Basin area by the LDS pioneers. Although it is without parallel in the annals of LDS pioneer lore, it is a relatively unknown episode that deserves much more attention than it has so far received. It was a desperate and successful attempt to obtain relief for the starving settlers of Panguitch during the severe winter of 1864.

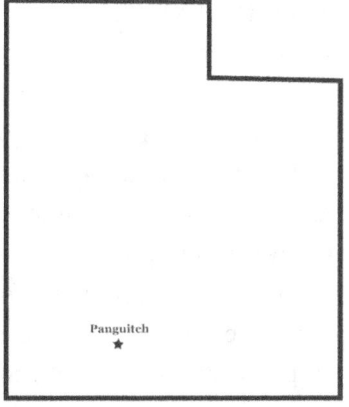

As part of Brigham Young's colonizing process, a company of Mormon pioneers from the Salt Lake Valley moved down to southern Utah in 1851 and established the community of Parowan. After having done so, some of these same colonizers moved eastward in 1864 and founded Panguitch (originally known as Fairview). But the Panguitch pioneers, who were in a more isolated location between the

Markagunt and Paunsaugunt Plateaus, had a very difficult time getting established.

That first winter in Panguitch was bitterly cold. The snow was deep, and communication between the two settlements had ceased because of the difficulty of travel. The Panguitch settlers had not had a good fall crop, and food supplies were becoming exhausted. As a result, the Panguitch settlers were on the verge of starvation. Relief had to be obtained from neighboring Parowan, but it required that someone travel to Parowan to inform the people there of the desperate situation in Panguitch.

It's only about 40 miles, as the crow flies, from Panguitch to Parowan. But a 40-mile trek by land won't quite get you there. Today's roads go around the mountains that are in between. And taking the direct route by foot or wagon is a challenge for the hardiest of men, especially if the winter snow is on the ground. Although the deep snows and the cold temperature made such a trip seem like an impossibility, it was clear that it had to be attempted by a relief party.

The community leaders in Panguitch organized a relief party to be led by Jesse Lowder, a counselor in the local bishopric. Many of the local men responded to a call for volunteers, and six were selected to accompany Lowder on the desperate and dangerous mission. In addition to Jesse Lowder, the relief party consisted of Thomas Jefferson Adair, Jr.; John Lowe Butler, II; Alexander Matheson; Thomas Morgan Richards; John Paul Smith; and William Talbot. With a wagon pulled by a pair of oxen and with quilts intended for warmth while sleeping, the group set out for Bear Valley, hoping to go from there over the crest of the hills and then down into Parowan.

Every step in the deep snow was a struggle for the rescue missionaries. Upon reaching the head of Bear Valley, they found further wagon travel to be impossible, so, abandoning the wagon, they proceeded on by foot. In those areas where the snow was relatively shallow, they made progress, but when encountering the soft and deep snow at the higher altitudes, they sank in up to their hips. It soon became apparent that they could not go any further and that their attempt to obtain relief for their starving community would end in failure. It was now time to plead with the Lord for help.

Spreading a quilt on top of the snow, the seven men knelt in a circle on top of the quilt, and they prayed for the way to be opened for them to complete their mission. As they finished their prayer, they realized that while they were on top of the quilt, they were not sinking into the snow. The answer to their prayer became clear, and they now knew how to proceed. Laying quilts down in front of them, they resumed their trek by walking on the quilts. After walking across one quilt, they laid another down, and then another, and they walked on this moving platform of quilts without sinking into the snow. In this manner, the seven men made their way across areas where the snow was too deep for normal walking, and they succeeded in arriving in Parowan and alerting the people there of the plight of the Panguitch settlers.

The people of Parowan immediately made food and other supplies available. The seven men of the relief party embarked on their homeward journey carrying sacks of flour and other foods, and the citizens of Parowan promised to follow up with further supplies as quickly as possible.

The homeward journey for the relief party was different from their original journey in two respects. In one respect, it was even more difficult because the seven men were now carrying heavy sacks of food supplies. But in another sense, it was an easier journey because the relief party members now knew that the trip could be done. Again, it was their quilts that enabled them to traverse the areas of deep snow and arrive successfully back in Panguitch. This rescue mission has become known in Panguitch as "The Great Quilt Walk."

In his journal, one of the quilt walkers, Alexander Matheson, recorded the following account of the overall experience:

> We decided that if we had faith as big as a mustard seed, we could make it and bring flour to our starving families. So we began the quilt laying in prayerful earnestness. The return trip was harder with the weight of the flour, but we finally made it to our wagon and oxen and on home with thankfulness. The whole settlement welcomed us because we had been gone longer than expected. There had been prayers, tears, and fears which turned to rejoicing and cheers.

In memory of the seven-member relief party and of the unusual way in which they made the trip, an annual Quilt Walk Festival is now held on the second weekend of June in Panguitch. It is a gala affair with a parade, quilt displays, quilting classes, and an "all you can eat" pancake breakfast. The highlight of the occasion is a dinner theater in which the story of The Great Quilt Walk is impressively dramatized. They wisely hold the festival in the summer, however, rather than in winter.

Reference:

Panguitch Quilt Walk Festival Brochures and Dinner Theater.

THE DONNER PARTY LEAVES A VITAL LEGACY
- HENEFER, UT -

ONE OF THE EPIC TRAGEDIES IN America's westward movement occurred in 1846 when the Donner Party became trapped in the snow while trying to cross the Sierra Nevada Mountains into California. Only one day from the summit, a heavy snowstorm halted their progress and resulted in a frozen isolation leading to starvation and death of several party members along with a degree of cannibalism by survivors.

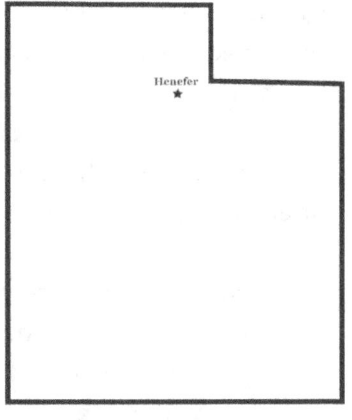

Bound for California, the Donner Party was given a choice between two possible routes after reaching Fort Laramie (in present-day Wyoming). An established route led northwest along the Oregon Trail to Fort Hall (in present-day Idaho), then westward, and then along the Humboldt River to a crossing point of the Sierra Nevada. But an explorer, Lansford W. Hastings, urged the Donner Party leaders to take a shortcut leading to Fort Bridger, then over and through the Wasatch Mountains, along the southern shore of the

Great Salt Lake, and through the desert to the same crossing point into California.

Choosing the short cut, the Donner Party found the Wasatch Mountains to be almost impassable. To get through with their wagons, they had to cut trees, remove boulders, and hew wider passages through narrow corridors of granite. Fortunately, they had the necessary equipment, but their progress was extremely slow. From present-day Henefer in Utah, the 30-mile trek through and over the mountains into the Salt Lake Valley was a 30-day ordeal. The trail they blazed is the legacy that they left.

The following year, in 1847, Brigham Young and the pioneers followed the same route as the Donner Party. But because they traveled a route that had already been blazed and cleared by the Donners a year earlier, Brigham Young's advance party received the gift of time. Even though the Saints had to do some additional cutting and clearing themselves, their trek through and over the Wasatch Mountains took only four days instead of the 30 days required by the Donner Party.

In commenting on the Donner Party's legacy to the Saints, George Albert Smith, eighth president of The Church of Jesus Christ of Latter-day Saints, wrote:

> But for the success of the well-equipped Donner Party blazing a road from Henefer over the mountains to the valley of the Great Salt Lake in 1846, consuming thirty days, the Mormon Pioneers who came over the same trail a year later in only four days could not have reached the Valley until too late to plant their crops and preserve their seed, particularly potatoes.

Lest it be thought very unfair and cruel that the Donners should suffer such a tragic fate in the Sierras after leaving such an invaluable legacy for the Mormons, it should be pointed out that because of disorganization and squabbles within their own ranks, the Donners lost several more days of time after entering the Salt Lake Valley. Had these internal problems not occurred, they would have reached the Sierras in ample time for safe passage into California.

References:

Walter M. Stookey, *Fatal Decision* (Salt Lake City: Deseret Book Company, 1950).

C. F. McGlashan, *The History of the Donner Party* (Stanford: Stanford University Press, 1954).

YOU DON'T MESS WITH THOMAS GROVER
- CENTERVILLE, UT -

There are some people in this world you just don't mess with. Thomas Grover was one such person. Tall and large in stature, Grover was solidly built. As a former bodyguard of Joseph Smith, he knew how to use weapons, and he knew how to react to challenges. Grover wasn't afraid to stand up to anyone, not even to Brigham Young, which he did on one occasion.

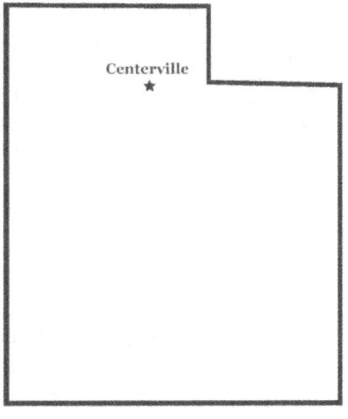

Because Thomas Grover was a polygamist in early Utah, he was subject to arrest by federal marshals. Authorized by the 1887 Edmunds-Tucker Act outlawing polygamy, federal marshals roamed Utah searching for polygamous husbands and arresting all they could find.

Finding the husbands of plural wives proved to be a formidable task. Some of the men went into hiding. Others had the knack of disappearing just before the marshals arrived. But some were taken by surprise.

Thomas Grover may have been taken by surprise. He was at home one day when a stranger knocked at his door.

"Thomas, there is a stranger here to see you," his wife Laduska announced.

"Show him in, show him in!" Grover responded.

As the man entered the house, Grover greeted him with, "How are you, brother?"

Perhaps Grover failed to recognize the stranger as a marshal, or perhaps he felt no need of fearing the stranger. At any rate, when the visitor announced his intentions of arresting Grover and taking him away, Thomas showed his true colors.

"Doiska (his pet name for his wife), get me Brother Joseph's sword, and watch while I cut this man's head off."

Standing tall with a resolute pose and with the sword in his large hand, Grover presented an invincible appearance. The stranger turned and left the house—alone.

Thomas and Laduska then had a hearty laugh, and over the years, Thomas' descendants also laugh when they recall the incident.

Reference:

Joel P. Grover, The Ancestry and Genealogy of Thomas Grover.

INTRODUCTION

THE INDIANS WERE HERE FIRST. THIS WAS THEIR LAND. BUT WESTWARD expansion under the rationalization of "Manifest Destiny" was not to stop until the Americans reached the Pacific Ocean.

At first, the Indians were willing to coexist if only the white men would allow the Indians to continue living as they had lived for centuries. But this was not to be. To the whites, the Indians were an inferior race—uncivilized, primitive, and unchristianized. They could not be considered as equals. And their presence, especially in the Great Plains, was an impediment to western expansion.

In the East and in the Northwest, the Indians practiced a degree of agriculture, and they were more permanently settled than their counterparts on the Great Plains. Indians of the Great Plains were nomadic, following the buffalo up and down the country. As the white men usurped the lands and built roads and erected fences, it was not just a matter of restricting the Indian's way of life, it was a matter of destroying a whole culture. Broken promises and treaty violations on the part of the white men further inflamed the situation. Indian resistance on the Great Plains was only natural.

It was frequently the whites who initiated the problems. The encroachment onto Indian lands, the wanton killing of the buffalo, and senseless massacres were infuriating to the Indians. Indian retaliations further inflamed the situation. Raids, thievery, and murders by the Indians became an expected part of frontier life

In addition to retaliatory raids, the Indians would steal horses and cattle, and they liked to kidnap white women and children. These they could sell to other tribes or keep for themselves. In more than one case, the captives assimilated into the Indian way of life and resisted efforts to be brought back to white civilization. Cynthia Ann Parker, who became the mother of Comanche Chief Quanah Parker, was the most famous of these converts.

Scalping of victims was considered to be a unique and barbaric Indian custom, although the Europeans practiced scalping during the French-Indian War. The act of scalping was a guarantee that the spirit of the victim would be dispatched down to the Indian version of hell.

Still, it was not all warfare. Peaceful relations frequently prevailed until one side provoked the other by an act of treachery. Friendly competitions, such as between the Comanches, who were superb horsemen, and the whites, were not infrequent. And on rare occasions, an Indian leader, such as Quanah Parker, would adopt the white man's ways and would become wealthy and prominent in the white man's world.

Yielding at last to the inevitable, the Indians accepted life on reservations. In so doing, they set their hopes and dreams on a future time when they would be restored to the dignity and nobility they had once enjoyed, a day when they would gain rightful ascendancy over the whites. This hope, while seemingly dormant, has never ceased.

WAY OF LIFE

NEVER BET AGAINST THE COMANCHES IN A HORSE RACE
- BRONTE, TX -

THE SPANISH BROUGHT CATTLE AND horses into what is now the American southwest. As Spanish control ebbed, particularly in what is now Texas, large numbers of these animals either escaped or were set free to wander. They survived and multiplied and became a major attraction to incoming American colonizers. The  horses, because of the speed and mobility they offered, were particularly valued by the Indian tribes of the Midwest. In fact, horses gave the Indians, particularly the Comanches and Apaches, the means of revolutionizing their methods of hunting and fighting.

The Spanish taught their Indian slaves how to tame wild horses. Recognizing the advantages of using horses in war and in hunting, the Apaches then learned the arts of capturing and taming. From the Apaches, these practices passed to the Comanches, then to the Kiowas, then on to other tribes. In the minds of many, the Comanches became the best horsemen in the world.

Before their introduction to horses, the Indians had only two ways of killing buffalo. One way was to drive the buffalo off of cliffs. The other way was to disguise themselves in animal skins, stalk the buffalo, and shoot their arrows whenever they could get close enough.

The horse revolutionized the hunting of buffalo. Armed with lances and bows and arrows and wearing bison hide shields, the Comanches (and soon men of other tribes) learned to fire a barrage of arrows from fast horses while hanging concealed on the opposite side of their mounts from their targets. Other Indians on horses assisted by circling the buffalo herds to prevent their escape from the hunters. Although explicit statistics are not available, the success of buffalo hunting expeditions increased significantly after the introduction of horses.

The Comanches were the best riders on the plains. They were masters of good horsemanship in battle and in hunting. During in-between periods, they enjoyed the sport of horse racing, and when in competition with the whites, they were also good con artists.

At Fort Chadbourne in the late 1800s, a shave-tail lieutenant just out of West Point was bragging about the prowess and speed of his horse and offering to bet that his horse could beat any other horse in Texas in a match race. When the Comanches heard of the lieutenant's boasts, about twenty of them showed up at Fort Chadbourne with a little mustang, shaggy-haired, pitifully thin, and only fourteen hands high. Not being aware that the mustangs, a blend of African, Arabian, and Spanish breeds, were very fast horses, the soldiers thought that their horses could easily beat the little critter standing before them.

Although feeling insulted about racing his sleek cavalry horse against such a nag as the Indian challenger appeared to be, the lieutenant acquiesced to the urging of his comrades and reluctantly accepted the challenge. Bets were placed, with the Indians wagering buffalo robes, buckskins, and turquoise and silver jewelry against the soldiers' silver dollars. The race was run, and the little mustang barely won, outrunning the lieutenant's horse by a neck. Anxious to recoup their losses, the soldiers brought out another horse and challenged the Comanches to another race. Again bets were placed, and this time the mustang barely won by a nose.

The humiliated soldiers then brought out a third horse, a fine Kentucky racing mare, the fastest horse in the fort. They knew that this horse could run faster than the mustang had run in the two previous races. This time the soldiers were betting almost all their personal belongings, and they were going to fleece the Indians at their own game and recover their pride, their honor, and their prior losses. The Kentucky mare was fast. The soldiers failed to notice, however, that after two races, the mustang was not winded.

The race began with the Comanche rider whooping piercingly into his horse's ear, and the mustang jumped to a quick lead. This time the mustang was running at full speed, and as the gap between the two horses widened with every hoof beat, the Kentucky mare was hopelessly outclassed. For the last fifty yards of the quarter-mile race, the Comanche rider sat backwards on his horse shouting taunts to the cursing white rider who was falling farther behind.

After the Indians had left with all their booty, a half-breed interpreter told the dazed soldiers how they had been duped. That Comanche mustang was the fastest horse in all the South Plains and had already won fortunes for its Comanche owners.

References:

Jack Loftin, *Trails Through Archer* (Burnet, Texas: Eakins Publications, 1979).

Jeff Adams, "Comanche Tricksters," *True West,* September-October 1958.

SQUAW FIGHTS
- SANTA CLARA, UT -

SQUAW FIGHTS WERE NOT FIGHTS among Indian women. Instead, when two Indian braves sought the same girl as a wife, a fight between the braves was sometimes needed to determine who would get the girl. White men had given the name "squaw fight" to this practice.

Among the Paiute nation of Nevada and southern Utah, the overall procedure for settling rivalries over the same girl went as follows. One brave would offer the girl's father a certain number of ponies depending on the brave's estimate of the girl's beauty and worth. The rival brave would then match the offer. The girl's father was usually pleased to be getting double pay for his daughter. Then the two braves would fight one another, usually with fists and without weapons, with the winner getting the girl. However, in the event of an obvious mismatch, like a big strong brave against a smaller and weaker one, the two rivals were allowed to

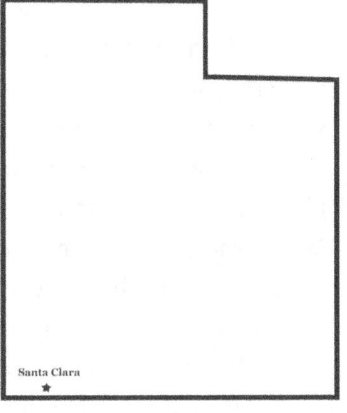

organize their comrades into teams, and the fight became a team fight.

In 1861, at Three-Mile Place, just west of the Santa Clara fort in southern Utah, a squaw fight occurred that ended with unexpected results. The girl in question, a member of the Santa Clara tribe, has been described as young, slender, and delicate looking—a beauty who seemed excited by the fuss being made over her. But Panimeto, the suitor she preferred, was young and slightly built. From another Paiute band, the rival, Ankawakeets, was older, larger, and more muscular. With the joint approvals of the girl's father and also of Chief Tutsegavits, each suitor selected twenty husky braves to aid in the battle. The rest of the Indians, along with a few white men, gathered as spectators.

The Indians marked off a large square of ground to serve as the battle arena, with a creek forming the southern boundary. The rule was that any Indian forced down and held long enough for an imaginary scalping to take place would have to leave the arena, and whichever side vanquished the other in this manner would be declared the winner. After getting started, the battle raged for over an hour with neither side showing any advantage. The combatants were tired, and it became accepted that neither side was going to vanquish the other. Paiute tradition dictated another type of contest in such cases.

There would have to be a tug of war. But it was not a tug of war using a rope. It was a tug of war using the girl herself. One Indian grabbed her right wrist, and another grabbed her left wrist. Then with fifteen Indians pulling on each side, they gyrated around. Losing balance, but without letting go, the Indians and the girl tumbled into the creek. With her joints pulled out of their sockets and her head below water, the thirty Indians still tugged in opposite directions.

One of the onlookers, Andrew Gibbons, a Mormon missionary to the Indians, could stand it no longer. Plunging into the water, he scattered the young braves and lifted the girl onto dry land where she lay. Ankawakeets was enraged that Gibbons should interfere. Three times he charged Gibbons, and three times Gibbons threw the big Indian to the ground. Although defeated, Ankawakeets showed a degree of the nobility that is ingrained in the Indian culture. He picked up the unresisting girl and handed her to Gibbons, the victor. Then Andrew Gibbons unwittingly committed another violation of Indian protocol. He led the girl to Panimeto, the man of her choice, and gave her to him. Instantly, all the Indians let out war whoops. Only a victorious warrior could deserve this squaw. Ankawakeets and his allies raced for their guns, but Thales Haskell, another Mormon missionary, stepped in front of the big warrior and said, "Put up your gun and be a man."

At that point they all heard the loud voice of Chief Tutsegavits ordering the father to lead the girl back into the arena for another tug of war. As the father and the girl were slowly walking forward, the girl's young brother knew that she could not survive another tugging. Springing out from the crowd, he plunged a knife deeply into his sister's bosom before anyone could stop him. Then turning to the crowd, he cried, "I loved my sister too well to see her suffer more. You call me a boy, but if there is a brave who thinks I have done wrong, let him take the knife and plunge it into my heart; so I will join my sister and lead her to the red man's happy hunting ground. I am not afraid to die."

One by one the Indians slipped away to their camps. The next day after the burial, the Mormons urged, and the Indians promised, that there would be no more squaw fights.

Reference:

Helen Bay Gibbons, *Saint and Savage* (Salt Lake City: Deseret Book Company, 1965).

IT MAY BE BETTER FOR THE DEAD TO STAY DEAD
~ PAWHUSKA, OK ~

HE SHOULD HAVE STAYED DEAD. THE remaining thirty years of Ho-To-Moie's life were filled with loneliness because his fellow Osage Indians would have nothing more to do with this "out-of-place-dead-spirit" who had returned to haunt them.

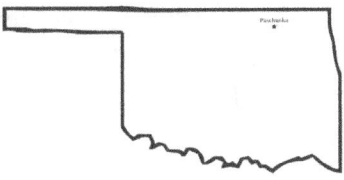

It all started in 1909 on a blustery, snowy day in the neighborhood of Pawhuska, Oklahoma. Walking on the snowy ground after imbibing a few too many drinks, John Stink (as he was known to white people) fell, passed out, and lay half buried in the snow. When his Osage friends finally found him, he was cold, stiff, and motionless. Deciding that John was dead, his friends built a platform on which to transport the body to a grave. The sun was beaming down that day, and as the burial procession arrived at the grave site, John's body thawed and he revived and sat up, fully conscious. None of the escorting Indians took time to welcome John back to the land of the living, for they scattered to the four winds as soon as he began to stir.

From that point on, John was an outcast. Eventually he began relieving his loneliness by gathering the stray dogs of Pawhuska and making them his companions. Almost every day, John could be seen walking with his dogs on the prairies outside of town. And almost every day, John would come into town seeking sustenance for himself and his dogs. They slept out in the open, and on cold winter nights, John would frequently be huddled against the side of a building in Pawhuska with his dogs around him.

After the Pawhuska sheriff shot some of John's dogs, suspecting them of having rabies, John moved into a tent outside of Pawhuska. A few years later he permitted himself to be moved into a log hut adjacent to the country club. Watching a man playing golf one day, John muttered, "White man's a crazy fool."

Over the years, John's ostracism continued. He tried to caution the Osages about what would happen after oil was discovered on their lands. "White man's greed and lust for gold will bring big trouble to the Indians," he declared. But no one wanted to listen to this "dead spirit."

In his 79th year, John fell and broke his leg. It refused to heal, and John died again, this time for good, with court-appointed guardians holding his hands and dogs sleeping peacefully at his feet.

Reference:

Davilla Bright, "The Indian Who Came Back From the Dead," *True Frontier*, March 1969.

MORMONS AVERT A PAIUTE MASSACRE
- LAS VEGAS, NV -

FOR THE MOST PART, THE PAIUTE Indians of Nevada and southern Utah sought to maintain friendly relations with the Mormon settlers of the area. The Mormons sent missionaries to work with the Indians, and in addition to their spiritual callings, the missionaries were good for food, blankets, and clothing. But more importantly, the Mormons did not have the reputation of speaking with forked tongues. To the Paiutes, there were two classes of white men: Mormons and Mericats (all other white men). So it should not be surprising when a group of angry Indians approached two Mormon missionaries at Las Vegas Spring and asked permission to kill some white men who had earlier killed an Indian. One can easily imagine the dilemma such a request placed upon the missionaries.

While sleeping in their wagon, Andrew Gibbons and Sidney Burton were suddenly awakened in the night by the Indians.

"You friends?" asked Chief Patsearump.

"You know we are friends," Gibbons responded in the Paiute language.

"If you friends, you let us go kill enemies."

Adding further explanation, Chief Patsearump said, "White men camped at spring. They killed our brave! Gave him poison! We take revenge while they sleep."

Gibbons and Burton looked at one another. "They're asking our permission to commit a massacre."

"It's the U.S. mail party," Burton whispered to Gibbons.

"One of us must go with you." Gibbons was stalling for time.

"No! You'd warn enemies. If you friends, you let us go kill."

In a further effort to stall for time, Gibbons then suggested that they all talk about it. It was a good suggestion because to the Indians, "talk" meant an unhurried council in which everyone could speak his mind. So two bearded missionaries and ninety angry Indians sat down together to discuss the situation.

Benjamin Hulse, president of the Las Vegas Mission, arrived and joined the discussion. "Brother Ebenezer Hanks is with the mail party," Hulse explained. "If you kill him, Brother Brigham would be very angry."

"We not kill him, but we kill all the others," Patsearump responded.

The three missionaries managed to keep the discussion going, thinking that the mail party would soon arrive. Finally they did arrive, and the Mormons almost lost control of the situation when the ninety Indians surrounded the mail party members with the intent of killing them.

As soon as the mail contractor, Mr. Yaff, understood the situation, he explained. "We didn't poison him. He was sick when he first came into our camp. We could do nothing for him, so we left him there."

"We'll wait here," said another, "while someone goes back to find him."

Believing that they were hearing the truth, the Indians agreed to wait while President Hulse went in search of the missing brave. But Chief Patsearump was not yet finished. Turning to Mr. Yaff, Patsearump demanded, "If brave is dead, you give me one horse and a blanket."

After traveling some ten or twelve miles, Hulse found the sick Indian and performed the Mormon ordinance of administering to the sick. The Indian became well again, and the two returned to the camp. Peace was restored, and the Indians rejoiced in the power of God that had once again been made manifest to them. Andrew Gibbons also had cause to rejoice, as the fervent prayers he had been offering all through the ordeal had apparently been answered.

Reference:

Helen Bay Gibbons, *Saint and Savage,* (Salt Lake City: Deseret Book Company, 1965).

CHIEF KICKING BIRD WAS NO COWARD

- JACKSBORO, TX -

CHIEF KICKING BIRD, AN OUTSPOKEN spokesman for peace with the Whites, was content to live on the Kiowa reservation in Indian Territory. He recognized that the Indians' only hope for survival lay in peaceful coexistence with the Whites, not with continued warfare. But thinking of Kicking Bird as a coward, the more warlike Comanches and Kiowas began to mock him and discredit him. Kicking Bird knew that his influence over his tribesmen was weakening, and he recognized that he had to do something about it. He had to exhibit an act of bravery to regain his patriarchal posture.

Gathering a force of 100 Kiowa warriors in July 1870, Kicking Bird headed south into Texas, and there he encountered a 56-member contingent of U.S. Cavalry on the Little Wichita River south of Wichita Falls. Kicking Bird and his warriors attacked, and the battle raged for half a day. Finding themselves nearly surrounded, the soldiers retreated to a strong defensive position and held their ground. They fought back gallantly, but Chief Kicking Bird and the

Kiowas were ferocious, and the soldiers were being decimated. Then, just as suddenly as the battle had started, it ended. The Indians had almost annihilated the cavalry patrol, and Kicking Bird had proved his bravery. There was no need for further fighting. He then called off his warriors, and let the few surviving cavalry men return to their base at Fort Richardson.

Returning to the reservation in Indian Territory, Chief Kicking Bird used his regained position of influence to continue urging peaceful coexistence with the Whites.

Reference:

Displays at the Ft. Richardson Interpretive Center, Jacksboro, Texas.

RELATIONSHIP WITH WHITE MEN

BILLY BOWLEGS, THE SEMINOLE CHIEF WHO COULD NOT BE CONQUERED
- FT. GIBSON, OK -

BILLY BOWLEGS, WHOSE INDIAN NAME was Halpatter-Micco, was the last chief of the Florida Seminoles. He was also a warrior, and as such he gave the U.S. Army fits. Of all the 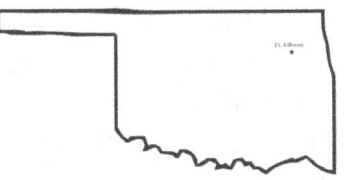 Indian tribes in the Southeast, the Seminoles were the most resistant to Andrew Jackson's policy of removing them to Indian Territory in present day Oklahoma. Against Federal troops, the Seminoles fought and won three wars, one of which lasted seven years. Although pushed back into the swampy Everglades, Bowlegs and his forces thwarted every attempt to dislodge them. Bowlegs beat Colonel William S. Harney. He also beat General Zachary Taylor. On May 10, 1842, President Polk finally announced: "The further pursuit of these miserable beings by a large military force seems to be as injudicious as it is unavailing."

Following the second war, the government attempted to coax the remaining Seminoles out of Florida. Bowlegs and two others were even taken to Washington, D.C. and wined and dined at government expense. They enjoyed the trip, but they still saw no reason to move out of Florida.

The Third Seminole War, also known as the Billy Bowlegs War, lasted only two years, with the Indians again the victors. Jefferson Davis, Union Secretary of War, admitted that the Seminoles "had baffled the energetic efforts of our army to effect their subjugation and removal."

Following this third war, the government offered Bowlegs $6,500 plus $100 for each of his four sub-chiefs, plus $500 for each warrior and $100 for each woman and child. Being weary from so much fighting, Billy and all but about 300 Seminoles accepted the offer. The 300 remained in the swamps, and their descendants are in Florida to this day.

Billy Bowlegs arrived in New Orleans in May, 1858 with a company that included two wives, one son, five daughters, 50 slaves, and $100,000 cold hard cash. A Harper's Weekly correspondent described the 50-year-old Billy as "about 160 pounds, fine forehead, keen black eyes, and somewhat above medium height." Visiting a local museum, Bowlegs was attracted to the wax figures of prominent U.S. Army officers. "Scott and Taylor," he said, "were great men and fought me mighty hard." But of Harney, Bowlegs said he made him "run like hell."

Headstone for Billy Bowlegs, National Cemetery in Ft. Gibson, Oklahoma

From New Orleans, Bowlegs and his company traveled by boat to Ft. Gibson, Oklahoma, where they settled with other Seminoles who had migrated earlier. Bowlegs' story becomes cloudy at this point, and there are conflicting accounts of his remaining activities. When the American Civil War broke out in 1861, the Seminoles and the Creeks sided with the Union, and disputed accounts say that Billy Bowlegs and over a hundred of his warriors joined with Union forces, and that Bowlegs was commissioned a Captain. His activities as a Union soldier are not known.

It is clear, however, that Bowlegs' heritage lives on in place names in Florida and Oklahoma. Bowlegs Town, Bowlegs Creek, and Bowlegs Landing are Florida place names. In Oklahoma, there is a Bowlegs Oil Field, and a town named Bowlegs is located in Seminole County. A tombstone bearing the name of Billy Bowlegs stands in the Officers' Circle of the National Cemetery at Ft. Gibson, although there is doubt by some that the great Seminole warrior and chief is actually buried there.

An undisputed honor is that a portrait of Chief Billy Bowlegs, this Seminole warrior who had earlier fought so bitterly and successfully against Federal forces in Florida, hangs in the Smithsonian Institute in Washington, D.C. And he is proudly remembered to this day by a numerous posterity in both Florida and Oklahoma.

Reference:

George U. Hubbard, "Billy Bowlegs: The Seminole Chief Who Wouldn't Be Subdued," *Old West,* Winter 1998.

THE MEDICINE LODGE PEACE COUNCIL
- JACKSBORO, TX -

WITH THE CIVIL WAR OUT OF THE way, the Federal government could now turn its attention to the war-like Indians on the western plains. If at all possible, peaceful relations had to be established so that whites and Indians could co-exist in harmony.

In 1867, President Andrew Johnson called for a council meeting to be attended by representatives of all the Plains Indian tribes and by government officials. The Indians, who were asked to pick the location, chose an area now known as Medicine Lodge, Kansas, at the confluence of the Medicine River and Elm Creek. It was an area sacred to members of the Kiowa tribe, who made annual pilgrimages to bathe in the healing waters of the river.

It is estimated that anywhere from 5,000 to 15,000 Indians came and camped around the council site. They came primarily from the Kiowa, Comanche, Kiowa-Apache, Cheyenne, and Arapaho tribes. Santanta, Little Raven, Ten Bears, and Black Kettle were among the chiefs who attended. The U.S. 7th Cavalry was there also to protect the government commissioners and other white attendees. Reporters from the East were there, including Henry M. Stanley, who was later to find Dr. Livingston in Africa.

The government plan was to get the Indians to agree on life on reservations. The government would build houses for them, teach them to farm, and provide them with food, clothing, and medicine as needed. Schools, churches, and farming tools would also be provided.

The Indians just wanted to be left alone to continue their normal way of life as nomadic hunters and to live at peace with their white brothers. They did not understand, nor did they like, the civilization being forced upon them. Chief Ten Bears of the Comanches, who longed for peace, expressed the Indian viewpoint succinctly.

> My heart is filled with joy when I see you here…. My people have never first drawn a bow or fired a gun against the whites. … It was you who sent the first soldier and we who sent out the second. Two years ago I came upon this road following the buffalo that my wives and children might have their cheeks plump and their bodies warm. But the soldiers fired on us, and since that time there has been a noise like that of a thunderstorm, and we have not known which way to go.

The whites could not understand that the Indians could not happily exist in the "superior" environment of white civilization. The Indians were essentially being asked to give up the nomadic way of life they had followed for centuries and assume an existence completely foreign to their nature. They were to become farmers rather than hunters, and they were to learn to live the way the white people lived. There seemed to be no peaceful alternative, but Chief Santanta of the Kiowa tribe was very outspoken in his opposition to the government's proposals.

All the land south of the Arkansas belongs to the Kiowa and Comanche, and I don't want to give away any of it. I love the land and the buffalo and will not part with it. I don't want any of the churches within the country. I want the children raised as I was.

This building of houses for us is all nonsense. We don't want you to build any for us; we would all die. I want all my land, even from the Arkansas south to Red River. My country is small already. If you build us houses, the land will be smaller.

Although the government commissioners listened to the Indian viewpoints, their minds were already made up. This would be the beginning of the policy of putting all Indian tribes onto reservations. After three weeks of negotiating, the Indian leaders agreed to sign the proposed treaty. Actually, there were three signings. The Kiowa and Comanche tribes signed first on October 21, 1867. The Kiowa-Apache tribe signed later that day. The Cheyenne and Arapaho tribes held out but signed a week later. Thus was born the system of placing the American Indians on reservations. The Indians were also given the choice of whether the reservations would be to the north or the south of the Red River. They chose the north.

The treaty, though well intended, was doomed to failure. Many bands of Indians had boycotted the council and refused to be bound by the terms of the treaty. Other bands of Indians, who truly tried to live according to the agreed upon precepts, became disillusioned by the government's failure to guarantee peace and safety and by the government's further failure to deliver promised food, clothing, and supplies. Warfare on the plains resumed, and the Medicine Lodge Treaty became just a historical document.

References:

Highway historical marker at Medicine Lodge, Kansas.

Tawnya Herman, "Lawton: A Child of the Prairie," found on Google.com.

Displays at Fort Richardson museum, Jacksboro, Texas.

THE QUAKERS TRY TO CIVILIZE THE INDIANS
- JACKSBORO, TX -

FOLLOWING THE CIVIL WAR, President Ulysses S. Grant recognized that things were not going well with the Indians on the western frontier. The U.S. Cavalry, with their policies of retaliation, had not succeeded in stopping Indian raids on western settlements. The Society of Friends (Quakers) applied to President Grant, and gained his approval, for the opportunity to try more peaceful and compassionate methods.

In 1869, Grant transferred the responsibility for "civilizing" the Indians and administering the reservations to the Quakers. Lawrie Tatum became the Quaker Indian Agent.

Hoping to establish a sense of dignity and security on the reservations, the Quakers insisted that the cavalry could not enter the Indian reservations for any reason. The Quakers were unable to conceive that kindness would beget anything other than kindness in return.

This policy had its effect, but not in the way the Quakers had intended. The reservations became havens of refuge for marauding

Indians who would venture out on raids and then retreat into the safety of their reservations where Federal forces could not go. On the plains, this became the Indians' pattern during the summer months. During the winters, the Indians would stay on their reservations and accept government rations delivered by the Quakers.

Sadly, the Quaker Peace Policy turned out to be a failure. After trying it for four years, President Grant terminated the experiment and returned control of the Indian affairs to the U.S. Cavalry.

Reference:

Displays at the Ft. Richardson Interpretive Center, Jacksboro, Texas.

BUFFALO BILL TAKES ON CHIEF YELLOW HAND
~ WARBONNET CREEK, NE ~

BUFFALO BILL CODY (WHOSE GIVEN name was William) was for real. Before becoming a master showman, he was one of the best frontiersman ever to roam the western plains.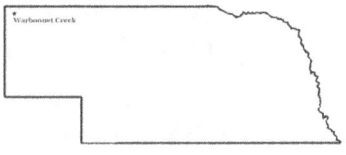
Chief Yellow Hand was also for real. As one of the leading Sioux chieftains, Chief Yellow Hand was one of the more prominent chiefs leading the Indians in massacring General George Custer's forces at Little Big Horn on June 25, 1876.

Buffalo Bill and Yellow Hand knew and respected one another, which is one of the reasons Buffalo Bill got away with calling this Sioux chieftain Yellow Hand instead of his correct name, Yellow Hair. Therefore, it was only natural they would eventually vie for supremacy. Shortly after the Custer massacre, Buffalo Bill and a group of U.S. soldiers came upon a group of Indians led by Chief Yellow Hand at Warbonnet Creek. Yellow Hand dispatched a messenger with a challenge. Riding up to Buffalo Bill, the messenger cried out, saying Yellow Hand was the greatest of their warriors and would like to fight Pahaska (Buffalo Bill), as he was the bravest of the palefaces.

"That suits me fine," Cody responded.

Buffalo Bill and Yellow Hand both put their horses into a full gallop and raced toward each other. The following description of the confrontation comes from Buffalo Bill's own mouth as related later to Frederick Bonfils, one of the owners and publishers of *The Denver Post*.

 When we had come within about fifty yards of each other, we simultaneously raised our rifles and fired. My horse stepped a forefoot into a gopher hole and turned a complete somersault. I fell and rolled, losing my rifle. I was on my feet immediately, however, and shouted to let my comrades know I had been uninjured. I ran forward, drawing my bowie knife. I noticed now that Yellow Hand also was on foot. My shot had killed his horse, and the Chief had been thrown and had lost his rifle. He was brandishing a tomahawk.

As we closed in, I crouched to get inside the arc of his blow. He had his left hand extended to ward off any thrust I might make. Instead of stabbing at him, however, I feinted and dashed inside the arc of his blow, just as his tomahawk began its descent. I grappled with him, caught his right wrist, twisted him about, and then sank my bowie knife between his ribs beneath the left armpit. He fell, his mouth open and his eyes staring.

Moved by the thought of what had earlier happened to Custer, Buffalo Bill jerked off Yellow Hand's war bonnet, grabbed his hair, and scalped the fallen chief. And what did he do with the scalp? He sent it to his wife, who immediately fainted upon seeing it.

Some critics have tried to minimize the significance of Buffalo Bill's victory, saying Yellow Hand was in the last stages of tuberculosis at the time. But Buffalo Bill attested that "Yellow Hand was anything but an invalid."

Reference:

Gene Fowler, Timberline (New York: Garden City Books, 1933).

CHIEF WASHAKIE WAS A FRIEND OF THE WHITE MEN
~ FORT WASKAKIE, WY ~

"My son, rather than see you take up arms against the white man, I will strike you dead at my feet."

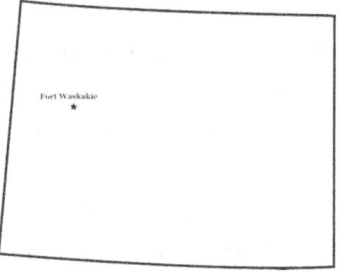

These words from Chief Washakie of the Eastern Shoshoni tribe to his son stemmed from an attitude that was very different from the more prevalent Indian attitudes toward the encroaching and untrustworthy whites. As a respected and powerful chief, and a staunch proponent of peaceful relations with the whites, Washakie had no tolerance for any deviations from this policy of peaceful coexistence, not even from his own son.

Because of the frequent inter-tribal raids and wars in the west, the only hope for survival for the smaller and weaker tribes lay in forming protective alliances with larger and more powerful tribes. Tribes also banded together in defiance of the white men. But to the Shoshonis in general and to Washakie in particular, an alliance with the powerful and numerically superior white men offered the ultimate in protection. The federal government's promises of food, protection, and instruction in agricultural pursuits further influenced the Shoshonis to seek peaceful relations with the whites.

The friendly relations between the Shoshonis and the whites began in 1805 (about the time of Washakie's birth) with the visit of the Lewis and Clark expedition, and they continued throughout Washakie's life. When the fur trappers met annually for their rendezvous, the Shoshonis were there, trading their own pelts for food, clothing, and guns. When the mountain men needed supplies and shelter, the Shoshonis came to their aid. Washakie encouraged these relations, although he did not like the Shoshoni practice of making their young women available to the whites.

On their westward migrations in the 1840s and 1850s, emigrants to Oregon, California, and the Salt Lake Valley felt an added sense of security when traveling through Shoshoni territory. The Mormon colonists, while making special efforts for friendly relations with the Indians of the plains, looked to the Shoshonis as friends and allies. In later years, one of Brigham Young's daughters was quoted as recalling: "Washakie, I remember, was located near the Sweetwater mining country at the time two of my uncles were Pony Express riders, and as a child I heard them say many times, when the Indians were bad on the trails, 'If we can only make Washakie's camp we are safe.'"

At one point of time, some of the younger Indians began to whisper that Washakie was becoming soft and weak because of his adamant stance of avoiding warfare with the Whites. Upon overhearing one of these conversations, Washakie quietly disappeared from his village, only to return a few days later carrying seven scalps he had taken from a band of hostile Indians. Waving the scalps for all to see, Washakie challenged the younger braves, "Let him who would take my place count as many scalps." There were no takers.

In the summer of 1883, President Chester Arthur spent a holiday hunting and fishing at Yellowstone National Park. Stopping at the Shoshoni agency headquarters, Fort Waskakie, the president visited Chief Washakie in his lodge and witnessed a mock battle between Indians and cavalrymen staged for the president. As part of the occasion, Washakie presented President Arthur with a fine pinto pony.

Arthur's only gift in return was the designation of Washakie as an honorary army scout.

One of Washakie's happier moments came on July 4, 1868, when he signed a treaty designating Wyoming's Wind River valley as a permanent home for the Shoshonis. He made sure that a school, instructors, a church, a mill, a hospital, farm implements and seed, and a protective army post were included. "I am laughing because 1 am happy because my heart is good."

Along with Quanah Parker of the Comanches, Chief Washakie saw the future and recognized the only course of action that could bring peace and prosperity to his people.

Reference:

The Great Chiefs (Alexandria, Virginia: Time-Life Books, 1975).

THE INDIANS HELP PETER SHIRT PLOW HIS FIELDS

~ PAROWAN, UT ~

PIONEER LIFE WAS DIFFICULT AND perilous on southern Utah's frontier. It was difficult because of the uncertain success of growing crops in that desert region with its infrequent rainfall. Despite the arid conditions, spring floods caused by the melting snow in the mountains frequently wiped out hastily constructed dams and sometimes destroyed entire settlements with loss of life to livestock and to humans. The relative isolation of the settlements from the more settled northern colonies added to the difficulties.

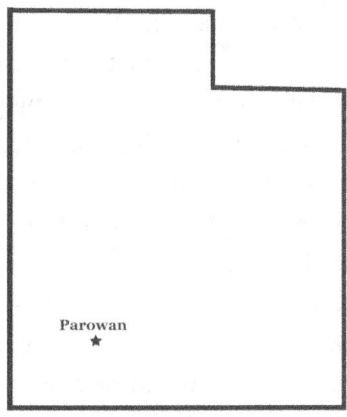

Life could also be perilous in southern Utah because the Indians, on the verge of starvation each winter, would steal, plunder, and even murder for food they needed to sustain themselves. Brigham Young's philosophy toward the Indians was that it was better to feed them than fight them. This policy worked as long as food was available to the Indians, and thus the Saints provided large amounts of food and clothing for the deprived Paiute Indians of that area. In their missionary zeal, the Saints also attempted to convert and baptize as many Indians as possible. Because the baptism of an Indian was usually accompanied by a gift of a blanket or a shirt, many of the Indians repeatedly showed up each spring to be re-baptized.

The Peter Shirts family settled in this environment, out on the southern Utah desert away from any settlement. With thrift, industry, and plain hard work, they managed to eke out a living sufficient to sustain themselves. To protect themselves from the plundering of hungry Indians, they built a wall around their gardens and living area, and thus they lived inside of a makeshift fort.

One spring after a particularly hard winter, a band of hungry Paiutes came seeking food and clothing. "I will share a little food with you, but I can't give you much. We didn't have much this year," Shirts told them. Although taking what was offered, the still-hungry Indians were dissatisfied. Convinced that Shirts was holding out on them, they attacked and tried to force their way into his fort. In the ensuing battle, one of Shirts' two oxen was killed. Even if he and his family survived the attacks, spring plowing would now be impossible.

Somehow, Shirts managed to communicate with the Indians and convince them that since he could not plow and plant seed, no one was going to have enough food that year. "You killed one of my oxen," Shirts told them. "Now we are all going to go hungry." Recognizing the gravity of the situation, the Indians laid down their weapons and agreed to cooperate. They allowed Shirts to hitch six of them to the plow, and thus these same Indians who had been trying to kill Shirts and his family were now pulling his plow and plowing his fields. Dire circumstances on the frontier had turned deadly enemies into cooperating allies.

Reference:

Juanita Brooks, *A Mormon Chronicle: The Diaries of John D. Lee* (San Marino: The Huntington Library, 1955), Vol. 2, pp 255-256.

EMMA LEE IS TERRIFIED BY SOME NAVAJO INDIANS
- MARBLE CANYON, AZ -

EMMA WAS SCARED. ALL ALONE AT Lonely Dell, site of Lee's Ferry across the Colorado River in northern Arizona, Emma knew that the Indians in the area were acting strangely. Knowing that Emma's husband, John D. Lee, was in jail for his role in the Mountain Meadows Massacre, the Indians in the Navajo camp near Lonely Dell appeared to be plotting mischief rather than their usual practice of trading or asking for food. At least, that was Emma's perception.

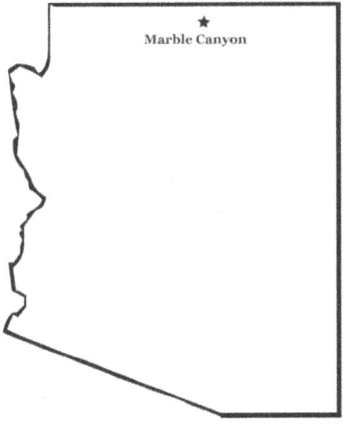

Alone with her six young children, Emma, became terrified when night approached. She knew that a locked door on her home would not be sufficient protection should the Indians decide to break in. Calling the children together for their usual evening prayer, she prayed differently this time. She prayed with an intense fervor for guidance and protection. The impression that came upon her surprised her.

Gathering quilts and pillows, Emma marched her children directly into the Indian camp and approached the chief. The chief was a friend of Emma's husband, John D. Lee, whom the Indians called Yawgett.

"I am afraid," she told him in a combination of Navajo and English. "See all my papooses. Yawgett's papooses. They are afraid, too. You are a big, brave chief. You are Yawgett's friend. Let us make our bed down here, close to your camp, so that you can watch over my tiny papooses."

Moved by Emma's appeal, the chief motioned to a smooth place in a clearing, and the family made their beds and slept there unmolested. The next morning when Emma awoke, the Indians were gone. She saw them in the distance walking single file toward Kanab.

At a later date, that same Navajo chief told Jacob Hamblin of the incident, and he concluded by saying that Emma was a "heap brave squaw."

Reference:

Juanita Brooks, *John Doyle Lee* (Glendale: The Arthur H. Clark Company, 1962).

SALINE SMITHSON WAS A SPECIAL PIONEER
~ WOODRUFF, AZ ~

SARAH ANN SALINA SMITHSON WAS the third of thirteen children in a family that helped settle the Mormon community of Woodruff, Arizona. The family engaged in farming, and Saline, as Sarah was called, assisted in all the chores. She plowed, cut, raked, and hauled hay. She hired out for twenty-five cents a day to help her neighbors, and she also did washing and house cleaning.

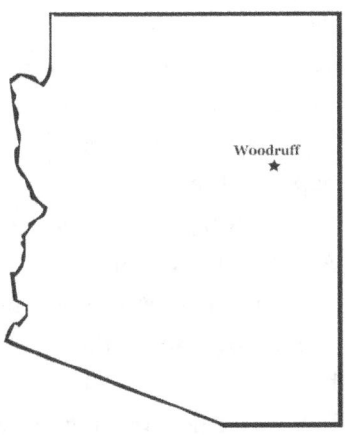

To earn money, her father and brothers drove wagons of freight to be delivered to Fort Apache, and Saline also became a freighter with skills equal to any of the men.

While resting on one of their trips to Fort Apache, the freighters encountered some Indians, one of whom took a great liking to Saline, who looked very pretty wearing a red dress trimmed with white braid. Riding up to one of the men in the company, the Indian offered ten horses for Saline. An offer of ten horses was indeed a tribute, but the Indian was talking to a man who did not understand the magnitude nor the seriousness of the offer.

"You can have her for two horses," the man jokingly countered. At that, the Indian rode away, but a short while later he returned leading two horses for his part of the bargain.

Riding up to Saline's wagon, the Indian motioned her to get on his horse behind him, and Saline, who knew nothing about the "deal" that had been made, refused. But a deal is a deal, and the Indian, who now considered Saline to be his property, grabbed her and attempted to pull her out of the wagon. As Saline struggled, the Indian grabbed her by her dress and was pulling with all his might when she picked up her black whip and struck both the Indian and his horse. The startled horse bolted and ran off with just the Indian on his back. By the time the Indian got his horse turned around, the male freighters, who had been away from their wagons during Saline's struggle, returned and were waiting at Saline's wagon when the Indian made a second approach. One of Saline's brothers, with pistol in hand, ordered the Indian to leave, and the wagon train proceeded on to Fort Apache.

When the commanding officer at Fort Apache learned what had happened, he became very concerned, and he advised the freighters not to stop on their return trip until they were completely out of the Apache reservation.

Saline's parents were not physically well, and when her mother was dying, the mother had Saline promise never to marry as long as her father lived. As the oldest child still at home, Saline cared lovingly for her father and her nine younger siblings until he also died. She then married Theodore W. Turley, a widower, who also had a large motherless family. It was a happy marriage, and Saline loved her new "children." At the age of forty-two, Saline finally had a child of her own who brought her great joy, although the daughter lived only twenty-six months.

At a later date, one of Saline's brothers paid her this tribute: "No one, no matter who or where they are, could have kept house better and taken better care of the children than she did."

Reference:

Marguerite Romney Pyper, contained in *An Enduring Legacy,* Vol. 5 (Salt Lake City: Daughters of the Utah Pioneers, 1982).

RELIGION AND CUSTOMS

THE LAST MAN TO DIE BY CREEK LAW
~ OKMULGUEE, OK ~

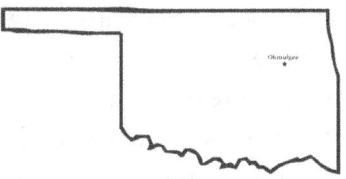

ON JANUARY 1, 1896, TIMMIE JACK, A Creek Indian, killed his friend, James Brown, in a drunken brawl at an Indian dance on the Creek reservation in Oklahoma. At Timmie Jack's trial, held on April 28, he was found guilty and sentenced to die on May 1. Creek law required execution for such a crime, and by Creek custom, death by shooting was the only acceptable method. White men may be pardoned or paroled for murder, but not so within the Indians' own laws.

The unique aspect of this episode is that Timmie Jack was never arrested nor held in jail. He was simply told to be on hand for the trial at the Creek District Court House in Okmulgee. On the appointed day he was there. After the guilty verdict and the sentencing, he was told to go home and settle his affairs, but to be at the Council House on May 1 prepared to pay his penalty. Again, he was there.

The day of execution was almost a gala occasion. Indians gathered from miles around with their families. White settlers and cowboys came. Picnic lunches were eaten under the shady elm trees. Timmie Jack mingled among the throng all day, introduced himself to those he did not know, and exchanged pleasantries with all. He could not say goodbye because there is no such word in the Creek language. But he did use a phrase which means "I will see you again, some where, some time."

Creek custom allowed Timmie Jack to name the time of execution and to name the executioner. Timmie chose Pleasant Berryhill, a captain in the Creek tribal police and one of the best shots in the Creek nation. Timmie wanted it to be as quick and painless as possible. Five o'clock was the designated hour.

Berryhill asked to borrow a rifle, because his own was in a scabbard on his horse over a block away. But Timmie said no. "Get your own Winchester. You know how it shoots." Timmie then embraced his family and friends for the last time, seated himself on a box, and leaned back against one of the elms. No blindfold nor bands were offered, nor would they have been accepted. A white doctor used his stethoscope to locate the exact position of Timmie's heart, and pinned a piece of white paper on the spot. Berryhill, 15 feet away, braced his Winchester on an elm tree, and for almost a full minute he and Timmie looked at each other eye to eye. Then Berryhill's rifle cracked, Timmie slumped forward, and the execution was consummated. Because the Creek nation was submitting itself to the laws of the recently formed Territory of Oklahoma, this was the last execution under Creek law.

Reference:

Museum of the Five Civilized Tribes at Muskogee, Oklahoma.

ARE THE TONKAWAS A FORGOTTEN PEOPLE?
- BASTROP, TX -

THE TONKAWA INDIANS WERE A peace-loving people in central Texas, but they were frequently at war defending themselves from their Comanche enemies. With the influx of Anglos into Texas, the White Men and the Tonkawas became allies in opposing the Comanches.

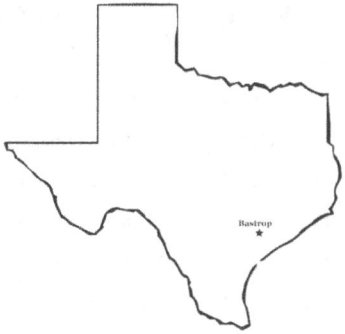

These two groups of allies coexisted for many years, but without either group assimilating the other. In fact, in their pride, the Tonkawas always maintained, "They joined us. We didn't join them." Despite their different ways of life, the two groups had much love and respect for one another.

The Tonkawas were also a spiritual people who took their religion seriously. As one example, their concepts included the belief that when they die, their spirit would leave the body through the head and would travel in a westerly direction to their ultimate destination. Therefore, when lying down to sleep at night, the Tonkawa would not lie with his head to the west lest his spirit be tempted to make a premature departure.

The Tonkawas feel they have a spiritual heritage binding them to Texas. For centuries, before their forced removal to Indian Territory in what is now Oklahoma, Texas was their home. Central Texas is where they were created by the Great Spirit, and it is the land of their birthright. It is the only place where their relationship with their Creator can fully flower without constraint. They maintain that their spiritual harmony cannot resume its natural condition as long as they are separated from their birthright home.

When the Federal government, in trying to rid Texas of Indians, moved the Tonkawas to a reservation in Indian Territory in the late 1870s, many of the Texan friends of the tribe promised that they would come up to Indian Territory and bring the Tonkawas back to Texas. But these words of intent were never backed up by action. Again, promises made to the Indians have been ignored, and again, the Indians feel betrayed. According to Terry Allen, a modern-day Tonkawan and historian for his tribe, "Many of the old people were really hurt and let down by the fact that the Texans never even contacted them once they were removed from the state."

Other problems have plagued the transplanted Tonkawas also. Without the protection of the Texans, their enemies have killed and decimated them as a nation. "And the Texans to this day," stated Henry Allen, a former chief, in a 1986 interview, "have not lifted a finger to help the Tonkawas out."

Reference:

Historical Museum, Bastrop, Texas.

THE GHOST DANCE SYMBOLIZED THE INDIANS' LAST GREAT HOPE
~ MASON VALLEY, NV ~

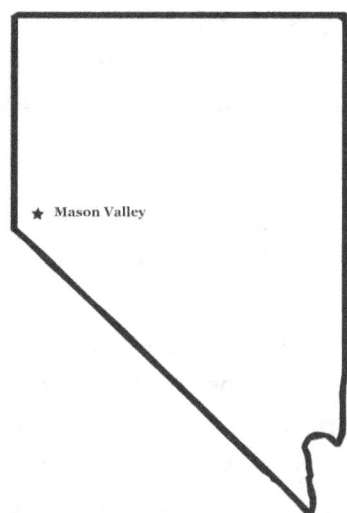

IN THE LATE 1880S, A RELATIVELY unknown and nondescript Paiute Indian went to heaven, was instructed by God, and returned to introduce a Messianic religion among the Indians of the western United States. Although Wovoka, whose Anglo name was Jack Wilson, never ventured outside his reservation in Nevada's Mason Valley, he became known throughout the West as the Indian Messiah.

Wovoka was a visionary man as his father had been, and over the years he had several experiences that established his reputation as a seer and a prophet among the Indians of western Nevada.

"If Paiutes need a prophet, I am that prophet," Wovoka preached. "Paiutes should have a Paiute prophet. I, Wovoka—on of Tavibo—am that man."

After visiting Wovoka in the winter of 1891-92, James Mooney, a

U.S. Government anthropologist, described him as "a young man, a dark full-blood, compactly built and taller than the Paiute generally, six feet in height." Mooney added that Wovoka's countenance was "open and expressive of firmness and decision."

Although accounts vary, it appears that Wovoka's first vision occurred in 1887 as he was sitting at home. With his head between his knees, he fell into a trance and gave every appearance of having died. Although his wife, Mary, and many friends made efforts to revive him, they worked in vain.

"He is dead," some claimed. "He must be buried."

"He is not dead," Mary insisted. "If he is dead, where is the stink of death? Why is there a warm spot near his heart?"

Mary's insistence prevailed, and Wovoka remained transfigured until the third day, when he began to revive. Two days later, after gaining sufficient strength, he called his people together to tell them about his three-day sojourn in heaven.

Wovoka spoke for over an hour about his experience in heaven and the things he had been commanded to teach to his people. He taught that the time was near for the Indians to become a united people.

"I saw Indians of every tribe, of every nation, walking arm-in-arm like brothers. One time they were enemies. Now they are as one."

Wovoka also taught that the Indians would soon be restored to their former state of glory. They would stand tall and handsome, and free from the oppressions of the white men. There would be no sickness, death, nor old age. And their final state would be a state of eternal bliss. To bring about this restoration the Indians would have to become a cleaner, more industrious, and more moral people.

"You must wash your sins away," Wovoka declared. "You must make yourselves pure before God and all the spirits that have gone before. For to you, my people, God has revealed a wonder that will go to Indians everywhere."

Wovoka then instructed the people in more specific terms.

"You must be good and love one another, have no quarreling, and live in peace with the whites. You must work, and not lie or steal. You must put away old practices that lead of war."

Thus, even though Wovoka preached a doctrine of eventual Indian supremacy, it was also a doctrine of peace and righteousness.

Along with these instructions, God instructed Wovoka to introduce a new dance among the Indians as a symbolic representation of their coming restoration. It was a dance that was to be performed at intervals for five consecutive days each time. By faithfully performing this dance, the Indians would secure their promised happiness and hasten the time of their ascendency over the white men. And thus was born the Ghost Dance.

Wovoka experienced additional trances over the next two years, and further instructions from on high emphasized those that had already been delivered.

Many Indian tribes believed Wovoka, and his new doctrine became a new great hope for them. From the east and from the north, tribe after tribe sent delegates to Mason Valley to meet Wovoka and learn first-hand of his religion and of the Ghost Dance. The Bannocks and the Shoshones in Idaho played major roles in spreading the message. From as far away as Indian Territory (now Oklahoma), the Arapahos sent a delegation. The Sioux in the Dakotas became fervent adherents, along with the Cheyenne, Mandan, Ute, Caddo Comanche, Kiowa, Pawnee, Delaware, Iowa, Kansas, Kickapoo, Wichita, and many others. Throughout the West, Indian tribes looked to the new Messiah and sought to hasten the fulfillment of his promises by dancing the Ghost Dance.

According to Mooney, who became an authority on the Ghost Dance, "The great underlying principle of the Ghost Dance doctrine is that the time will come when the whole Indian race, living and dead, will be reunited upon a regenerated earth, to live a life of aboriginal happiness, forever free of death, disease, and misery."

The dance is a circular dance of both males and females. Some tribes dance around a pole or a tree, while others use nothing in the center of the circle. Slowly the circle rotates in a clockwise direction as the dancers, with holy symbols painted in their faces, entwine their hands and move from right to left. The steps are simple and stately. As the left foot advances to the left, the right foot moves to where the left had been, while keeping time to the songs.

As the various tribes conducted their Ghost Dance ceremonies, a few variations naturally developed. Some tribes performed the dance on ground hallowed by a pre-dance dedication ceremony. Other tribes preceded the dance with song and with a purification ritual referred to by whites as a "sweat bath." In many tribes, the dance required fasting by the participants. In almost all tribes, the ritual included a ceremonial garment, or shirt, which constituted a protective shield for the wearer. After participating in the dance, the Indians could continue wearing these decorated shirts as a sacred protection against harm or death from the white men.

Although the Indians' intentions, as taught by Wovoka, were noble and peaceful, government officials looked upon the rapid spread of the Ghost Dance with considerable alarm. They became especially wary as they watched the infusion of the dance into the rebellious Sioux nation.

Within the Sioux nation, Sitting Bull and Red Cloud had accepted Wovoka's messiahship, and they looked upon the movement as a beginning of the liberation they so desperately wanted. Believing that by peaceful means they would finally be freed of the white man's oppression and double-dealing, they made the Ghost Dance a popular feature on their Pine Ridge and Rosebud reservations. But the Indian agent, already apprehensive of the Sioux's warlike tendencies, feared that another uprising might be forming, and he ordered the dance stopped. For a while the Sioux complied with the cease and desist order, but upon noting changes and indecisiveness among the government agents, they resumed the dance.

In October 1890, Sitting Bull invited Kicking Bear, the chief high priest of the Ghost Dance among the Sioux, to introduce the dance on Sitting Bull's own reservation of Standing Rock. Refusing new government orders to abandon the dance, Sitting Bull added to the government's long-standing mistrust of him. So in the midst of preparations to inaugurate the Ghost Dance at Standing Rock, government agents and Indian police swept in on December 15, 1890, in an attempt to arrest Sitting Bull. In the ensuing fracas, they shot and killed him.

Two weeks later, the Battle of Wounded Knee occurred. Riding into battle wearing their ceremonial protective garments which were supposed to protect them from harm and death, the Indian warriors were massacred. Short Bull, who had been one of the original Sioux delegates to Wovoka, later asked, "Who would have thought that dancing could make such trouble? The message I brought was peace. And that message was given by the Father to all the tribes."

With these two tragedies among the Sioux, the Ghost Dance began to fade in popularity, and the Indians' last hope of redemption from the oppression of the white men died.

References:

James Mooney, *The Ghost-Dance Religion and the Sioux Outbreak of 1890* (Washington, D. C.: Fourteenth Annual Report of the United States Bureau of Ethnology to the Secretary of the Smithsonian Institution, 1892-93).

Paul Bailey, *Ghost Dance Messiah* (Los Angeles: Westernlore Press, 1970).

Paul Bailey, *Wovoka, the Indian Messiah* (Los Angeles: Westernlore Press, 1957).

Harold Peterson, Ed., *I Wear the Morning Star* (Minneapolis: The Minneapolis Institute of Arts, 1976).

Russell Thornton, *We Shall Live Again* (Cambridge: Cambridge University Press, 1986).

INTRODUCTION

In the early and mid-1800s, a great gulf existed between the eastern states of America and the settlements of the west and southwest. In their relatively isolated environments, miners and other settlers of the southwest were starved for communication with relatives and friends and for news of happenings in the east. It took weeks for mail to be transported and delivered, and newspapers, when they did come, were weeks, or even months, out of date.

The early miners lived, not only for gold and silver, but also for mail from home, and local delivery systems came into being for connecting the mining camps of California and Nevada with San Francisco, which had become a distribution center for mail and messages. The people and the nation wanted a faster solution, and the pony express service came into being to provide that solution.

The pony express service operated between St. Joseph, Missouri and Sacramento, California, a 2,000-mile stretch through wild, unsettled country. Weather, terrain, and hostile Indians made it a treacherous journey. Although this service operated less than two years, it was an enterprise of exemplary bravery, endurance, and dedication. The riders were young, the Indians were a constant threat, and to say that the weather and terrain were challenges is a gross understatement. But the mail had to go through, and the young, mostly teenage riders made it happen. Depending on the weather, the trip took anywhere from ten to sixteen days with riders galloping full speed for shifts of 75 to 100 miles while changing horses every 10 to 15 miles. The pony express service was a glorious enterprise, but it was cut short by the completion of the transcontinental telegraph in 1861. Messages could now be transmitted instantly.

Overland travel for people and freight was also slow in the 1800s. Travel by stagecoach, uncomfortable at best, took many days depending on one's destination, and it was fraught with danger, especially in the west. Indians attacked for a variety of reasons, not the least of which was revenge for broken treaties and unfulfilled promises. Bandits attacked for wealth, as the stagecoaches frequently carried gold and silver as well as passengers. The Conestoga wagon became the symbol of overland transportation of people and freight. Machinery and heavy freight that could not be hauled overland made the journey by ship, traveling down the Atlantic, around Cape Horn, and up the Pacific to California. Whether overland or by sea, transportation of freight took weeks, sometimes months

With the completion of the transcontinental railroad in 1869, things changed dramatically. Effectively, two nations became one nation. Travel time between New York and California was now reduced to about seven days. Travel by stagecoach or by Conestoga wagon waned and eventually disappeared as rail lines spread out like spider webs. The completion of the telegraph from coast to coast in 1861 signaled the end of delayed communications, and now the completion of the transcontinental railroad in 1869 heralded a new era in coast to coast transportation.

MESSAGES

MAIL SERVICE WAS IMPORTANT TO THE WESTERN MINERS
- AMARGOSA, NV -

PEOPLE WHO COMPLAIN ABOUT THE U.S. Post Office in these modem times should have lived in the mining camps that proliferated the west a century and a half ago. Mail service then was sporadic and uncertain at best.

Mailboxes were unknown in all but the more established camps, and when the mail did arrive by mule or by wagon, some local person would do the distributing. With everyone gathered around in hopes of receiving something, he would shout out the name of each lucky recipient. When the last item was handed out, those who had received mail were the envy of the disappointed remainder. Coveted were the messages from home; even more coveted was the money occasionally included with the messages.

Sending mail out was also a problem. Stamps had to be purchased at a post office which might be miles away. And they had to be purchased with legal tender, not with company scrip that miners usually received as pay.

In 1904, a cluster of mining camps existed in southwestern Nevada. Amargosa, Bullfrog, South Bullfrog, and Rhyolite were all in close proximity with each other. When mail arrived by stagecoach from Goldfield, over 100 miles away, it would be put off at the general merchandise store in Amargosa. There the mail was deposited into a large box, and miners from their various locations would gather to Amargosa to sort through the box and pick out anything belonging to them.

Early in 1905, Bill Parker opened the Nye County Grocery Store, and when the mail arrived, Bill would climb onto a box and shout out names to the men, women, and children gathered around. If Bill became tired, another person would mount the box and continue the procedure until all the mail was "delivered." Once a month, the citizens would take up a collection, usually around $200, to pay the stage company for delivering the mail.

Special post office functions, such as money orders, registered mail, etc., could only be performed at established post offices. From the Amargosa area, miners had to travel five miles to Beatty for these services.

In June 1905, the postal service established a post office at Rhyolite. Mrs. Anna B. Moore was the postmistress, and her office was in a 10' x 12' tent. Whenever the stage came in with mail, the usual crowd gathered, and Mrs. Moore called out the names of recipients, even though the hour was sometimes approaching midnight.

Eventually Mrs. Moore procured a set of mail boxes, but her tent was not large enough to accommodate the mail boxes along with her other functions. Citizens then made a larger tent available in which Mrs. Moore could sort the mail and deposit it into the rented mail boxes. Within one day, all the mail boxes were rented, and bounties were offered to anyone who would give up a box.

Even though Rhyolite now had a post office, it could not get stamps from the postal service. Mrs. Moore had to make an arrangement with the Goldfield postmaster to order more stamps than he needed and send the surplus to Rhyolite. Whenever Rhyolite ran out of stamps, which was frequently, the miner were unable to send out any mail. At the end of 1905, many Christmas letters were not sent out of Rhyolite until the following February.

Although the postal service in Rhyolite improved over the next two years, the mines began to play out, and the miners began moving on. By 1908 they were looking for their mail in other locations, and mail service to Rhyolite was just a memory.

Reference:

Roberta M. Starry, "Christmas was Slim in Bullfrog," *Frontier Times*, December-January, 1973.

THE JACKASS EXPRESS PRECEDES THE PONY EXPRESS

- SUTTER CREEK, CA -

IN THEIR INITIAL YEARS OF EXISTENCE, the mining camps of the Sierra Nevada Mountains were almost completely isolated from the rest of the world. Although tons of mail traveled by sea around Cape Horn to the San Francisco post office, it sat as dead mail except when some person going to the mines was willing to add some mail to his otherwise full load of supplies. The miners were starved for news from the east, and when it did come, it was old news.

A young miner named Alexander Todd decided to take advantage of the situation. Touring the mining camps, he collected a dollar from every person who wanted him to bring mail back from San Francisco. His enterprise became known as the "Jackass Express."

Todd's enterprise showed itself in additional ways. As he passed through Stockton on his initial journey, merchants there asked him to carry their gold to San Francisco. Upon his agreement, they handed him $150,000 worth of gold dust to be transported at a five per cent carrying charge. In San Francisco, Todd got himself sworn in as a postal clerk and paid the post office twenty-five cents for each letter he picked up for his subscribers. He then bought a whale boat and filled it with passengers who paid him one ounce of gold for passage across the bay to Oakland. And the passengers had to do all the rowing.

Once across the bay, Todd stored the boat and loaded his saddlebags with hundreds of pieces of mail for his subscribers in the mines. Back on his mule once again, he headed back to the mountain mining camps where he delivered letters for $4.00 each and eastern newspapers for $8.00 each.

Although Todd continued this enterprise for a short time, it was not long before every camp and town in the gold mining region had its own "jackass express" in operation.

Reference:

Irving Stone, *Men to Match My Mountains* (Garden City: Doubleday & Company, Inc., 1956).

PONY EXPRESS RIDERS NEVER TURNED BACK
- SCHELLBOURNE, NV -

THE PONY EXPRESS SERVICE WAS ONE of the more glamorous aspects of America's westward expansion. Although it lasted less than two years (April 1860 to October 1861), this unique mail service gave rise to countless episodes of bravery and endurance. With the completion of the coast-to-coast telegraph line, this heroic service was no longer needed.

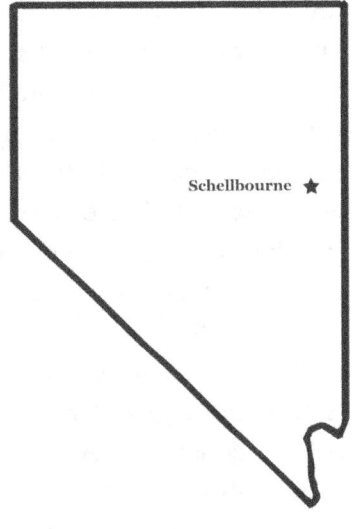

Pony Express riders had to be special. Physical stamina and personal bravery and integrity were essentials. Every Pony Express rider signed a contract of service and took an oath of allegiance to the company and its goals. The oath included the following provisions:

- At no time, except when carrying the mail, would the rider ever be more than one hundred yards from a relay station.

- The rider must be prepared to make his run at top speed, day or night, rain or snow, Indians or no Indians.
- Once on his run, the rider should never, under any circumstances, turn back.

Nick Wilson became a Pony Express rider at the age of fifteen. He was not afraid of Indians because he had just spent four years living with a group of Shoshone Indians as an adopted son of Chief Washakie's mother. He was already brave beyond his years.

As a Pony Express rider between relay stations in Utah and Nevada, Wilson drew an assignment to make runs between the Schell Creek Station (Fort Schellbourne) in Nevada and the Deep Creek Station near Toelle, Utah. His runs were through territory occupied by hostile Paiute Indians, who frequently staged uprisings.

On one of Wilson's mail runs westward from Deep Creek, his progress was suddenly interrupted by four Paiute warriors who jumped out from behind some large rocks. Whirling his horse to go around them, Wilson found his way blocked by three other Indians with arrows and a gun aimed at him. Having no other alternative, Wilson obeyed the Indians' order to dismount. A mean-looking one-eyed chief took Wilson's revolver and the reins of Wilson's horse. The Indians were tired of white trespassers on their land, and they had no intention of letting Wilson pass through.

Fortunately one of the Indians, an elderly warrior named Tabby, had been a friend of Wilson's father. Remaining flint-faced, Tabby showed no signs of having recognized Wilson, but Wilson knew that their eyes had met. As the Indians backed off and went into a pow-wow, Wilson was also aware that they were deciding whether or not to kill him. Hoping for the best, Wilson knew a unanimous vote would be required.

After a brief parley, Tabby walked over to where Wilson was waiting and explained that they would not allow Wilson to proceed, but also they would not kill him if he would turn and go back.

Appealing to Tabby, Wilson insisted the mail must go through, and if the Indians would let him proceed, he would never ride that trail again. Again the Indians went into a pow-wow, and again Tabby walked back to Wilson with a decision. The Indians, admiring Wilson's courage, agreed to let him pass onward provided he keep his promise never to ride that trail again.

Nick Wilson mounted his horse and sped away at a gallop. He delivered the mail successfully, and he kept his promise. Continuing to ride for the Pony Express, he left Utah and signed on for a different route in Nevada.

Reference:

Joseph J. DiCertto, *The Saga of the Pony Express* (Missoula, Montana: Mountain Press Publishing Company, 2002).

BUFFALO BILL RODE HARD FOR THE PONY EXPRESS
NEBRASKA AND WYOMING

WILLIAM F. CODY, LATER KNOWN AS "Buffalo Bill," got an early start on life. Orphaned at the age of eleven, Cody took a job with the western freight and transportation company 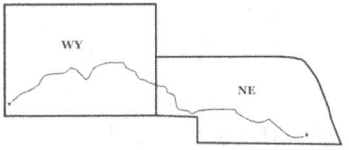 of Russell, Majors, and Waddell. In this first job, he helped haul freight for Johnston's Army on its march to quell a supposed Mormon rebellion in Utah. At the age of fourteen, Cody reached virtual manhood riding for the Pony Express during its brief but illustrious existence.

One of Cody's rides involved transporting a large sum of money, and "road agents" were out to steal the money. Arriving safely at a relay station with his saddle pouches still full of the money, Bill reasoned that on the next leg of his journey, he would pass through the most likely place for a holdup. He had to find a way to get past the expected bandits.

After walking longer than usual around the relay station, Bill devised his plan. He folded the precious pouches into his saddle blanket so they could not be seen. He next obtained another set of pouches, and after filling them with worthless material, he set out on the next leg of his journey. Arriving at the spot where he thought a robbery might be attempted, Bill found that his assumptions were correct. Two "road agents" were there waiting for him. As Bill approached, the two bandits jumped out of the brush and accosted him. One of the bandits held a rifle on Cody while the other took the reins of Cody's horse.

"Hold up, Pony Express boy," they yelled as they forced Cody and his horse to stop. "We know who you are and what you are carrying."

"What I have is worthless, and you will both be hung if you interfere with me," Cody retorted.

"We'll take our chances. Hand over your pouches."

Upon being commanded a second time to hand over the money, Cody raised the pouches of worthless material high and then slung them with force at the bandit holding the rifle. The bandit ducked, and as he bent over to pick up the pouches, Cody whipped out his pistol and shot the other bandit in the arm. He then spurred his horse into action and charged straight into the first bandit who was still bending over. With both bandits down, Cody kept his horse running at a gallop and eventually reached the next relay station safely and with the money still intact.

For a fourteen-year-old boy, this was an auspicious beginning of a life that made Buffalo Bill a living legend.

Reference:

William Lightfoot Visscher, *The Pony Express* (Golden: Outbooks, 1980).

TRANSPORTATION

THAT WAS NO LADY
~ RIVERSIDE, AZ ~

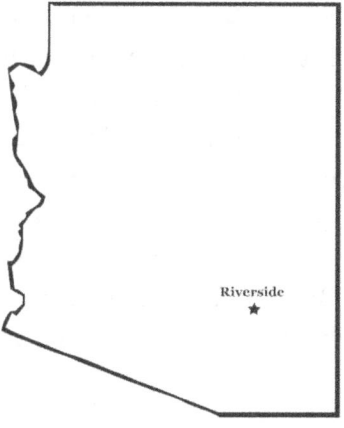

THE COMMAND, "THROW DOWN THAT BOX!' heard frequently along stagecoach routes, meant that the stagecoach was being robbed and the robbers were demanding the strongbox in which they expected to find money or precious ore. In hopes of being allowed to go free, the driver and the guard would usually throw the box down without resistance. Occasionally, however, they would try to outwit or outshoot the bandits.

The bandits sometimes had tricks of their own. One example occurred near Riverside, Arizona on August 10, 1883. Bandits stopped a stagecoach and called for the box, whereupon the Wells Fargo guard claimed that there was no gold being carried. At this point a lady passenger jumped from the stage and called the guard a liar.

"1 saw you putting gold into that box," she shouted.

As the guard reached for his gun, the female passenger pulled her gun from under her skirts and shot the guard dead.

It turned out that the lady wasn't really a lady after all. She, or rather he, was Jack "Red Jack" Almer, leader of the gang that was robbing the stage. Disguised as a woman, Red Jack had watched the gold being placed on the stage, and as a passenger, he signaled to his gang to attack. Red Jack and his gang fled with almost $3,000 in gold and currency.

Red Jack enjoyed a series of successful stagecoach robberies, particularly along the San Pedro River in southern Arizona, until finally one of the local sheriffs decided to rise to the occasion. With a large posse, Sheriff Bob Paul tracked down the gang and found Red Jack hiding near Wilcox, Arizona. In the gun fight that ensued, Sheriff Paul shot and killed Red Jack.

But the story is not quite over. Legend has it that over the years Red Jack had hidden about $8,000 in gold coins somewhere near Prescott, Arizona. As yet, this treasure has not been found.

The last stagecoach robbery in America took place on December 5, 1916 near Jarbridge, Nevada. The robber killed the driver and escaped with almost $4,000 in gold coins. But he left behind a telling clue - a bloody handprint on one of the letters in one of the mail sacks. From this clue, law authorities managed to find and identify Ben Kuhl, a local miner, as the culprit. Kuhl was tried and executed, but the stolen money was never recovered.

References:

"Legends of the High Desert" in the Legends of America Website, http://legendsofamerica.com.

"Dangers of the Trail," in the U. S. Postal Website.

THE POETIC STAGECOACH ROBBER
~ SAN FRANCISCO, CA ~

HIS NAME WAS CHARLES E. BOLES. HE was a gentleman who occasionally wrote poems, and he was highly respected by those who knew him. He also robbed stagecoaches. Known throughout central California as Black Bart, Boles's robberies netted him about $6,000 a year, a nice sum of money in those times.

Boles liked to read the serial adventure stories that appeared in the local newspapers, and he was particularly enthralled by one serial called "The Case of Summerfield" in which one of the villains is dressed in black and is known as Black Bart. This character became Boles's hero, and Boles used the name of Black Bart when on his stagecoach robbing escapades. Boles (a.k.a. Black Bart) perpetrated his robberies in gentlemanly style. His command to "throw down the box" was always preceded by the word, "please." He never asked the stagecoach passengers to step out, explaining that he did not intend to rob them. And after sending the stagecoach on its way, Bart sometimes tacked to a tree a piece of paper on which he had written a poem. Californians knew him as a daring, but unusual, bandit.

Born in England in 1829, Boles came to America with his parents two years later. In 1849, Boles and a cousin made their way to California, where they mined for gold with some success. After a trip back to the east, Boles returned to California and resumed mining for a few more years. Then he gave it up, returned to his home in Decatur, Illinois, and married. By 1861, he was the father of two daughters. He then served three years in the Union army during the Civil War. Returning to the west, something unknown happened between Boles and the Wells Fargo company which left Boles very bitter toward Wells Fargo. He vowed he would get even.

Boles is credited with 28 stagecoach robberies, with all but the last being successful. On July 25, 1878, after robbing a stagecoach of $379 and a diamond ring worth $200, he left the following poem:

> *Here I lay me down to sleep*
> *To wait the coming morrow*
> *Perhaps success perhaps defeat*
> *And everlasting Sorrow*
> *Let come what will I'll try it on*
> *My condition can't be worse*
> *And if theres (sic) money in that box*
> *Tis money in my purse*

The poem was signed "Black Bart."

Black Bart's last robbery occurred on November 3, 1883. On the Sonora to Milton route in California's Calaveras County, a stagecoach driven by Reason E. McConnell was struggling up a particularly steep hill when Black Bart stepped out onto the road and stopped it. McConnell's companion, nineteen-year-old Jimmy Rolleri, had gotten off the stagecoach a short while earlier to do some hunting with his repeating rifle. Black Bart told McConnell to start walking while he (Bart) attempted to pound open the money box. McConnell found Rolleri, and together they ran back to the stage and opened fire with their repeating rifle. Carrying some gold but dropping the mail, Black Bart ran for the bushes and made his escape.

Black Bart dropped more than mail, however. He dropped his derby hat, and he left food, field glasses, and other items behind a rock. He also dropped a handkerchief containing a laundry mark, FX07, and that was his undoing. Wells Fargo detective James B. Hume queried 91 San Francisco laundries and finally found one that could identify the owner of the laundry mark. It belonged to Charles Bolton, a respected mining engineer living only four blocks from the Wells Fargo office. Hume then made the arrest, and found that Bolton was really Charles E. Boles.

After being tried and convicted, Boles received a six-year sentence in San Quentin penitentiary; however, he was out in four years for good behavior. Upon his release, a bevy of reporters met him as he emerged from the prison. One asked "Do you plan to rob any more stagecoaches?"

"No, gentlemen," Boles responded, "I'm all through with crime."

"Are you going to write any more poetry?" another asked.

"Same answer," Boles said. "I'm all through with crime."

The ultimate fate of Boles is unknown. He was last seen on February 28, 1888 at the Nevada House in San Francisco. The next day he was gone, having left his belongings behind. He simply disappeared

Reference:

"Black Bart" in the Shadows of the Past Website.

WHEN THE RIO GRANDE RAILROAD BUILT INTO ROLLINSVILLE
~ ROLLINSVILLE, CO ~

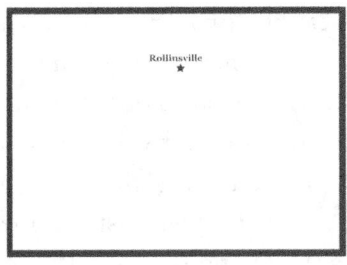

CELEBRATIONS WERE USUALLY IN order whenever a railroad built into an existing town, and the Denver and Rio Grande's 1904 entry into Rollinsville, Colorado, was no exception. The arrival of a railroad meant prosperity for a frontier town, and it meant another measure of accomplishment for the railroaders. The Rio Grande's work crew had built up through rugged Boulder Canyon, had fought snowstorms and snowdrifts, and had crossed the Continental Divide by tunneling under it. They overcame incredible difficulties, and they maintained their schedule while doing it. When they arrived in Rollinsville, they were ready to celebrate.

The last spike was scheduled to be driven on a Saturday evening, but when the Rio Grande crew learned that two barrels of whiskey were on hand and that twenty ladies of "assorted ages" had arrived from Denver, they got renewed energy and the work schedule was suddenly accelerated. With their renewed vigor, they hammered the last spike into place six hours early. Taking the town by surprise, the brass band hired for the occasion was not ready, the whiskey was locked up somewhere, and most of the town's men were still at work in the mines. But the celebration began anyway, and it was a celebration to beat all celebrations.

Only three gallons of whiskey could be found, but that was enough until the two barrels could be located. The work crew lined up and politely passed the jugs from mouth to mouth, but the politeness didn't last much longer than that. They broke into singing and dancing, speech-making, and yelling. One of the crew, John Christiansen, wanted to do a parachute jump, so he climbed a 50-foot precipice behind the saloon and with a yell, leaped into the air. Although he was not critically injured, his fellow celebrants hauled him to Dr. Baughman's in a wheelbarrow for temporary repairs.

Every celebration needs explosions, so the work crew located the gunpowder supply, and in a couple of hours there was not an ounce left in town. Then someone thought of the gasoline, and in spite of its scarcity, two drums were set off with appropriate ceremony.

Darkness finally came, and fireworks from Denver were set off to finish the day. For fifteen minutes the air was filled with displays of all colors. But not very many of the work crew were in any condition to appreciate the sight.

The Denver Post summed up the celebration as follows: "The rails are laid and the casualties can be summed up as follows: One man in hospital. Eighty-seven men who should be there. All the liquor in town consumed. Not an ounce of powder to explode and probably all the gasoline gone up in smoke." Rollinsville had had its celebration.

Reference:

The Denver Post, May 2, 1904.

THE HARVEY HOUSES WERE AN AMERICAN INSTITUTION
- TEMPLE, TX -

FOLLOWING THE CIVIL WAR, FRED Harvey was appalled at the poor food services available to train travelers in America. Trains at that time had no dining cars. At, or near, meal times, trains would stop at a convenient station, and passengers would step off the train and go into a local eatery for their meal. The available food was often cold and stale. And even if it had been good food, there usually was not enough time to eat it. After a stop of thirty minutes or less, the engineer would blow the whistle, and the passengers would have to scurry immediately back to the train. Walking to the eatery, ordering, and waiting for the food to be prepared and served frequently left passengers with no time at all to eat. In some cases, the cafe merely put the uneaten food away and served it to passengers on the next train.

Harvey set about to change all that. A native of England, Harvey had come to the United States at the age of fifteen, and he immediately found work in a New York City restaurant. After becoming a successful restaurateur, Harvey migrated to the railroad industry where he also ascended to the upper echelons. His knowledge of what could be done in providing quality food service, coupled with his observations of how little was actually being done for railroad passengers, led Harvey to a meeting in 1870 with Charlie Morse, president of the Atchison, Topeka, and Santa Fe Railroad.

"You provide the train service," Harvey proposed, "and I'll provide the food service." They shook hands, and Harvey went to work.

Harvey established restaurants in major Santa Fe depots. At a variety of other stations along the Santa Fe's line, Harvey established restaurants in separate buildings adjacent to Santa Fe depots. His concept was to treat train travelers to good food at reasonable prices in clean, elegant restaurants, and he succeeded in a grand way. The Harvey Houses soon became an American tradition along with baseball and apple pie. At its peak, the Harvey Company had 84 such establishments.

Harvey's procedure was to have the passengers place their food orders while still on the moving trains before reaching the next Harvey House. The orders would then be telegraphed ahead, and hot, delicious food would be ready and waiting for instant consumption. The plan worked beautifully.

Harvey Houses were noted for their pleasingly elegant decor. Another feature of the Harvey Houses were the waitresses—Harvey girls wearing black dresses with white aprons. Although the Harvey Houses were mostly in the West, the waitresses were usually hired from the East. They received $17.50 per month, free room and board, and clean uniforms. They also received many offers of marriage.

Although the Harvey Girls were part of the ambience, it may surprise some to know that Harvey started initially with local men as waiters. This did not last very long, however. One night at the Harvey House at Raton, New Mexico, the male waiters had a little too much to drink, and they got into a brawl that emptied the establishment. Harvey quickly determined that young women were much less likely to act in such a manner, and besides, they would bring an ambience that male waiters could not provide.

COMMUNICATION LINKS

When the Santa Fe railroad began including dining cars on its trains in the 1890s, Fred Harvey met the challenge by getting the contract to provide the dining car food. His company continued to thrive, and the established Harvey Houses began catering to the general public as well as to train passengers. But with the decline of railroad passenger travel after World War II, the demise of the Harvey Company followed.

Old traditions die slowly, however, and the tradition of the Harvey Houses is being revitalized by a number of restoration projects in former Harvey House facilities. Museums, bed and breakfast services, and soon some restaurants will keep the tradition from fading away.

Reference:

Chris Cooper, "Comfort on the Line," *Texas Journey*, May/Jun3 2005.

Displays at the Santa Fe Depot Museum, Temple, Texas.

"Harvey Houses" Website.

MINNIE ISGREEN TWICE ESCAPED DEATH

- SALT LAKE CITY, UT -

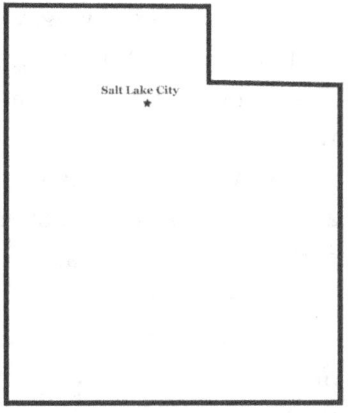

BEFORE THE ISGREEN FAMILY emigrated from Sweden to Utah, Minnie Isgreen, while still an infant, became ill and was believed to be dying. Minnie's young mother, however, was sure the Lord would answer her prayers and restore the child to health. Despite her prayers, the child did die, but the mother still refused to accept that verdict. Then looking out the window, the mother saw two LDS missionaries walking by, and she called to them to come in and administer to Minnie. They did so, and Minnie was restored to life.

Two years later, the Isgreen family left Sweden for Hamburg, Germany, where they boarded a ship bound for America. Shortly after setting sail, measles broke out among the passengers, and as there was no way to establish a quarantine area, most of the children contracted the disease. Many of the children, including Minnie, died. The ship's doctor pronounced Minnie to be dead and had her body prepared for burial at sea.

After a number of dead bodies were gently slid on a long plank into the sea, Minnie was scheduled to be the next to go. Again, Minnie's mother could not accept the death of her child, and again she called for the Elders. The ship's captain, impressed with the mother's plea, found two LDS missionaries on the ship and gave them the opportunity to administer to Minnie. And again, she was restored to life.

When the family arrived in Utah, they settled in Tooele. After a few years, there were seven children in the family, and Minnie was especially fond of her three younger sisters. She was devastated when these three sisters contracted diphtheria and died within a few weeks of one another. In an effort to help Minnie overcome her grief, the family sent her to Salt Lake City to live with some friends.

Minnie, still grieving, was surprised late one night when she realized she was not alone in her room. There stood her three sisters. They had a long conversation in which Minnie asked them if they were happy.

"We would be," they responded, "if you wouldn't grieve for us—we are all right. You can join us later, but you have a mission to perform first on earth. You will be the mother of a large family, and you will live to be an old woman."

The next morning when Minnie came down to breakfast, the lady of the house asked her, "Who did you have in your room last night? We heard children's voices." That was confirmation to Minnie that she had not been dreaming.

Minnie Isgreen eventually married Charles Peacock. She became the mother of ten children, and she died at the age of eighty-one.

Reference:

Jennie B. Huffaker, contained in Kate B. Carter, *Heartthrobs of the West,* Vol. 10 (Salt Lake City: Daughters of the Utah Pioneers, 1932).

EZEKIEL SAW THE WHEEL, AND REVEREND CANNON SAW THE FLYING MACHINE
~ PITTSBURG, TX ~

IN 1902, FULLY A YEAR BEFORE THE Wright brothers' flight, the Reverend Burrell Cannon built a flying machine that flew in a field outside of Pittsburg, Texas. The airship looked like a giant mushroom with a series of large wheels under a 26-foot circular canvass canopy. A gasoline powered engine turned four sets of  paddles mounted on wheels, and the pilot, sitting in the center of the machine, could control the angles of the paddles with a lever. The machine had no resemblance to a conventional airplane, but no one then knew what a conventional airplane should look like. Cannon, who designed the airship, got his inspiration from the Book of Ezekiel in the Holy Bible.

> *The appearance of the wheels and their work was like unto the color of beryl; and they four had one likeness; and their appearance was as it were a wheel within the middle of the wheel.*

--Ezekiel 1: 16

And when the living creatures went, the wheels went by them; and when the living creatures were lifted up from the earth, the wheels were lifted up.
--Ezekiel 1: 19

In addition to being an ordained Baptist minister, Cannon was an expert carriage maker, gunsmith, blacksmith, and machinist. Starting in 1883 with these verses from Ezekiel, Rev. Cannon developed a mental picture of a flying machine, and he spent the next 20 years modeling and refining his design. Needing money with which to finish the project, Cannon managed to convince friends that his machine could actually fly, and in August 1901, they organized the Ezekiel Airship Manufacturing Company, which was capitalized at $20,000 by selling stock at $25 per share. Cannon and a Mr. Stamps built the airship in the upper floor of P. W. Thorsell's machine shop in Pittsburg.

Although the Ezekiel airship's first (and only) flight occurred in 1902, the exact date has been lost. With Stamps as pilot, the airship made its maiden flight from a pasture owned by Thorsell. Stamps started the engine, and the ship jumped forward and then rose vertically 10 to 12 feet into the air where it stayed. It even moved forward while in the air. Severe engine vibrations, however, caused Stamps to bring the ship back down to earth. Even though refinements were needed, Cannon and his backers were ecstatic. Stock prices rose to $1,000 per share.

Cannon's next move was to load the Ezekiel airship onto a railroad flat car bound for the 1903 Sl. Louis World's Fair where a $100,000 prize awaited the first person who could make a "sustained controlled flight." Cannon's dreams were dashed when a violent wind blew the Ezekiel off the railroad car near Texarkana, Texas, and smashed it to pieces. The airship never made it to St. Louis.

The crestfallen Cannon is said to have muttered, "God never

willed that this airship should fly; I want nothing more to do with it." He never even tried to recover the pieces. Angry feelings existed for many years in Pittsburg among holders of the now worthless stock certificates, and Cannon went to work as a sawmill operator in order to support himself.

Cannon was down, but he was not out. Five years after his first experiment, he was ready to try it again. From 1908 until 1913 he sold stock in Longview, Texas, to finance a second airship which he built in Chicago. A pilot named Wilder flew this second version of the Ezekiel airship in 1913. But as the machine rose into the air, it hit the top of a utility pole and came crashing down. This ended forever Cannon's attempts with flying machines.

Burrell Cannon spent the remainder of his life in Longview and in nearby Marshall. He died in Marshall in 1922 at the age of 74. At the time of his death, he was in the process of perfecting a cotton picker and a boll weevil destroyer.

A post script reference to Cannon's Ezekiel airship in Pittsburg must be added here. In 1977, the Texas Historical Commission erected a historical marker at the edge of the pasture where the airship flew. Then in the 1980s, townsfolk banded together and had a local carpenter build a full-size replica of the airship which is now on display at the Northeast Texas Rural Heritage Museum in downtown Pittsburg. The beautiful model is an awe-inspiring thing to behold.

References:

The Ezekiel Airship, brochure of the Pittsburg/Camp County (Texas) Museum Association.

Denton Record Chronicle, December 3, 2003.

Dallas Morning News, November 25, 1901.

GEORGE U. HUBBARD

Wall Street Journal, November 20, 2002.

Texas Monthly, January 2003.

Texas Highways, May 2003.

THE SANTA FE TRAIL HAD NO COMFORTS

- BENT'S FORT, CO -

THE 1846 JOURNEY FROM INDEPENDENCE, Missouri to Santa Fe, New Mexico was supposed to be a comfortable and pleasant experience for Susan Magoffin, the eighteen-year-old wife of a wealthy Santa Fe trader. Because his wife was pregnant at the time, Mr. Magoffin provided her with a "tent house," private carriage, books, notions, a maid, a driver, and at least two servant boys. It can be assumed that no one was better provided for on such a journey.

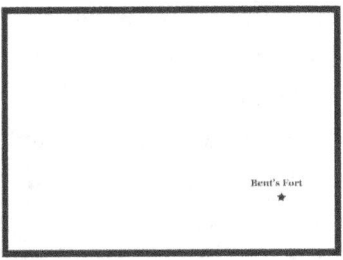

Bent's Fort

Mr. Magoffin had done everything he knew to do to provide for his wife's comfort. But there were elements on the trail that he couldn't guard against. The mosquitoes were relentless. Although Susan slept under mosquito netting, she was still covered with large red welts, some of which were "quite as large as a pea," she recorded in her diary.

At the Ash Creek crossing in Kansas, Susan's carriage overturned going down the steep creek bank. In her diary she wrote that the damaged carriage was a "perfect mess." Although shaken up and with a sore back and side, Susan seemed not to be seriously hurt.

Two weeks later, the party experienced a prairie thunderstorm. Words cannot adequately describe the violent intensity of such storms nor the terror a person may experience when caught in such a storm. With a succession of lightning bolts striking the ground accompanied by deafening claps of thunder, one can be truly awed by the ferocity that nature can assume.

"The lightning flashed its awful tongue in all directions," she wrote, "till the whole heavens seemed in one light blaze. The angry thunder raised its course notes, peal after peal. And the dark clouds poured down the rain. The tent shook violently, and without a groan sunk to the flooded Earth!" A poetic description of a dreadful experience.

After finally arriving at Bent's Fort in southern Colorado, Susan celebrated her nineteenth birthday. She also gave birth to the child she had been carrying. However, it was born several months too early, and it died.

Susan and her husband spent an additional twelve days at Bent's Fort while she recovered some of her strength. They then resumed their journey to Santa Fe. Except for spending five days to cross Raton Pass, the rest of their journey was uneventful, and they arrived in Santa Fe in the middle of August 1846.

While traveling between Santa Fe and Mexico with her husband on trading ventures, Susan contracted yellow fever, and she lost another child. The couple eventually returned to Missouri to live. Susan, however, never fully regained her strength, and she died in 1855 at the age of twenty-eight after successfully giving birth to a baby girl.

Reference:

"Susan Magoffin," *Trail Traveler*.

TRAIN TRAVEL IN THE LATE 1800S HAD ITS INTERESTING ASPECTS
- GRENADA, CO -

WHEN ONE THINKS OF THE excitement and perils of train travel in the late 1800s, one usually thinks of robberies and wrecks, but there were a lot of other things that helped make the trips memorable. A case in point is the Santa Fe railroad in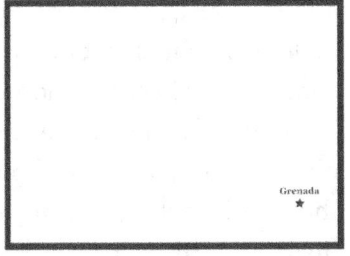
southeastern Colorado in 1870s. Building west from Dodge City, Kansas, the line reached the town of Grenada in the southeast corner of Colorado in 1873. With Grenada being at the end of the line, passengers going farther westward would have to continue their journey by taking wagons or stagecoaches. The trip from Dodge City to Grenada, however, frequently had interesting occurrences.

Night trains out of Dodge City ran without lights, and as a result, they could not run safely at full speed. This was a defensive measure by the railroad because a favorite sport of Dodge City citizens was to shoot the headlights out of passing trains.

Passengers on the trains did their share of shooting also. When passing through a herd of buffalo, passengers would break out the windows of the train cars, and then fire their rifles on the buffalo for sport. In the winter time, this sport had its consequences because the coal stoves in the cars were not up to the task of keeping the cars warm when the cold air rushed in through the windows that had been shot out.

There were no fences alongside of the track to keep cows and buffalo off the track. The engine headlight, if it worked at all, was not strong enough to illuminate more than 100 feet of track at night. Whenever a herd of cattle were sighted, the fireman put down his shovel and picked up a pike-pole and ran ahead of the train prodding the cattle off the track. As might be expected, the trains ran slowly under such conditions.

Keeping enough water in the tender tank for the engine to generate needed steam could also be a problem. When the water in the tender tank became too low, the train would stop alongside of the Arkansas River, or some other stream, and the train crew would form a bucket brigade to 'jerk" water from the river and into the tender tank. Passengers frequently assisted. As a result, that portion of the Santa Fe line became known as the Jerkwater Line.

Somehow the Santa Fe persevered and overcame these many obstacles, and the route from Dodge City to Granada became a part of the overall system carrying the famous Super Chief and other streamliners and freight trains that eventually ran between Chicago and Los Angeles.

Reference:

Ava Betz, *A Prowers County History* (Lamar, Colorado: The Prowers County Historical Society, 1986).

WHO STOLE MY DEPOT?
- LAMAR, CO -

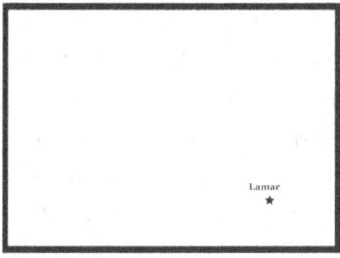

WHEN A NEW GROUP OF LAND promoters from Garden City, Kansas, decided in 1886 to organize the town of Lamar in southeastern Colorado, they entered into competition with an earlier group of promoters who had already established several successful town sites.

Although the Lamar site, situated on the Santa Fe railroad, was one of the last areas still available along the railroad, its promoters considered it a perfect site. It was also on the Arkansas River, and the fertile land was good for farming and for ranching. Only one thing was lacking—a railroad stop.

The Santa Fe railroad already had a depot, Blackwell Station, four miles to the east of the proposed Lamar site. It was on a ranch owned by Amos R. Black, one of the earlier land promoters. Even though the Santa Fe railroad officials favored the Lamar site and its promoters, it was understood by all that the railroad would never allow two railroad stops within four miles of one another.

Black had no desire to see another depot within four miles from the one he already had, and he refused to cooperate in any way with this new group of promoters who he recognized as competitors. Black denied their request to move the depot, and he also denied their request to purchase the property on which his depot stood.

The new group of promoters, however, were not to be denied. They arranged for a telegram to be delivered to Black on May 22, 1886, summoning him to Pueblo for some "important business." Black obliged by boarding the westbound train that day. That evening a work train steamed into Blackwell Station loaded with all the able-bodied men that could be recruited for ten dollars plus all the beer and whiskey they could drink at a dance after the work was completed. At midnight, the work was under way. Equipped with picks, shovels, jacks, and other tools, the workers lifted the Blackwell Station depot and loaded it onto the flat cars of the work train. It was a two-story frame structure, and living in the upper floor was Black's foreman, J. A. MacDowell, and his family. Despite their protests, the MacDowells were left standing by the empty tracks as the work train and the depot departed for Lamar.

Not only did the men move the depot, they also moved necessary outbuildings, cattle loading facilities, and equipment. The move was so timed that they reassembled everything in Lamar on a Sunday so that no court order nor injunction could be filed to stop the work.

When Amos Black returned from Pueblo, he was angry about being summoned there for nothing. Then when he stepped off the train onto what he thought was his ranch, he exploded. It was his depot all right, but the surroundings were not the same.

"Who stole my depot?" he roared. "Who is responsible for this?" With pistol in hand, he went in search of the responsible persons, but no one seemed to know anything. In the end, Black went home, walking the four miles to get there, and Lamar, with its "new" depot, was on its way to becoming the major city in southeastern Colorado.

Reference:

Ava Betz, *A Prowers County History* (Lamar, Colorado: The Prowers County Historical Society, 1986), 190-193.

INTRODUCTION

In the emerging development of the American West, the "law west of the Pecos" was more than just a clever phrase. Law and order, where it existed, took a variety of forms. Court sessions and sworn testimonies could be extremely informal. If a court house did not yet exist, trial sessions were held in barrooms, on front porches, under trees, or anywhere else where shade and protection from weather conditions was needed.

Where authorized law enforcement personnel were not available, citizens took the law into their own hands. Vigilante committees were formed as needed to take care of specific situations, and then when their action was completed, they would disband. At least a modicum of organization and order normally prevailed. Justice was usually swift, with trial and punishment frequently not taking more than an hour or two.

As more formal processes such as courts and designated officials began to replace the vigilante committees and direct citizen action, the crime rate increased rather than decreased. This is because the court systems slowed the process of justice, and many of the designated officials were either weak or were as corrupt as anyone else. For example, Officer Jack Williams of Virginia City, Nevada was believed to be one of that camp's most notorious criminals. Bribery of judges and jurors became a common practice.

Gunslingers abounded. Cattle rustling and the robbery of banks, trains, and stagecoaches led the list of perpetrated crimes, and hanging seems to have been the preferred means of punishment. It is believed that face-to-face shoot outs, seen so frequently in the movies, were extremely rare. Most shootouts were from hidden assailants or in situations where the outcome was fairly certain. Still, many of the gunslingers exhibited a considerable degree of braveness and daring, and several are legends to this day.

In the long run, law and order prevailed in the developing southwest, although it did have its growing pains.

FRONTIER JUSTICE

FRONTIER COURTS GOT THE JOB DONE
- NEVADA CITY, NV -

THE FRONTIER SYSTEMS OF JUSTICE didn't waste time or words on lengthy trials or legal jargon. In their states of relative isolation, they got the job done quickly and then went about their normal business.

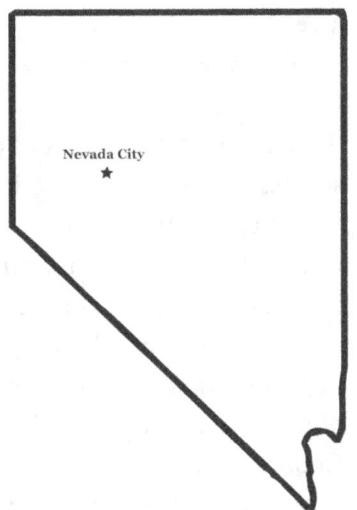

The "Rules and Regulations" adopted by the miners at Gold Hill, Nevada give a good example of the lack of confusing legal jargon.

Section 1 -- Any person who shall willfully and with malice aforethought take the life of any person shall, upon being duly convicted thereof, suffer the penalty of death by hanging.

Section 2 -- Any person who shall willfully wound another shall, upon conviction thereof, suffer such penalty as the jury may designate.

Section 3 -- Any person found guilty of robbery or theft shall, upon conviction thereof, be punished with stripes or banishment as the jury may determine.

Section 4 -- Any person found guilty of assault and battery, or exhibiting deadly weapons, shall upon conviction, be fined or banished as the jury may determine.

Section 5 -- No banking game under any consideration shall be allowed in this district, under penalty of final banishment from the district.

No involved definitions were needed. Everyone knew that punishment with stripes meant a back lashing. Everyone also knew that banking games were schemes to defraud a person of his money or assets.

The rules were simple, and the punishment was sure. One Nevada City pioneer was quoted as saying, "1 saw Charley Williams whack three of our fellow citizens over their bare backs twenty-one to forty strokes for stealing a neighbor's money."

Although there were many cases in which judges and jurors yielded to bribery or intimidation, there were many other situations in which judges exhibited the integrity and devotion to justice expected of those holding such offices. Justice was usually more important than formality, and many judges put up with no foolishness of any kind. A case in point is a Dr. Gally, Justice of the Peace in Nye County, Nevada.

In a trial held in his own log cabin, Gally presided over a case between Harry Newton, a mining operator, and Alexander McVey, a rancher. The two antagonists had been in a quarrel in which Newton had threatened McVey with a revolver. McVey had Newton arrested, and the two, along with their wives, were now before Justice of the Peace Gally. Newton was displaying an ugly temper, and McVey was in no good mood either. At one point, the situation became overly heated, and when Newton made a move as if to draw a gun, McVey grabbed a satchel his wife had been holding.

"Hold it," roared Gally, and when the two antagonists looked, they saw Gally with a shotgun aimed at both of them.

The two men sat down, and Newton's gun was taken from him. McVey claimed that he had no gun, but upon Gally's order, his satchel was opened and inside was a large revolver. The trial ended with Gally ordering Newton to appear before a higher court at Belmont, the county seat, and Gally fixed Newton's bail at $1,000. Newton said he would not pay such a bail, so with shotgun in hand again, Gally said, "You will pay or go to jail."

Newton paid, later explaining that he could not refuse to obey the order of a court that was run with a shotgun.

Reference:

W. A. Chalfant, *Gold, Guns, & Ghost Towns* (Stanford: Stanford University Press, 1958).

MARY MCCANN WAS TOO BUSY TO STAND TRIAL
~ BODIE, CA ~

FRONTIER JUSTICE WAS USUALLY METED out without frills and without time-consuming formality. Before courts could be established in a community, vigilante committees took care of criminal offences with speed and informality. Once court systems were established, speed suffered somewhat, but much informality remained until the judicial process "matured." Often, court sessions had to be held at the convenience of the defendant as well as of the plaintiff. An example of inconvenient scheduling is found in the mining town of Bodie, California in the mid-1800s.

Mary McCann, a janitor at the school house, was tough. She was usually seen wearing a beat-up man's hat, a man's vest, and a woman's skirt. Her language was as salty as it could be, and she could be physically abusive when provoked. On one occasion, when a neighbor suggested that she marry him, he got his answer in the form of two black eyes and a broken nose.

For reasons unknown, Mary had a running feud with the owner of a brewery next door to where she lived in Bodie. On one occasion she clogged the sewer so that it backed up into the brewery's cellar, and the brewer had her arrested. There was a running stream between where Mary lived and where her court hearing was to take place. When the constable arrived to escort Mary to the hearing, she insisted that he carry her across the stream. He did so, to the vocal amusement of nearby spectators.

The hearing took place in the late afternoon, and as the hour of four o'clock approached, Mary rose from her chair and started walking out.

"Come back here," called the justice of the peace.

"Them kids is gittin' out of school. I have me work to do, and ye kin hold yer court some other time," she called back.

Out she went, and no one offered any further opposition.

Reference:

W. A. Chalfant, *Gold, Guns, & Ghost Towns* (Stanford: Stanford University Press, 1958).

WE NEED MORE JAILS
- BISHOP, CA -

It seems that jails were in short supply in many parts of the early southwest, and prisoners were held in custody in a variety of ways. In Bishop, California, for example, local officers chained their prisoners to the wheels of freight wagons. On one occasion when there was no wagon available, the sheriff handcuffed his prisoner's arms around a small tree. The joke was on the sheriff, however, for when he arrived the next morning to reclaim his prisoner, the tree was still there, but the prisoner was gone. During the night, the prisoner had climbed the tree until his weight caused it to bend over and he was able to slip over the top of it. Thus, the sheriff lost both his prisoner and his handcuffs.

In eastern Nevada, the sheriff of one of the towns used his home as the jail. One night, two men, Abbott and Sullivan, got into a fight during a card game, and when it was over, Abbott lay dead. The sheriff took Sullivan, who was badly wounded, home and gave him all the privileges of a guest. As days passed and Sullivan's wounds healed, he was allowed to come and go as he pleased. In fact, whenever the sheriff was out in a late-night card game, he would give Sullivan the house key with instructions to go home and lock himself in. Sullivan was a model prisoner.

Finally, the time came for Sullivan's trial, and he was sentenced to be hung. The court then ordered the sheriff to keep Sullivan in confinement. This aroused the sheriff's ire, and he retorted that he didn't intend to treat a friend that way, and when the time came for the hanging, he and Sullivan would be present. Further, if the court didn't like the current arrangement, he (the sheriff) would resign.

Knowing that his own demise was imminent, and not wanting to be a further problem to the sheriff who had nursed him and befriended him, Sullivan took one of the sheriff's pistols and shot himself. In so doing, he wrote the following note. "Tell the boys good-bye. You needn't resign. Better lock up the others who come along. They may not think as much of you as 1 do."

Eureka, Nevada was another town without a jail, and although the citizens were clamoring for a jail, the county authorities didn't want to spend the money to build one. A County Commissioner named Burgess was the leading voice against building the jail. If he could be induced to change his mind, the jail would become a reality.

One day when Burgess drove into town with a load of ore and two sacks of grain on his wagon, a local citizen paid a "tinhorn" gambler to steal the grain. Upon discovering the loss, Burgess burst into the citizen's place of business yelling, "I think we do need a jail in this town. Someone just stole the grain off my wagon."

"That's nothing," the citizen replied. "You're lucky they didn't steal the shoes off your mules."

Eureka got its jail.

Reference:

W. A. Chalfant, *Gold, Guns, & Ghost Towns* (Stanford: Stanford University Press, 1958).

JUSTICE, EVEN IF INFORMAL, WAS SURE

~ MOUNT PLEASANT, TX ~

AN AIR OF INFORMALITY USUALLY pervaded the early frontier court rooms. This was true both of location and procedure. Early court venues were located wherever the presiding official wanted them—in saloons, on front porches, under shade trees. Even in the courthouses of established county seats, an air of infor-  mality could be expected, and rituals from earlier times could also be expected. A prime example is the Texas town of Mount Pleasant in Titus County at the turn of the century.

In Mount Pleasant, the ritual (no longer followed) for opening a court session was as follows. After the judge was seated, he would announce to the sheriff, "Sheriff, will you open court."

The sheriff would then go to a nearby window, open it if necessary, and shout as loudly as possible, "Oh, yes. Oh yes. The Honorable District Court of Titus County is now in session."

This ritual was a holdover from early England when a traveling judge would come into a village to hold court and would be preceded by the Town Crier announcing the convening of the court.

The nature of the court cases frequently had a touch of humor associated with them. As an example, a case of statuary rape was scheduled to come before the Titus County court. A man named Edward (last name not recorded) was the accused culprit.

When the judge asked if Edward was in the courtroom. a young feminine voice responded. "Judge, me and Eddard (as he was called) done got married, and I don't want nothing done to Eddard because I want to keep Eddard here."

The victim came walking down the aisle holding hands with Edward. "Are you and this man married?" the judge asked.

"Yes. Judge." she responded. "Me and Eddard done got married and I don't want nothing to happen to Eddard because I want to keep Eddard."

"Edward, are you married?"

"Yes sir." he meekly replied.

The judge had no choice but to dismiss the case.

Standing in the back of the courtroom with a self-satisfied look on his face was a man named Graf Pollen. Graf had arranged the marriage. "There wasn't no need of prosecuting that boy," he explained. "They both got what they wanted—that is, she got Eddard, and Eddard got out of trouble."

Courtroom humor could be found in many places. On one occasion in nearby Jefferson, Texas, two brothers were prosecuted for making whiskey. As they stood before the judge in tattered overalls and jumpers and with shoes held together with baling wire, they looked as impoverished as they were frightened.

"How do you fellows plead?" the judge asked.

"Judge, we is guilty." one of them responded.

The judge then asked, "Do you want a lawyer to represent you?"

"Naw suh, Judge. We'd rather have the mercies of the court than to have a lawyer."

It had been a long day for the judge, and after thinking the matter over, he said, "I must tell you that the mercies of this court have been used up for the day."

The two brothers looked at one another. "Did you hear what the Judge said?"

"I sho' did."

Then turning back to the judge, one of the brothers said, "Judge, can't we wait on this matter 'til tomorrow?"

Law and order were alive and well in East Texas, even if sometimes rather informal.

Reference:

Traylor Russell, *History of Titus County, Texas.* Vol. II (Waco: W. M. Morrison, 1965).

"MY NAME IS BAT MASTERSON"
- LAMAR, CO -

As a young boy in Lamar, Colorado, in 1888, Tom Hoover stood on a board sidewalk at the intersection of Main and Olive streets and watched a group of about twenty cowboys ride into town. To Tom, it looked like trouble approaching, and he stood transfixed. The cowboys were from an XIT trail drive, and they were ready for some diversion.

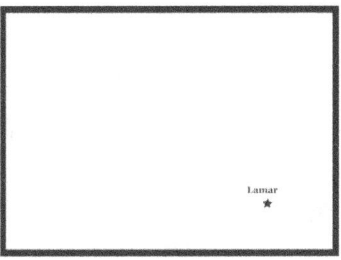

The next thing Tom saw was a solitary man, with his gun belt strapped on, walking out of one of the buildings to meet the cowboys.

"Glad to see you boys," the solitary man exclaimed. "Heard you were coming this way. Also heard about you roping outhouses and stove pipes at Vilas and Springfield and riding your horses into saloons and up to the bars. We have sixteen saloons and two red light districts here and all the gambling you want."

Now that he had their attention, the solitary man delivered his real message. "There will be no gunplay or monkey-shines here or your horses will go back to your outfit with empty saddles." Then he added the final touch to his warning. "My name is Bat Masterson."

That was all the cowboys needed to hear. According to Tom, they dispersed quietly as he ran home to tell what he had just witnessed. The XIT cowboys enjoyed Lamar, and they caused no trouble.

Reference:

Ava Betz, *A Prowers County History* (Lamar, Colorado: The Prowers County Historical Society, 1986), 217.

WEAPONS

THE COLT REVOLVER REVOLUTIONIZED FRONTIER WARFARE
- WASHINGTON, TX -

WITH THEIR SINGLE-SHOT MUZZLE-LOADING MUSKETS, the Texas frontiersmen, and even the Texas Rangers, were no match for marauding Comanches. The Comanche tactics were to encircle a numerically inferior group of Texans and induce them to fire their muskets. Then before the Texans could reload, the Comanches would charge and engage in hand-to-hand combat with knives and clubs. With their superior numbers, the Comanches were usually victorious. But in one skirmish on the banks of the Pedernales River in 1844, the attacking Comanches got a real surprise.

A group of sixteen Texas Rangers led by Captain Jack Hays had recently been armed with a new type of weapon—the Colt Paterson revolver. With its revolving cartridge, the revolver could fire several shots in rapid succession without being reloaded after each shot. The revolver was named after Samuel Colt, who invented it, and after Paterson, New Jersey, where it was manufactured.

When Hays and his men found themselves surrounded by a fierce band of Comanches, Hays told his men to fire their muskets and then hold their fire with their new revolvers until he gave the signal. The Comanches taunted as usual, and the Texans fired their muskets as usual. The Comanches then charged, fully expecting to exterminate the small band of Rangers. But as the Indians closed in for the kill, Hays gave the signal. The Rangers opened fire with their revolvers, and the surprised Comanches met their fate. Half of the 80 warriors were killed or wounded, and the rest fled from the unexpected turn of events. There were no Ranger casualties.

With the introduction of the Colt Paterson revolver, armed skirmishes between Whites and Indians, and between lawmen and gunslingers, changed forever.

Reference:

Displays at the Washington-on-the-Brazos State Museum, Washington, Texas.

THE WINCHESTER RIFLE TOOK ITS TOLL IN MORE THAN ONE WAY

~ SAN JOSE, CA ~

THE WINCHESTER RIFLE, INTRODUCED in 1860 by Oliver F. Winchester, is said to have "killed more game, more Indians, and more U.S. soldiers than any other weapon in the nation's history." Nicknamed the Henry after its designer, Benjamin T. Henry, this rapid-firing repeating rifle revolutionized western fire-power. It became known as "the gun that won the West," and Oliver Winchester (and the Winchester Repeating Arms Company) amassed a huge fortune from its sales.

The Winchester family, with the exception of one, enjoyed their new-found wealth. But Sarah Pardee Winchester, widow of Oliver Winchester's only son and heiress of the family fortune, looked upon the rifle as an instrument of doom. Early into her marriage Sarah had lost a one-month old child, and fifteen years later her husband, William, died. Devastated by these two deaths, Sarah was also greatly troubled by all the deaths attributed to the rifle her family had produced. When she received her $20,000,000 inheritance following Oliver's death in 1880, the conscious-stricken widow became even more troubled by the spirits of those slain by the rifle, and these specters haunted her the rest of her life.

Believing that the spirits of the dead were tormenting her, Sarah sought the help of a medium who advised her that the spirits had placed a curse on her and that her only escape was to move west, build a house, and keep building. As long as the house was in the construction phase, Sarah would be protected against the angry spirits. So that is what she did.

Sarah moved to San Jose, California in 1884, bought a farmhouse, and began remodeling. Thirty-eight years later, at her death, the remodeling was still underway, and the eight-room farmhouse had been turned into an enormous mansion containing hundreds of rooms and innumerable architectural quirks. It is believed that about 750 rooms were constructed at one time or another, with most of them ripped out and rebuilt with a different design. The important thing was that the construction never be allowed to stop. Today, the house stands with 160 rooms, and it serves as a prominent tourist attraction in San Jose.

Sarah's idiosyncrasies are quite evident in the home which contains winding, twisting, and bewildering corridors that snake through its interior. Secret passageways are concealed within the walls. Some of these passages lead to other rooms, while others lead nowhere. In the rooms, some doors open into other rooms, into closets, or into halls, while other doors open to blank walls. One staircase goes down seven steps and then up eleven steps. Another staircase with two-inch risers requires 100 linear feet to rise just one story. A tall cupboard has shelves an inch and a half deep.

Sarah spent many nights in one particular room designed as a séance room. Harry Houdini, the great escape artist, joined her in the room on one occasion, but he left disappointed the next day.

Despite her idiosyncrasies, Sarah also relied on good taste, and she incorporated several architectural innovations into the house. Many of the floors are made of beautiful hand-inlaid parquet, chandeliers contain real gold and silver, and many windows are made of Tiffany glass. The house has 47 fireplaces, three elevators, gas lights that are operated by pushing a button, and modern heating and sewer systems. The home is built on a "floating" foundation designed to resist earthquakes.

Sarah Winchester's home is certainly a mystery house. The Winchester rifle took its toll in more than just one way.

Reference:

Materials available at the Winchester Mystery House in San Jose, California.

DID AL PACKER EAT HIS COMPANIONS?
- GUNNISON, CO -

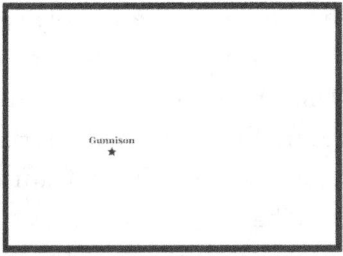

FREQUENTLY, OCCURRENCES IN THE early southwest assume legendary proportions that grow with the passage of time. Such was the case with "The Great Diamond Hoax" which was recounted in a different vignette. This vignette will deal with Al Packer, who was accused of cannibalism in Colorado in 1874.

In November 1873, Packer and twenty others left Provo, Utah, to prospect for gold in Colorado. Near Montrose, Colorado, they encountered the famous Ute chieftain, Ouray, who advised them to wait until the spring thaws before proceeding farther. Although most of the party heeded Ouray's advice, the impatient Packer along with five others struck out for Gunnison. Along the way, they got hopelessly lost and snowbound, and they ran out of provisions. Starvation became imminent.

What happened next becomes conjecture and legend. It is a fact, however, that on April 16, 1874, Al Packer showed up alone at the Los Pinos Indian Agency near Gunnison. His claim was that while he was out scouting for an escape route, one of his party, Shannon Bell, killed the other four members of the party, and when Packer returned to the camp, Bell was eating some flesh from one of his victims. Bell then rushed at Packer, who shot and killed Bell in self-defense. Packer's story, however, was not believed by anyone.

Upon being arrested, Packer signed a confession, was jailed, and then manager to escape. Nine years later (in 1883), Packer was discovered to be in Cheyenne, Wyoming. After being re-arrested, he signed a second confession. He was then tried and convicted of manslaughter and sentenced to death, but he managed again to escape. At the same time, the Colorado Supreme Court overturned the sentence.

Caught and arrested a third time, Packer was convicted of manslaughter and sentenced to 40 years in prison. Although the Supreme Court upheld this ruling, the Governor later paroled him. Packer then went to work as a guard at the *Denver Post* newspaper building in Denver. He died as a free man in 1907 at the age of 65. But by reputation, he also died as a cannibal.

It is interesting to note that in the Student Union Building at the University of Colorado in Boulder, the cafeteria grill is named the "Alfred G. Packer Memorial Grill," and its printed slogan is "Have a friend for lunch." A featured dish is a meat-filled snack called "El Canibal."

Another aspect of the legend that has grown out of the incident is that at Packer's first trial at Lake City near Gunnison, Judge M.B. Gerry thoroughly chastised Packer, saying, "When you came to Hinsdale County, there were seven Democrats here, and you ate five of them."

Truth is truth and legend is legend. We can't always tell them apart.

References:

"Alfred Packer," Wikipedia (en.wikipedia.org/wiki/Alfred_Packer)

REYNOLDS GOT THERE JUST IN TIME

- DENVER, CO -

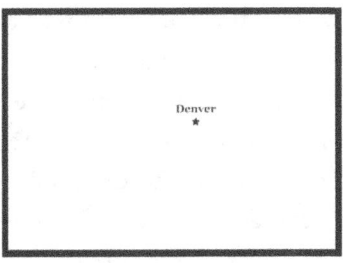

THERE WAS A CERTAIN AURA OF romanticism about railroading in the Rocky Mountains of Colorado during the last century. There was also a certain amount of peril and danger, especially during harsh winters.

Mr. A.D.F. Reynolds, a railroad bookkeeper riding in the caboose of a Denver and Rio Grande Western narrow-gauge freight train, had an experience one evening that he never forgot. Reynolds' westbound train pulled onto a semi-circular siding to allow an eastbound passenger train to pass on the main line. Responding to a whim, Reynolds hopped out of the caboose and climbed a hill to look over the whole situation. Ahead, he saw that the switch was set correctly for the passenger train to pass that point. But when looking back, Reynolds' blood froze in his veins. It appeared that the switch had not been reset after his freight train had passed onto the siding. Andrews, the brakeman, had opened the switch for the siding and then had gone on to perform some other tasks on the freight train as it waited for the passenger train to pass. Had Andrews forgotten to reset the switch to be open for the main line?

Reynolds started running, and upon hearing the whistle of the approaching passenger train, he ran for his life, or rather for the lives of the 200 passengers that the passenger train seemed always to carry. Reynolds hoped that the engineer of the passenger train would notice his desperate run, sense that something was wrong, and apply the brakes. But it didn't happen that way. The passenger train continued coming at full speed.

Reynolds and the passenger train both reached the switch at the same time, and Reynolds managed to pull the lever and get the switch reset just as the engine's front wheels arrived at the points. Not having had time to lock the lever in place, Reynolds then held it in place by wrapping his legs around the lever and the body of the switch mechanism. With Reynolds' legs locked tightly, the passenger train passed over at full speed and without incident.

They say that "what you don't know won't hurt you." About 200 passengers that evening never knew about the wreck they almost had. And Reynolds and Andrews saw no need to report the incident (except in Reynolds' memoirs). So Reynolds never received the hero's accolades that were his due. But he always remembered the incident with a large measure of satisfaction.

Reference:

A. D. F. Reynolds, "Last Days of Narrow Gauge," *Railroad Magazine*.

THE ORIGINAL SONS OF KATIE ELDER
~ RIDGWAY, CO ~

To those familiar with the movie *The Sons of Katie Elder* starring John Wayne and Dean Martin, it might be interesting to know that the movie was based on real people living just outside the town of Ridgway in Ouray County, Colorado. Katie Elder 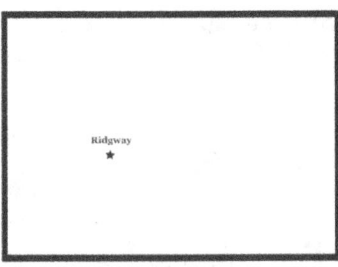 was really Martha Jane Marlow, who is buried in a small private grave at the far end of Billy Creek in Ouray County.

Martha had five sons who were pursued and hunted from Texas to California on charges based on false evidence. In the process, three of the sons were murdered. After finally proving their innocence, Martha and her remaining two sons, George and Charles, came in 1888 to Ridgway hoping to settle down. They purchased 160 acres of land, and the boys opened a blacksmith shop in town.

For three years, they were respected and well-liked citizens of the area. Then on a fateful day in June of 1891, two Texas Rangers stepped off a train in Ridgway with the intent of arresting George and Charles and taking them back to Texas for complicity in the killing of a Sheriff Wallace by their brother, Boone Marlow. J.H. Bradley, sheriff of Ouray County and a friend of the Marlows, went to the Marlow's cabin and advised them to come with him to have a talk with the Rangers. George and Charles made it clear that they would not go back to Texas unless they had "fifty strong armed government men" for protection. Otherwise they were sure they would never be allowed to return home.

The citizens of Ridgway rallied around the Marlows and let it be known that if the Texas Rangers wanted George and Charles, they had better send 2,000 men instead of two. The Marlows appealed by telegram to the governor of Colorado, who immediately wired back that they were under his protection. The two Rangers returned to Texas empty-handed. Shortly thereafter, George and Charles were cleared of all charges in federal courts.

The next year, in 1892, George and Charles became deputies to the county sheriff. They spent the rest of their lives in Ridgway, loved and respected by all.

Reference:

Doris Gregory, *Ridgway, the Town that Refused to Die* (Ouray: Cascade Publications, 1992).

GUN SLINGERS

ELFEGO BACA HAD MORE LIVES THAN A CAT
~ RESERVE, NM ~

ELFEGO BACA KNEW HOW TO USE A gun. After all, he had learned his skills from no less than Billy the Kid. Unlike the Kid, however, Baca tried to stay on the right side of the law. While still in his teens, Baca pinned a badge on himself and became a self-appointed deputy sheriff in Socorro County, New Mexico.

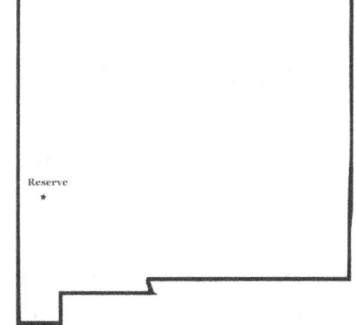

Saturday evenings were wild times in most frontier towns, as cowboys filled the saloons seeking relaxation and excitement. The nineteen-year-old Baca inadvertently happened to be visiting the town of Frisco (now Reserve) in western New Mexico on a Saturday when an overly drunk cowboy named McCarty was being especially troublesome. After shooting up the saloon, McCarty was riding back and forth in the street shooting at everything and everyone in sight.

When asked by Baca why they weren't doing anything to stop McCarty, the Justice of the Peace and other citizens explained that they feared retaliation by McCarty's fellow cowboys at the nearby

Slaughter Ranch. Since Frisco was at that time in Socorro County, the young Baca took it upon himself to go out and confront McCarty. Baca succeeded in disarming and arresting McCarty, but because it was late in the day, Baca decided to wait until morning before taking his prisoner to Socorro. This delay gave time for word of McCarty's arrest to spread to the Slaughter Ranch, and a number of cowboys rode into town to rescue their fellow worker.

Responding to the demands for McCarty's immediate release, Baca said he would give the cowboys the time it took to count to three to get out of town. Counting "one, two, three," he then opened fire with his pistol. The leader of the cowboys, Mr. Perlman, was killed and another was wounded. The cowboys left, and Baca still had his prisoner.

The next morning, a crowd of eighty cowboys, headed by Jim Heme, rode in from the ranch to settle things. Baca, in the meantime, had sequestered himself in a jacal, a house made of sticks and mud. Heme, who hated Mexicans, advanced on the jacal with rifle in hand shouting, "Come out of there, and come out quick." With two quick pistol shots, Baca killed Heme, and a siege was underway.

All during the day, Baca held off his attackers. Toward evening, a part of the building weakened by bullets fell on him, and he lay there for two hours protected while bullets still flew above. That night, after dark, Baca got up and found that the cook stove in the jacal was still hot. So he made himself some coffee, cooked some meat and, of all things, made some tortillas.

About midnight the cowboys exploded some dynamite next to the jacal, and half of the house was destroyed. Baca, in the other half of the house, was not hurt. The next morning, the cowboys were astonished to see a thin trickle of smoke rising from the chimney in the remaining section of the jacal. Baca was calmly cooking and eating breakfast.

Concentrating a steady fire on the portion of the jacal still standing, the cowboys hit everything except Baca himself. About midmorning, one of the cowboys, using a cast iron section of an old stove as a shield, tried advancing on the house. Baca held his fire until he saw the cowboy peek out from behind the shield. One well-placed shot from Baca was all that was needed.

The siege terminated in a truce at the end of the second day when an American deputy sheriff named Ross showed up to take charge of the situation. It was estimated that over 4,000 bullets had been fired into the jacal. The front door, with 367 bullet holes, looked like a sieve. Yet, no bullet ever hit Baca. The Slaughter cowboys were tired of it all, having been held off for two days by one Mexican boy who seemed to have more than the nine lives of a cat. Ross arranged a compromise and coaxed Baca out of the jacal with assurances of safe passage back to Socorro.

In Socorro, Baca was tried twice for the Frisco killings, and he was acquitted both times. It was ruled that, even though he had been overzealous, he had acted within the law. One of the cowboys who testified in the trials gave it as his deliberate opinion that Baca was possessed of something from God or the devil and could not be killed.

Living for forty years after the Frisco incident, Elfego Baca went on to become a prominent attorney in New Mexico. Whatever happened to the cowboy, McCarty, about whom the entire incident was centered? McCarty's fate seems to have been forgotten by those who recorded the story.

Reference:

Kyle S. Crichton, *Law and Order; LId.* (Santa Fe: New Mexican Publishing Corporation, 1928).20

SAM DITTENHOEFER OUTWITS BILLY THE KID
~ SANTA FE, NM ~

IMMIGRANTS INTO THE GREAT American west came from all over Europe as well as from the United States itself. Scotch, Irish, English, French, and Germans were represented as well as other nationalities. Texas had an especially large Germanic population. Religiously ethnic groups were also present, the Jewish people being among the leaders numerically. Among a large number of Jews settling in New Mexico was one Samuel Dittenhoefer. A great friend of the Indians, Dittenhoefer was also known as Navajo Sam.

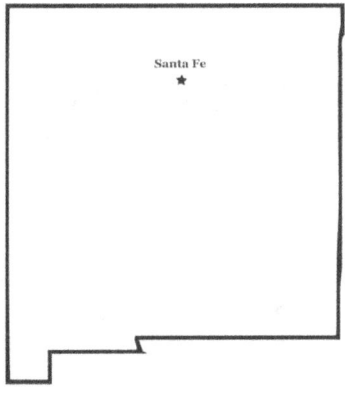

One time in 1877, Navajo Sam was delivering $25,000 in silver from Mexico to the Spiegelbergs' main store in Santa Fe. Transportation of hard cash was a common practice on the frontier, as banks were rare and currency was not standardized. Robberies were also common when it became known that money or bullion was being transported. As a precautionary measure, Sam concealed the coins in six large flour barrels that had false tops and bottoms. With the space between the tops and bottoms filled with flour, Sam's silver was well concealed from unsuspected eyes.

Along the way to Santa Fe, Sam encountered Billy the Kid, who stopped him with the intent of robbing him. "I don't have much money," Sam pleaded. "All I have is this cargo of flour."

"I've a good mind to help myself to a few pounds of this flour," responded the Kid. Then thinking the better of it, Billy turned and rode away.

Over the years as the story was told and retold, Samuel Dittenhoefer achieved the status of Jewish folk hero for having outwitted Billy the Kid.

Reference:

Kenneth Libo & Irving Howe, *We Lived There Too* (New York: 8t. Martin's/Marek, 1984).

THE THIRD TIME WAS NOT A CHARM FOR BLACK JACK KETCHUM
- CLAYTON, NM -

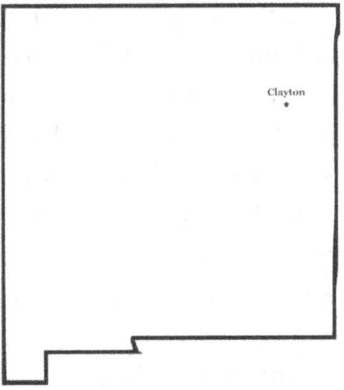

FRANK HARRINGTON WAS TIRED OF having his train held up and robbed. Twice now it had happened, and twice the bandits had gotten away. And when friends started making jokes about his being in league with the robbers, Harrington became even more upset. If the bandits should try it again, Harrington, who was a conductor on Colorado & Southern trains through New Mexico, would be ready.

Frank Harrington traveled frequently on C&S trains running between Denver and Ft. Worth. Crossing the northeastern corner of New Mexico, the trains had to slow to a crawl on a steep rise just south of Folsom. It was an ideal place for bandits to jump onto a train and force the engineer to bring it to a stop. Robberies at this location were so frequent that the area became known as Robbers Roost.

On September 3, 1897, Tom (Black Jack) Ketchum and his gang stopped and held up Harrington's southbound train. Boarding the engine at Robbers Roost, Ketchum ordered the engineer to stop the train. The other bandits then forced their way into the express car, where they knocked the express manager unconscious. Ketchum held off Conductor Harrington with a gun as the gang made their getaway with a bag containing $3,500 in silver.

So easy and successful had the robbery been that Ketchum and his gang tried it again the following July. Using the same technique, all went well except that this time the express manager cleverly dropped the money bags behind some fruit boxes, and all the robbers found were two crates of lemons and a saddle. The robbers made a successful escape, but without any money. A posse quickly formed at Folsom and caught up with the bandits the next morning. In the ensuing gun battle, two of the posse were killed. All of the bandits escaped, although two were later arrested in other parts of New Mexico.

At 10:15 on the night of August 16, 1899, a southbound train left Folsom with Conductor Harrington aboard. At Robbers Roost, Black Jack Ketchum struck for the third time, and Harrington, with a newly purchased sawed-off shotgun, was ready. During the ensuing fracas, Ketchum and Harrington found themselves face to face, and each fired directly at the other. Ketchum's rifle shot missed, but Harrington's shotgun blast hit Ketchum. As he fell, Ketchum rolled down the embankment of the tracks and became invisible in the darkness. Again the robbers were thwarted and Harrington had proved that he was not one of them.

The next day a posse arrived from Clayton, New Mexico, to search the area where the attempted holdup had occurred. Down the embankment from the tracks they found a man sitting, unable to move, with a blood-stained handkerchief tied around his right arm. "I wish that SOB had shot me through the head or the heart," he said. "Then all this would be over with." They took the man, who claimed to be George Stevens, first to Clayton and then to Trinidad, Colorado, where nuns removed forty-two shotgun pellets from his arm. The arm bone was so shattered that shortly thereafter the arm was amputated.

After a sheriff from San Angelo, Texas, came and identified "Stevens" as Black Jack Ketchum, officers sent the prisoner to the state penitentiary in Santa Fe. A law specifying hanging as the penalty for attempted train robbery had just been enacted in New Mexico, and Black Jack Ketchum was slated to be the first person executed under that new law. The execution would be in Clayton.

New Mexico Governor Otero liked to know the men awaiting execution under his authority, and Otero and his six-year-old son, Miguel, made several calls on Ketchum. Ketchum and the young Miguel became quite attached to one another, and the boy made additional visits on his own, frequently taking peanuts to the condemned prisoner. On one such occasion, Ketchum asked Miguel to deliver a message to his father, the Governor. "You tell your papa not to send me to Clayton. You tell him I'll go straight." Miguel faithfully delivered the message but was unable to bring back the hoped-for response.

Wearing a new derby hat and with his mustache parted and neatly combed, Black Jack Ketchum was executed on the gallows at Clayton on April 26, 1901. After one other train robbery by some easterners who were not familiar with New Mexico's laws, there were no more crimes of that sort in New Mexico.

Reference:

Erna Fergusson, *Murder and Mystery in New Mexico* (Albuquerque: Merle Armitage Editions, 1948)

IT TOOK TWO HANGINGS TO END BILL LONGLEY'S LIFE
~ EVERGREEN, TX ~

NOT MANY PEOPLE CAN CLAIM TO have been hung twice. Being hung once is bad enough, and the result is usually very final. But William Preston Longley, known more simply as Bill, survived a hanging and lived to be hung again.

Growing up in Evergreen, Texas, Bill became an excellent marksman. It was said by some that he could hit any target from a galloping horse. During his teenage and early adult years, Langley was involved in several shooting scrapes around Evergreen and throughout Texas. Over a ten-year period, he was credited with over thirty killings—mostly federal soldiers, Northern sympathizers, and posse members. A posse finally caught up with Longley, and he was captured and hung from the limb of a tree.

As Longley dangled from the noose, the posse members took shots at him. The first shot bounced off a gold belt around Longley's waist, and the second shot cut most of the strands of the rope around Longley's neck. As the posse rode away, a thirteen-year-old boy cut the rest of the rope, and Longley tumbled to the ground, still alive.

Recovering, Longley soon exacted retribution on one of the posse members by hanging him from the same tree. This time, it was Longley who fired shots into a dangling body, and his shots were right on the mark.

After being away for some time, Longley returned to Evergreen with the intent of killing Wilson Anderson, who Longley believed had murdered Longley's cousin. Captured and jailed, Longley was tried in Giddings, the county seat, and he was sentenced again to be hung. While awaiting his execution, Langley wrote a letter in which he complained of his unfair treatment since John Wesley Hardin, an equally prolific and notorious killer, had gotten off with only a twenty-five-year sentence. The plea fell on deaf ears, however, and the second hanging took place.

An old-timer in Giddings who later recalled witnessing the hanging reported Longley's last words of contriteness: "I see a lot of enemies out there and mighty few friends. I deserve this fate. It is a debt I owe for my wild reckless life. Goodbye, everybody."

Bill Langley was hung until dead. He was only twenty-seven years old.

Reference:

Ann Ruff, *Amazing Texas Monuments & Museums* (Houston: Lone Star Books, 1984).

NED CHRISTIE HELD OFF THE LAWMEN FOR SEVEN YEARS

- TAHLEQUAH, OK -

NED CHRISTIE, A CHEROKEE INDIAN living near Tahlequah, Oklahoma, was a jack-of-all-trades. He was a blacksmith, gunsmith, whiskey runner, and horse thief. Ned's life, 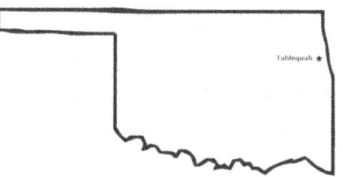 however, was relatively simple and peaceful until May 1885, when he shot and killed a lawman who was trying to arrest a companion of Christie's for running whiskey. Then followed a series of attempts to arrest Christie.

Deputy Joe Bowers approached Christie's cabin to make the first attempt, but rode away after receiving a gunshot wound in the leg. Deputy John Field tried next. Determined to talk Christie into surrendering, Field rode up to Christie's cabin, but galloped away after being shot in the neck. Christie was not at all cooperative about being arrested.

It was some time later, in 1886, when a third attempt was made to apprehend Christie. This time it was a posse instead of a lone individual. Christie wounded three of the posse members, and they finally withdrew in defeat. Christie was then left to himself for the next three years.

In 1889, it was decided to try again. Three deputy marshals approached Christie's cabin just before dawn, but Christie's dogs awakened the inhabitants inside. The marshals set fire to Christie's shop, and then they succeeded in driving Christie and his family into the open by setting fire to his cabin. Christie's wife and son ran to safety in the woods, although the boy was wounded in the process. Christie then made his dash, firing at the marshals as he ran. One of the marshals managed to shoot Christie in the face, shattering the bridge of his nose and putting out his right eye. Nevertheless, Christie made his escape as the cabin burned to the ground.

After recovering from his wounds, Christie moved a few miles to the east to a location on a precipice that was approachable from only one direction, and there he built a cabin that was really a fort. The walls were two logs thick and were lined with oak two-by-fours. It proved to be quite an effective bastion.

In 1891, Deputy Marshall Dave Rusk made another attempt to bring in Christie. Attacking with a posse of hired Indians, Rusk also failed, and he withdrew after four of his posse were wounded. Rusk made two additional attempts alone that also failed. In retaliation for being bothered so much by Rusk, Christie slipped out one night and burned down a store owned by Rusk.

A new posse assaulted the fort in October 1892. Filling a wagon with brush, they set it afire and shoved it toward the fort. At first the wagon traveled in the right direction, and then it swerved and crashed into an outhouse, burning it. The officers then threw several sticks of dynamite at the fort but they merely bounced off the walls. Two of the posse were wounded by Christie's gunfire, and they withdrew in disgust. Again, the underdog had prevailed.

It had now become a matter of honor to arrest Ned Christie. In November 1892, sixteen lawmen approached the fort with a three-pounder cannon and six sticks of dynamite. The cannon balls struck the walls of the fort with no effect, and after firing 30 rounds, the cannon barrel split. Next, the lawmen seized the rear axle and wheels of the burned-out wagon and built a portable barricade of scrap oak timbers. Advancing behind this barricade after dark, the officers approached the fort as Christie and a companion fired at them from second-story gun ports. Soon they were close enough, and Charley Copeland ran out and placed the six sticks of lighted dynamite against the southern wall of the fort. Copeland got back to safety just in time as the dynamite exploded and shattered the wall of the fort. Christie and Wolf had to evacuate, and as they ran toward the woods, one of the officers shot Christie and killed him on the spot. Wolf escaped but was apprehended a few weeks later.

Thus, after seven years, the side of law and order finally prevailed. But to many people, Ned Christie's long endurance against overwhelming odds makes him the hero of the story.

Reference:

Billy O'Neal, *Encyclopedia of Western Gunfighters* (Norman: University of Oklahoma Press, 1979).

"DOC" HOLLIDAY: IF YOU CAN FIND HIM, YOU CAN HAVE HIM
- GLENWOOD SPRINGS, CO -

THE NAME "DOC" HOLLIDAY IS WELL known in western lore. Besides winning enduring fame as a participant with Wyatt Earp in "the Gunfight at the OK Corral," Holliday was a legend in his own right, both as a gambler and a sharpshooter. 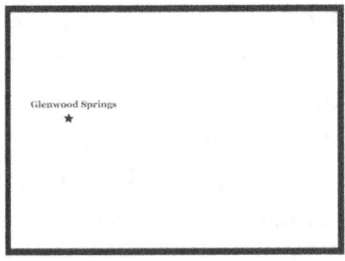 Although only one death has been conclusively attributed to Holliday, unofficial estimates of his victims run as high as 25.

John Henry Holliday was born in Valdosta, Georgia in 1852. Remaining in Georgia during his youth, he then attended dental school at the Pennsylvania College of Dental Surgery in Philadelphia where he was graduated in 1872. Drifting west seeking relief from consumption, Holliday actually did practice dentistry, although it soon became apparent that his primary interests were in saloons and gambling. This meant that in spite of chronic ill health, he had to become adept with guns and gun battles, which he did. He carried a six-shooter at his side, and he frequently had a small derringer concealed under his clothing. He also drank quite heavily, sometimes consuming three quarts of whiskey in a day.

In praise of Holliday's skills as a gunfighter, Wyatt Earp has been quoted as saying:

> Doc was a dentist whom necessity had made a gambler; a gentleman whom disease had made a frontier vagabond; a philosopher whom life had made a caustic wit; a long, lean, ash-blond fellow nearly dead with consumption and at the same time the most skillful gambler, and the nerviest, fastest, deadliest man with a six-gun I ever knew.

Doc Holliday arrived on the scene in Glenwood Springs, Colorado, in May, 1887. Although the reason for Holliday's choice of Glenwood Springs remains a mystery, there are two suggested explanations. One story says that he came hoping to benefit from the curative powers of the springs of mineral waters in the area. Another story has Holliday and Wyatt Earp arriving together in search of two outlaws who had offended them in some way. According to the story, the two outlaws were never able to offend anyone again.

Very little is known of Doc Holliday's life in Glenwood Springs. Although dying of consumption (now known as tuberculosis), Holliday practiced dentistry for a short time, and he also dealt poker and faro in several Glenwood saloons. His health, however, never improved, and he spent much of the time in bed. It is said that one of Doc's girl friends from the past, a prostitute named "Big Nose" Kate, came and nursed him during a part of his illness. Holliday died on November 8, 1887, six months following his arrival after lying in a coma for two of those six months. Just before dying, Holliday awoke from his coma, asked for a drink of whiskey, and said, "Isn't it funny." He may have been referring ironically to his long-standing expectation of dying a violent death from some gunman's bullets.

Headstone and Burial Plot for Doc. Holliday

Holliday's burial is also shrouded in mystery, for no one knows just where his body lies. It is said that when he died, a Midwestern gang wanted his body, so the funeral took place at the First Presbyterian Church with a casket of stones while the real burial was in the basement of a house at 8th and Palmer streets. Sometime later the body was supposedly moved to the Linwood Cemetery high on a mountainside overlooking Glenwood Springs from the east, but the location of the new grave remains unknown. A representative grave site, complete with monument, headstone, whiskey bottle, and fence has been established in Linwood Cemetery, but it serves only as a memorial, not as the actual grave site.

Some years ago, a group of Holliday's relatives from Georgia came to Glenwood Springs hoping to exhume the body and take it home with them. The mayor at that time, wishing to cooperate, told the group, "If you can find him, you can have him." After a few days they went home empty-handed.

References:

Jim Nelson, *Glenwood Springs: The History of a Rocky Mountain Resort* (Ouray, Colorado: Western Reflections, Inc., 1999).

GEORGE U. HUBBARD

Jim Nelson, *Glenwood Springs: A Quick History* (Fort Collins, Colorado: First Light Publishing, 1998).

"BIG NOSE" GEORGE COULDN'T WIN FOR LOSING
- RAWLINS, WY -

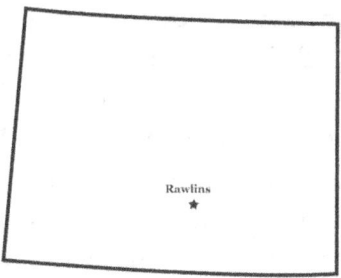

"BIG NOSE" GEORGE PARROTT WAS just another outlaw—that is, until he decided to try robbing a Union Pacific train in Wyoming. Not only did the attempt fail, but everything in George's remaining life, and even after his death, seemed to go wrong. Although his attempt brought him no money, it led to a series of bizarre circumstances that are still remembered.

George Parrott and his gang had gotten along fine stealing horses and robbing stagecoaches and pay wagons in the Powder River area of northeastern Wyoming. Then they decided it was time to move on to bigger ventures. Moving southward, they planned to derail and rob the eastbound UP No.4 train at a bridge about four miles east of the Medicine Bow station in Carbon County, Wyoming. The date was August 16, 1878, and the plan was simple. They would remove spikes and fishplates from one of the rails on the bridge, and as the train approached, they would jerk the rail out of place. But they miscalculated the time element, and the train came roaring through just as they were getting started. George, on the bridge, barely escaped being hit by the engine. The train sped past, unimpeded and unharmed.

Not to be denied, the gang finished loosening the rail, tied a long piece of telegraph wire to it so they could jerk it at the right time, and retired to some bushes to await the evening westbound UP No.3 train. But this time, a track maintenance crew came along, discovered the loose rail, and made repairs while the gang watched from their cover. The westbound train came along and also passed unimpeded and unharmed.

As the disgruntled robbers retreated to Rattlesnake Canyon on Elk Mountain, the Union Pacific repair crew notified officials that train robbers were in the area, and a two-man posse went out to look for the gang. Tracking the gang to Elk Mountain, Sheriff Robert Widdowfield and Railroad Detective Henry "Tip" Vincent came upon the hot remains of a campfire, and they knew they were close to their quarry. But the gang members, hiding behind rocks, opened fire and killed both pursuers. The gang then scattered and never worked together again. The Union Pacific and Carbon County combined to post a $20,000 reward for their capture.

Two years later, "Big Nose" George was enjoying his freedom in Miles City, Montana, until one night in 1880 when he got drunk and bragged about having participated in the attempted train robberies and subsequent murders. Local authorities arrested him, and Sheriff Rankin came up from Carbon County, Wyoming to bring George back for trial. When the train carrying the sheriff and his prisoner stopped in the town of Carbon, a vigilante mob boarded and took George into their own custody. As they were in the process of hanging him, George pled for his life, promising to tell all if they would let him live. The vigilantes allowed Sheriff Rankin to take George on to Rawlins for trial.

LAW AND ORDER

Old Prison Building in Rawlins, Wyoming

At his arraignment on September 13, 1880, George pled guilty to murder. Four days later, he changed his plea to not guilty. When the trial began on November 8, George again pled guilty and then not guilty. But the end result was a conviction and a sentence to be hanged the following April. Upon hearing the sentence, George burst into uncontrolled sobbing that required the support of two deputies to keep him from collapsing onto the floor.

Following the trial, George made one attempt at escaping jail. Somehow he had managed to remove the heavy shackles from his ankles, and the next time Sheriff Rankin came into the area, George came up behind him, and swinging the heavy shackles, hit Rankin on the head, fracturing his skull. It was a blow from which Rankin never fully recovered. Rankin, however, managed to call for his wife, Rosa, and with pistol in hand, she came running in, locked the cell block door, and forced George back into his cell. Rosa was later given a gold pocket watch for her bravery in preventing George's escape.

Stirred by news of George's attempted escape and attack on the sheriff, citizens of Rawlins decided it was time for them to take action. At ten o'clock the next evening, groups of two or three men began converging on the jail from all directions. Wearing masks and brandishing pistols, they entered, got the jail keys, and unlocked the cell block area. A deputy named Simms knew better than to resist, and he quietly disappeared. Then when the intruders told John Landon, a special guard hired to prevent such a mob takeover, that his health would be better if he "took a walk," Landon disappeared also.

Taking George down to East Front Street, the mob stood George on a barrel with one end of a rope around his neck and the other end thrown over the cross arm of a telegraph pole. Legend has it that it was Mrs. Elizabeth Widdowfield, sister-in-law of the murdered Sheriff Widdowfield, who kicked the barrel out from under George. At any rate, as George dropped, the rope broke, and George tumbled to the ground. Procuring a ladder and another rope, the mob forced George to climb the ladder, and they hung him again. By this time, George had managed to work his hands free, and as he dropped, he grabbed onto the telegraph pole and clung to it tenaciously with his arms and legs. But gravity and fatigue had their effects, and George gradually slid downward. It was a spectacle that would have been quite comical had it not been so tragic. As a crowd of 200 citizens watched, George desperately tried to hold on to the pole, but he helplessly continued sliding downward. In the end, he died of strangulation instead of having his neck snapped, as is usual in hangings.

Although now dead, George's story is far from over. Following George's expiration, two local doctors took possession of his body. Dr. John Osborne, later to become governor of the State of Wyoming, wanted to see if there was any anomaly in George's brain that might explain criminal tendencies. So Osborne, assisted by Dr. Thomas Maghee and Maghee's young assistant, Lillian Heath, sawed through the top of George's skull and removed the brain for study. But Osborne didn't stop there. He also cut away skin from George's chest and thighs, tanned it, and had a local shoemaker make a pair of shoes from the skin. It is reported that he wore the shoes frequently, and in 1893 when Osborne became governor, he even wore the shoes to the inaugural ball.

Nothing has been reported regarding any results of the study of George's brain. After finishing with the body, the two doctors stuffed the remains into an empty whiskey barrel, which they buried behind Dr. Maghee's office.

Lillian Heath eventually became Wyoming's first female doctor. She kept the top part of George's skull, called a skull cap, and for years, her husband used it upside down as an ashtray.

But this still wasn't the end of "Big Nose" George's story. In 1950, workmen excavating for a new building unearthed the barrel. Inside were human bones including a skull with the top sawed off. Instantly citizens of Rawlins remembered "Big Nose" George. Lillian Heath and her husband were still alive, and they were summoned to help with a positive identification. Bringing forth the skull cap they had kept for so many years, the Heath's applied it to the unearthed lower skull, and it fit perfectly. Later DNA testing added further certainty that the unearthed remains were those of "Big Nose" George.

Today, Osborne's shoes and the lower portion of George's skull are on display in the Carbon County Museum in Rawlins. Rosa's gold watch is also in the collection. The skull cap and the shackles with which George struck jailer Rankin are in the Union Pacific museum in Omaha, Nebraska. Although everything went wrong for him in robbing the train, being in jail, and being hanged, "Big Nose" George is still remembered in Wyoming as Carbon County's most infamous outlaw.

References:

The Legend of Big Nose George, published by the Carbon County (Wyoming) Museum.

"The Story of Big Nose George," Carbon County tourist bulletin.

Displays in the Carbon County Museum and in the Old Jailhouse Museum in Rawlins, Wyoming.

INTRODUCTION

ANYWHERE LARGE NUMBERS OF PEOPLE ARE TO BE FOUND, INTERESTING, eclectic characters will be included. This is especially true among the variety of people attracted to America's western frontier and its opportunities and challenges.

The trappers, explorers, prospectors, and settlers came from all walks of life. There were planters, woodsmen, cowboys, entrepreneurs, industrialists, fighters, outlaws, gamblers, healers, charlatans, and plain humbugs.

They came for all kinds of reasons, and they came from all kinds of places. Explorers came seeking adventure. Trappers and miners came seeking wealth. Farmers and ranchers came seeking free land along with the freedom just to live and work in the great outdoors. Some came to conquer and gain wealth; others were brought to serve. Still, they came.

They came from the eastern United States. They came from Europe. They came from the Orient. They came as builders and doers. They came as settlers. Some, particularly the Orientals, came almost as slaves. Many who came could not endure the challenges. But many others who came not only endured, they thrived and conquered.

Although many of the migrants were real characters on an individual basis, the blend of their individual traits produced an invigorated populace that accomplished wonders. As they battled the elements, competed with one another, and lived by their wits, they created a heritage of accomplishment against all odds. And when we get inside their accomplishments to view them as actual people, we find them sometimes funny, sometimes ingenious, but always interesting.

There is humor and drama to be found in the lives and actions of these people who tamed and developed the American West.

PIONEERS

A REMITTANCE WOMAN SUCCEEDS AT HOMESTEADING
~ WEED, NM ~

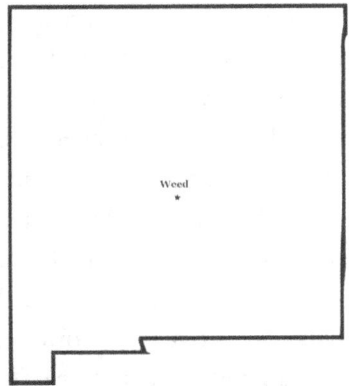

ONE OF THE UNIQUE CHARACTER TYPES on the American frontier was that of the "Remittance Man." Remittance Men were sons, other than the first-born, in prosperous European families who could not inherit the family estate. Therefore, with a lifelong allowance or remittance, they had to go elsewhere to make their way in life.

Because of the lure of adventure and opportunity in America, many of them came to this country, and some became homesteaders, ranchers, or merchants on the frontier. It should come as no surprise that many Remittance Men were the subjects of jokes and derision from hardened frontiersmen until they proved themselves equal to the rigorous life into which they had entered. One may imagine, then, the surprise felt by the citizens of Alamogordo, New Mexico, when a Remittance Woman arrived from Scotland to become a homesteader by herself.

All through her youth, Jessie MacMillan, who was born in Glasgow, Scotland in 1872, was enthralled by tales of the American frontier. Growing up on cowboy stories, her dream was to become a homesteader in America. Her wealthy family gave her a good education and provided the finer things of life, but Jessie's dream persisted. Having promised an aunt that she would remain in Scotland until thirty years old, Jessie came to America as soon as she could without breaking that promise.

Going east from Alamogordo to Weed in the Sacramento Mountains, Jessie obtained 160 acres of land and began fulfilling her dream. But because she was a single woman, she made it a point not to give any cause for gossip among the ladies of Weed. For example, Jessie had hired a number of men to build an adobe house for her. Promptly at 8:00 pm each evening, she sent the workmen to their tents and shacks on her property, and there they stayed until morning.

Jessie plowed, harrowed, rolled, and leveled her fields. She raised oats for her horses, and she fed chopped turnips and cabbage to the cattle, a practice she had learned in Scotland. The neighbors, who quickly learned to respect Jessie's integrity and courage, taught her to grow cabbage in raised mounds and to cover it with burlap bags on cold evenings. Help came from Scotland, also. A Scottish family named Broughall came to visit and stayed seven months helping Jessie through her first winter in New Mexico. With frugality and a careful balance between income and operating expenses over the years, Jessie's hard work bore fruit, and she became a successful homesteader.

In her late thirties, Jessie MacMillan fell in love and married. In so doing, she entered into a new kind of life, but only after successfully fulfilling her childhood dreams.

Reference:

Sandra Varney MacMahon, "Fine Hands for Sowing: The Homesteading Experiences of Remittance Woman Jessie de Prado MacMillan" (*New Mexico Historical Review,* June 1999).

EILLEY ORRUM: THE WASHOE SEERESS
- GOLD HILL, NV -

ALLISON EILLEY ORRUM AFFILIATED with the Mormon faith in Scotland at the age of fifteen. With her family, also converts, she migrated to Utah, where she married a Mormon bishop named Stephen Hunter. After ten years of marriage. Eilley had no children, but her husband had three additional wives.

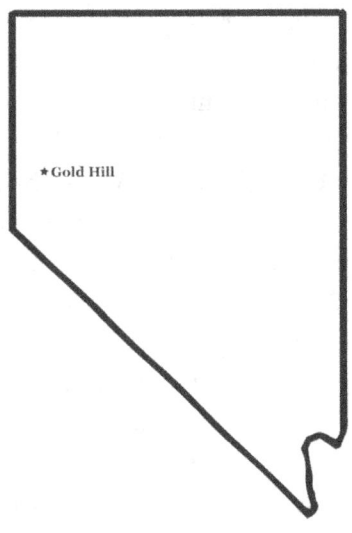

Divorcing Hunter, Eilley married Alexander Cowan, and the couple migrated with a company of Mormons to the Carson Valley area of what is now western Nevada. In 1855, the newlyweds settled at Gold Hill where they opened a boarding house. Although Eilley was now busy cooking for prospectors and washing their clothes, fate lured her into doing some prospecting on her own. One boarder, unable to pay his bill, got Eilley started by deeding her his undeveloped claim in the Comstock Lode.

Later that same year, because of the march of Johnston's army to

Utah, Brigham Young called all the Mormons west of Utah to come "home." Mr. Cowan heeded the call, but stubborn Eilley refused to budge. She liked the Washoe area where they had been living, she liked the prospect of becoming wealthy, and she was tired of moving.

Two years after Cowan's departure, Eilley assumed that she had been deserted. She obtained a divorce on those grounds, and she continued to eke out her own existence. She was tough, and she was resilient. She also had a special skill that she used to her advantage.

Eilley was a visionary person, and with a crystal ball she supplemented her meager income by "seeing" grand visions for the people who came to learn of their future. She predicted locations for digging, disasters such as fires in the mines, and other triumphs and disasters. She was correct enough times for her fame to spread, and she became known as the "Washoe Seeress."

It is recorded that Eilley also saw grand visions of herself as a millionaire and as the princess of the Washoe. Eilley was also an optimist, and heeding her crystal ball visions, she went out and staked additional mining claims throughout the Comstock area.

Husband number three soon came along, having staked claims next to Eillery's. After a brief stint at prospecting, this new husband, Lemuel "Sandy" Bowers, became discouraged with the prospect of finding gold, and he wanted himself and Eilley to sell their claims for $3,500. But Ellery's crystal ball showed that someday a big city would stand where their claims were located and that wealth would be theirs. Eilley's view prevailed, and Sandy joined in her optimism.

The rest is history. Virginia City, Nevada encompasses much of the land where Eilley and Sandy (and many others) had their claims, and the Comstock Lode became the richest bonanza of gold and silver in the world. Within five years of the initial discovery, the Comstock mines had yielded over $100,000,000. In 1863 alone, the mines sent more than $20,000,000 in bullion over the mountains to banks and owners in San Francisco.

Eilley and Sandy became millionaires, and Eilley's vision of becoming a princess came to fruition. As the social magnate of the area, she dubbed herself "Queen of the Comstock." While most of the

Comstock millionaires were busy building mansions on and around Nob Hill in San Francisco, Eilley and Sandy built theirs there in Nevada, about a third of the way from present-day Carson City to Reno. It was a large, two-story edifice built of solid sandstone.

It is only fitting that queens should regale queens. So while their mansion was being built, Eilley and Sandy traveled to England, hoping for an audience with Queen Victoria, but this could not occur because of Eilley's divorces. Although failing to get the desired audience, Eilley and Sandy traveled abroad for about two years, and they spent thousands of dollars for clothes and jewelry and for furniture and furnishings for their mansion. Eilley even imported a whole brass band from Scotland to entertain guests who would be coming for the opening of their new home.

Sandy died in 1868, and Eilley's demise began at that point. She had never learned how to handle wealth, and having lost her husband, she also lost her earlier flair for business. Eilley became prey to the unscrupulous, and she eventually lost everything. She was living in poverty when she died in 1903.

References:

Irving Stone, *Men to Match My Mountains* (Garden City: Doubleday & Company, Inc., 1956).

Ronald M. James and C. Elizabeth Raymond, *Comstock Women* (Reno: University of Nevada Press, 1998).

Thompson and West, *History of Nevada* (Berkeley: Howell and North, 1958).

WPA Writers' Project, *Nevada: A Guide to the Silver State* (Portland: Binfords & Mart, 1940).

HENRY FLIPPER IS DISMISSED FROM THE MILITARY
- FORT SILL, OK -

HENRY FLIPPER'S DREAM WAS TO SERVE a life-long career with the United States Army. Born in 1856 to a slave family on a Georgia plantation, Flipper grew up after the Civil War as 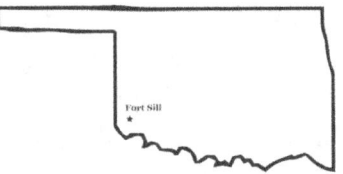 a free man determined to educate himself and to amount to something. The military was the career he wished to follow.

Following schooling at the American Missionary Association and at Atlanta University, Flipper succeeded in obtaining an appointment to the United States Military Academy at West Point. Although the fifth black cadet accepted into the Military Academy, he was the first African-American to graduate. His experiences at West Point, however, were not easy, as he had to struggle with prejudice and ostracism which he described in his book, *The Colored Cadet at West Point*. Nevertheless, Flipper endured and was graduated as a second lieutenant in 1877. He immediately accepted an assignment with Company A of the Tenth United States Cavalry in Texas and Oklahoma.

Flipper served with distinction in this assignment. In supervising the drainage of malarial ponds at Fort Sill in Oklahoma, he created what is known as Flipper's Ditch, a project that has now become a national historic landmark. He supervised the construction of a road from Gainesville to Fort Sill after a prior work crew from the Fourth Cavalry got drunk and walked off the job. Flipper also built a telegraph line from Fort Elliot to Fort Supply, scouted on the Llano Estacado, and assisted in returning Quanah Parker's band from Palo Duro Canyon to Fort Sill. In 1880, Flipper also fought in two battles against Indians at Eagle Springs, Texas. As a reward for these services, Flipper became post quartermaster and acting commissary of subsistence at Fort Davis in southwestern Texas.

Flipper's dream of an army career, however, was short lived. When Colonel William Shafter became commanding officer of Fort Davis in 1881, he immediately relieved Flipper as quartermaster and planned to relieve him as the commissary officer. Civilian employees at the fort warned Flipper of a plot by white officers to force him out of the army, and the plot materialized when Flipper discovered some post funds missing from his quarters. Knowing that he would be accused of the theft, Flipper made the decision to conceal the loss in hopes that he could find or replace the money. But as soon as Colonel Shaffer learned of the situation, he relieved Flipper of all his duties and had him court martialed.

The court martial board acquitted Flipper of embezzlement, but found him guilty of "conduct unbecoming an officer and a gentlemen." Thus, Flipper's army career came to an inglorious end as he received a dishonorable discharge on June 30, 1882. Maintaining his innocence until his death in 1940, Flipper waged a life-long battle for reinstatement in the army.

Although no longer a soldier, Henry Flipper nevertheless had a distinguished career as a mining engineer in the southwest United States, Mexico, and South America. He developed mines, he translated technical articles and books from Spanish to English, and he published numerous articles and books of his own. J. Frank Dobie took notice of Flipper and told a story about Flipper's research on the Lost Tayopa Mine in *Apache Gold and Yaqui Silver*. Flipper also spent two years serving as assistant to the secretary of the interior in the Department of the Interior in Washington, D.C.

In an effort to correct a wrong that had been done to one loyal to the United States, the army unveiled a bust of Henry Flipper at West Point in 1976 and awarded him an honorable discharge dated June 30, 1882. The Military Academy now honors Flipper each year by presenting an award to the graduate who best exemplifies "the highest qualities of leadership, self-discipline, and perseverance in the face of unusual difficulties while a cadet."

Reference:

The Handbook a/Texas Online (Austin: Texas State Historical Society).

BUFFALO BILL: MAY HE REST IN PEACE
- DENVER, CO -

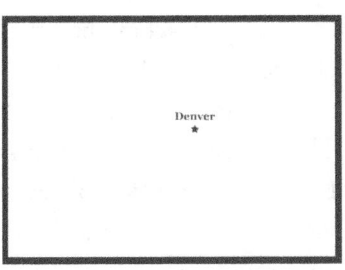

IF WILLIAM F. (BUFFALO BILL) CODY was a showman, at least he was an authentic showman. His fame rested on real exploits, including his killing of Yellow Hand, the Sioux chieftain who had earlier led the massacre of General George Custer and the 7th U.S. Cavalry. But showmanship during one's life is one thing. Showmanship after one's death can be quite another thing. Buffalo Bill's burial arrangements were packed with showmanship.

Toward the end of 1916, Buffalo Bill, having been ill for some time, sought relief at the home of his sister, May Cody Decker, in Denver. He also spent a few days at Glenwood Springs hoping to obtain relief from the mineral waters there. But suffering a relapse after returning to his sister's home, he summoned his attending physician, Dr. East, and asked how much time he had left.

"Thirty-six hours," the doctor responded after much hesitation and further prompting by Cody.

Then calling his brother-in-law, Lew, to his bedside, Cody said,

"The doc says I've got thirty-six hours. Let's forget about it and play some cards."

On the morning of January 9, 1917, Bill announced to all that his time had come. By mid-morning he had lost the ability to speak, so he communicated using the sign language he had learned from the Indians. At noon, he took his last breath.

The question now became, "Where would Buffalo Bill be buried?" Cody, Wyoming, named for Buffalo Bill, wanted the body. So did North Platte, Nebraska, where Bill had a large ranch that he often called home. In his will, Cody expressly had stated his desire to be buried "in some suitable plot of ground on Cedar Mountain, overlooking the town of Cody, Wyoming." He had further directed that "there shall be erected over my grave, a monument wrought from native red stone in the form of a mammoth buffalo." He even willed ten thousand dollars for the creation and upkeep of the grave site.

It would seem that there should have been no question about a choice of burial site. But Frederick Bonfils and Harry Tammen, the flamboyant owners and publishers of *The Denver Post*, had other plans. They were determined to keep Bill's body in Colorado and bury it on Lookout Mountain, a few miles west of Denver. With a spectacular view of Denver from the mountain top, the grave site would become an immense tourist attraction for the city.

History is still not clear as to how the Lookout Mountain site was justified. Bill's widow, Louisa, claimed that Cody had changed his mind toward the end of his life and that Lookout Mountain was his own idea. Johnny Baker, a close friend of the family, confirmed Louisa's report. But several sources claim that Tammen paid Louisa ten thousand dollars to say that Cody had changed his mind. Since Cody's estate was essentially penniless at his death, this might have been a very tempting offer. Regardless of how it was done, it became a fact that Buffalo Bill belonged to Denver.

Buffalo Bill's funeral on January 14 has been described as "the most impressive and most largely-attended ever seen in the West." The body was taken to the state capitol rotunda where it lay in state for three and a half hours. It was a bitterly cold day with deep snow on the ground, yet an estimated 18,000 people filed into the capitol to view the famous westerner. Viewers included the governors of Colorado and Wyoming and the lieutenant governor of Nebraska. Indians and old scouts were also included in the throng. Troopers from Fort Logan in ceremonial dress added dignity to the occasion, as did a delegation of Knights Templar from North Platte. Members of the Colorado National Guard, the Pioneer Society, Elks, and Civil War veterans constituted an honor guard.

Following the viewing, the body was transported on a horse-drawn caisson to the Elks Home for the funeral. Elks, Masons, a number of cowboys, and a crowd of 3,000 trudged through the snow in the procession. Two of the cowboys led a riderless horse, with stirrups reversed, and with Buffalo Bill's pistols hanging from the saddle horn.

In the funeral service, a quartet sang Buffalo Bill's favorite song, "Tenting Tonight on the Old Camp Ground." Eulogies were offered, and then the Rev. Charles H. Marshall, pastor of St. Barnabas Episcopal Church, read the funeral service. Following the funeral, the body went to Olinger's Mortuary where it was to wait five months for burial.

Harry Tammen's plans called for a spectacular burial ceremony on Lookout Mountain. The only problem was that there were not adequate roads for an elaborate funeral procession to reach the top of the mountain, and the necessary construction of a road had to wait for the spring thaws. So Tammen scheduled the burial for June 3, five months after Bill's death. In the meantime, the body lay in a temporary vault with guards hired to make sure it didn't leave town.

The burial was quite a production. According to Gene Fowler, noted reporter for *The Denver Post*, "There was a circus-like atmosphere about the whole thing." It is estimated that 25,000 people gathered at the gravesite on Lookout Mountain. Three thousand automobiles, including some Sells-Floto circus wagons, made the trip.

The Masonic lodge of Golden, Colorado, acting for the North Platte Masons, conducted the services. For two hours, men, women, and children passed by the open casket. The hot afternoon was further lengthened by a number of speeches, and then the ceremonies closed with a rendition of Taps followed by an eleven-gun salute. "No president could have been more honored by the presence of thousands," Fowler wrote.

Because of the heat, the glass protecting Cody's face in the open casket began to steam up on the inside. Inconsistent versions exist of how the casket was protected from the sun. Fowler reports that six elderly and obese Indian women, all claiming to have been Cody's wives, sat on camp chairs beside the grave and opposite from Louisa. With solemn dignity, one of these women rose and walked to the casket, and with her parasol, she shielded the open part of the casket from the sun throughout the service. "It was the gesture of a queen," Fowler later wrote. On the other hand, the aforementioned Johnny Baker claimed that the Indian women were not there and that the shading umbrella was a large beach-type umbrella provided by the mortuary.

It took several years for the concept of "rest in peace" to apply to Buffalo Bill's grave. Rumors persisted that people from Wyoming and also from Nebraska were going to steal the body and rebury it in their own locations. So prevalent were these rumors that at one point, the Colorado National Guard parked a World War I tank at the grave as protection. In 1921 following Louisa'a death and burial beside her husband, tons of concrete were poured onto the site for permanent protection. All those actions, however, are now in the past, and although thousands of visitors come to the grave site each year, it is assumed that Buffalo Bill is now resting in peace on Lookout Mountain.

References:

Gene Fowler, *Timberline* (New York: Garden City, 1933).

Henry Blackman Sell and Victor Weybright, *Buffalo Bill and the Wild West* (New York: Oxford University Press, 1955).

Robert A. Carter, *Buffalo Bill: The Man Behind the Legend* (New York: John Wiley & Sons, Inc, 2000).

John Burke, *Buffalo Bill: The Noblest Whiteskin* (New York: G. P. Putnam's Sons, 1973).

Robert N. Jenkins "Burying Buffalo Bill," *St. Petersburg (Fla.) Times,* March 26, 2000.

ENTREPRENEURS

FERRY CARPENTER BRINGS THE CATTLEMEN AND SHEEPMEN TOGETHER

- RIFLE, CO -

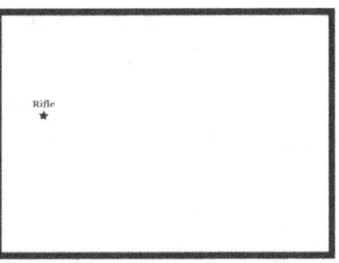

WHEN PRESIDENT ROOSEVELT SIGNED the Taylor Grazing Act in 1934, organization and order came to some 173 million acres of federally owned grazing lands west of the 100th meridian. Prior to this act, the western grazing lands were unmapped, unregulated, and unmanaged. Cattle and sheep grazed wherever water and grass could be found, but not without serious problems between the two factions. After sheep graze, there isn't enough grass for cattle, so when the sheep move in, the cattle have to go to another section of land. But if the sheepmen wanted a grazing section that the cattlemen were using, all they had to do was establish a homestead on it, and the government gave it to them. Needless to say, the two sides hated each other, and numerous range wars were fought.

The Taylor Grazing Act was created to bring about a peaceful and permanent solution to these problems, and Ferrington (Ferry) Carpenter was chosen to bring the cattlemen and sheepmen together to determine how the Act should be implemented. Carpenter, a Princeton graduate and a Harvard lawyer by training, and a Colorado cattleman by preference, understood the problems involved. He was a decisive person who liked to cut right through to the heart of a problem. But he was not a "yes" man, and thus he did not always get along with his boss, Harold Ickes, Roosevelt's Secretary of the Interior. "Ickes fired me three times," boasted Carpenter, "but he always brought me back."

Ferry Carpenter brought the cattlemen and sheepmen together in a series of meetings throughout the western states, beginning at Grand Junction, Colorado. In Grand Junction, the two sides would not meet nor speak with each other. Carpenter arranged for ten sheepmen representatives to assemble in the upstairs of the fire department in nearby Rifle, and he placed ten representatives of the cattlemen in a room of the Winchester Hotel in Rifle. Carpenter located himself in the chamber of commerce office where each side made proposals to him. After a lot of traveling between his office and the two meeting rooms, Carpenter saw that some other approach was needed. Both sides were unyielding, and progress was not being made.

So Carpenter went to a restaurant and secured a single table for 21 people. He put out place cards to specify a seating arrangement in which each cattleman was between two sheepmen, and vice versa. "They had to talk to each other," Carpenter later recalled. "I wanted each side to find out that the other side also puts their pants on one leg at a time."

The stratagem worked, and communication between the two sides began. And as the two sides began to realize that Carpenter intended to deal fairly and impartially with them, their trust in him took root, and the Taylor Grazing Act was implemented throughout the West without further serious problems.

Reference:

Personal conversations with Farrington Carpenter.

NO ONE IS GOING TO ROB THIS BANK
- DENVER, CO -

IN 1907 A SPECIAL KIND OF BUILDING was completed on Denver's 17th Street between Champa and Stout Streets. It was the first reinforced concrete high-rise building west of the Mississippi River. And it was built to be safe and permanent.

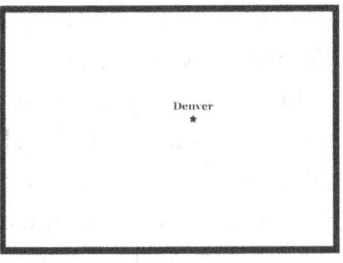

The builders were Charles Boettcher of the Colorado Portland Cement Company and Frederick Bonfils, the colorful publisher of *The Denver Post*. To Boettcher, the building would be a "poster building" intended to be a showplace leading to the sale of great amounts of cement. To Bonfils, it was another of his many ventures in exercising control over the business and politics of Denver.

Already well known for his flamboyant publicity stunts, Frederick Bonfils wanted to demonstrate the strength and permanence of the new building to prospective clients. To do this, he and Boettcher loaded 65,000 pounds of "stuff" onto the first floor of the building and then stoked a fire of 1,800 degrees in the basement below. After 75 minutes they extinguished the fire and demonstrated that no damage had been done. The building was strong, and it was safe.

Frederick Bonfils (left of elephant) and employees of The Denver Post

With the lower part of the building designed to house a bank, a vault of unusual characteristics was built in the basement. The vault served as part of the foundation on which the upper portion of the building rested. The vault had a round door weighing 23 tons through which no robber was going to penetrate. Built by the Diebold Company with alternate layers of stainless steel and copper, the different melting points of the two metals made it impossible to penetrate with a torch. The walls, floor, and ceiling of the vault consisted of 30 feet of concrete poured over reinforcing steel rods.

Several banks occupied the building, the last of which was the Denver National Bank, which bought the building in 1928. There was a lot of wealth in Denver in those years resulting from Colorado's gold and silver mining operations, and the Denver National Bank had to offer the utmost in security for its depositors.

The basement of the building is now occupied by an upscale restaurant called "The Broker," and the bank vault serves as one of the dining rooms. As an indication of the strength with which the vault was originally built, it took six weeks to cut a doorway from the vault to the kitchen.

Just as there has never been a successful escape from Stalag 13 on the TV series *Hogan's Heroes*, there was never a successful robbery of the Denver National Bank – not even an attempted one.

References:

Francis J. Pierson and Dennis J. Gallagher, *Getting to Know Denver* (books.google.com).

Menu of the Broker Restaurant. Denver, Colorado

Displays at the Ouray County Historical Museum.

Photo copyright granted to author by Denver Public Library, Western History Department, Reproduction and Print fee paid for Order #07791

EMPEROR NORTON
- SAN FRANCISCO, CA -

IN A VERY REAL SENSE, IT CAN BE SAID that there were two major cultures in the early American West: (1) the entrepreneurial culture in San Francisco, and (2) the rugged culture in the rest of the West. San Francisco was different—a diamond in the rough. San Francisco was a mecca for entrepreneurs who profited by proximity to the gold fields and by taking advantage of California's agricultural and other natural resources made possible by fertile land and a favorable climate. San Francisco was also the focal point for commerce with Asia, and ships to and from the rest of the world were continually sailing through the Golden Gate.

San Franciscans thought big. Millionaires were constantly being created. Many lost everything through further enterprises. Many became millionaires again. Many became "peculiar." The more peculiar a person became, the more the San Franciscans loved him. Of those who were so loved, one, Joshua Norton led the pack.

Born of Jewish parents in London, England, Joshua Norton made his way to San Francisco in 1849 when San Francisco was more a village than a city. Determined to accumulate wealth, Norton stayed in San Francisco while others rushed to find gold in the High Sierras. Norton bought lots: lots above the water, and lots below the water during high tides. He improved them and sold them at a profit. Having a Midas touch, he quickly became a millionaire. He also became a man from whom bankers and investors sought investment advice. They considered him a genius, and they referred to him informally as Emperor Norton.

Having established an enviable record of success, Norton turned toward more grandiose endeavors, and he embarked on a scheme to corner the rice market of the world. Because of the high regard others had for his business acumen, he had no trouble securing investors and seed money. But after a short period of success, something went wrong. The bubble burst, and his investors lost their money. Norton tried desperately to reimburse them, using his own money in the attempt, but all was lost. He was now penniless, a pauper.

Norton disappeared and then reappeared several months later, having lost his mind as well as his money. Clad in a red and blue military uniform with golden epaulets and with a feather in his cap, he declared himself Emperor of the United States and Protector of Mexico. Needing funds with which to buy food and other necessities, he went to a local printer and ordered certificates of various monetary denominations. Considering it all to be a joke, the printer printed a supply of certificates and gave them to Norton free of charge. It is said that all the restaurants and all the merchants of San Francisco honored Norton's certificates. There is a story, however, that the waiter in a Central Pacific dining car, who did not know of Norton and his situation, refused to honor one of his certificates. Flying into a rage, Norton made such a scene that the conductor rushed in, recognized Norton, and apologized to him. The Central Pacific Railroad pacified Norton by giving him a pass good on all their trains and with free service in their dining cars.

During this period of his life, Norton had two very close friends:

two mongrel dogs named Bummer and Lazarus. (The dogs are featured in their own story elsewhere in this collection.) Rarely was Norton seen without his dogs. When he attended synagogue each Saturday, Bummer and Lazarus were there with him, sleeping at his feet. When he attended Mass at Old St. Mary's Church on Sundays, the dogs were with him. At the opera and at the theater, three seats were always reserved for the Emperor and his retinue. Even at the state capitol in Sacramento, a seat in the gallery was reserved for Emperor Norton. At the end of each day, Norton returned to his royal palace, a flea-bag room rented at fifty cents a night.

After a few years Norton's uniform began to show signs of wear. Actually, it was ragged. Appearing before the San Francisco Board of Supervisors, Norton protested that it was a disgrace for the Emperor of the United States and Protector of Mexico to be seen in such shabby clothing. The Supervisors unanimously voted him a clothing allowance of $30 a year.

If Norton was going to be an emperor, he was going to act like an emperor. He regularly sent messages to the Kaiser and to the Czar suggesting to them how they should run their countries. Pranksters would occasionally respond, thus giving Norton the satisfaction that he was being heard. Concerned at one time about relations between the United States and Great Britain, Norton sent a telegram to Abraham Lincoln ordering him to marry the widowed Queen Victoria. Lincoln graciously responded that he would consider the matter.

Unfortunately, all good things must eventually come to an end. While walking along Kearny Street on a cold January morning in 1880, the aging Emperor Norton collapsed on the sidewalk. He died before passersby could get him to a hospital. The city went into mourning. Flags were flown at half mast. Thirty thousand people followed the funeral procession to a grave donated by The Pacific Club. San Franciscans would miss their Emperor.

Reference:

GEORGE U. HUBBARD

Samuel Dickson, *Tales of San Francisco* (Stanford, California: Stanford University Press, 1957).

William Drury, *Norton I Emperor of the United States A Biography of One of America's Most Colorful Eccentrics* (New York, Dodd, Mead, & Company, 1986).

POLITICIANS

HARRY TAMMEN ADJOURNS THE COLORADO LEGISLATURE
- DENVER, CO -

HARRY TAMMEN AND FREDERICK Bonfils were probably the most colorful and unconventional journalists in all the American West. As owners of *The Denver Post* during the early 1900's, they wielded extraordinary power and influence, 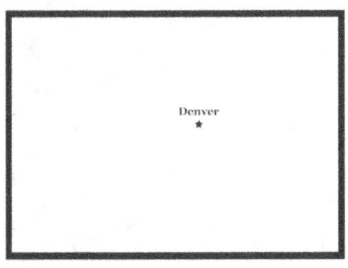 and they generally got their way. Bonfils was more of a businessman, but Tammen was a flamboyant entrepreneur and had been all his life. Tammen got his start in Colorado as a bartender at the Windsor Hotel. He showed his "stuff" on many early occasions, like when Spec Lyons came to town carrying with him a bag of "Peacock Ore," a worthless mineral that looked much like gold.

According to Gene Fowler in his book, *Timberline,* Spec immediately made his way to Madam Rogers' place for libations and feminine entertainment. Not liking the prices the Madam charged, Spec made a ruckus, and Rogers threw him out. But his bag was still inside, and the Madam wouldn't let him back in to get it. She was preparing to entertain the Colorado Legislature that evening, and she couldn't put up with the likes of Spec.

The Rocky Mountain News January 14, 1900

Bemoaning the loss of his bag, Spec told Tammen the whole story in the Windsor Hotel bar that evening. Even though "Peacock Ore" was worthless, Tammen thought he could make profitable use of it. So he also wanted to retrieve Spec's bag.

"We'll get that bag," said Tammen.

"How?" Spec asked. "She won't let me in, and she has the Legislature there tonight."

"That won't stop us. Come on."

The two men drove to a livery stable where, with a little bargaining, Tammen secured a wagonload of hay. Driving the wagon to Madam Rogers', they unloaded the hay on her doorstep.

"Now listen," Tammen said to Spec. "When the excitement begins, you run inside and grab that bag. Don't hesitate."

"But the Legislature's in there," Spec reminded him.

"They'll move to adjourn," Tammen replied as he put a lighted match to the hay.

The stone building was in no danger, but the fire and smoke nevertheless had their effect. Suddenly there were screams, and plunging from the building came the ladies followed by the solons in varying stages of undress.

In the excitement, Spec Lyons recovered his bag, and Harry Tammen was one up on the Colorado Legislature.

References:

Gene Fowler, *Timberline* (Garden City, New York: Garden City Books, 1933).

Photo copyright granted to author by Denver Public Library, Western History Department, Reproduction and Print fee paid for Order #07791

GOVERNOR GILPIN GETS HIS REWARD
- GLORIETA PASS, NM -

SOMETIMES THE REWARDS FOR NOBLE efforts seem not to measure up to the good that has been done. Such was the case on one occasion during the Civil War with Colorado's first territorial governor, William Gilpin.

The Confederacy needed money, and Confederate General Henry Sibley convinced Jefferson Davis that the Confederacy could gain access to the gold mines of Colorado and California. With this goal in mind, General Sibley led a Confederate force into New Mexico in 1861. They were bound for Colorado. Sensing the impending danger, Gilpin knew that a fighting force would have to be assembled in order to help federal forces in New Mexico stop the Rebels. But his efforts to obtain authorization and funding from Washington met with failure because federal officials could not accept the idea of danger from the Confederacy in that part of the nation.

Acting on his own initiative, Gilpin organized the First Colorado Regiment of Volunteers, and without authorization, he issued negotiable drafts on the national treasury to finance the acquisition of arms, ammunition, food, and supplies for this volunteer force. Colonel John Slough led the Coloradoans, and they met the Rebel forces in New Mexico. A major skirmish occurred at La Glorieta Pass (northeast of Albuquerque). Other skirmishes were fought at Fort Union, Peralta (south of Albuquerque), and at Valverde (near Fort Craig). Although both sides claimed victories in these skirmishes, the Confederate forces were nevertheless stopped, and they retreated back to Texas. Governor Gilpin had played a major role in saving Colorado and its vast resources for the Union.

And how was Governor Gilpin rewarded for his patriotic efforts? With a unanimous vote of approval by his cabinet members, President Lincoln fired Gilpin from his gubernatorial post for issuing notes for $375,000 in unauthorized federal debt.

References:

Display at the Cuerno Verde Rest Stop at Colorado City, Colorado.
Website: www.colorado.gov/dpalarchives/govs/gilpin.html.

"Civil War in New Mexico" (Brochure published by the Northeast New Mexico Regional Board).

SUNDAY SCHOOL IS DISMISSED
- AUSTIN, TX -

TO JAMES E. (JIM) FERGUSON GOES the dubious distinction of being the only Texas governor to be impeached and removed from office. Although just reelected for a second term, Ferguson's removal in 1917 came as a result of a serious disagreement with The University of Texas Board of Regents and also because of his "borrowing" $156,000 from a brewery association working to forestall prohibition. Lt. Governor William Hobby served as governor until 1921, and then Pat Neff occupied the governor's office from 1921 until 1925. But the Fergusons were never completely out of politics, and toward the close of Neff's term of office, Jim Ferguson decided that he was ready to come back despite his lifetime restriction from ever again holding public office in Texas. So his wife threw her hat into the ring.

The Ku Klux Klan was a powerful force in Texas at that time with Klan members being represented in law enforcement agencies, in the

Texas Legislature, and even in the ministry. Because two anti-Klan gubernatorial candidates had split the anti-Klan vote, Miriam (Ma) Ferguson gained a run-off position against Klan candidate Felix Robertson. To the Texas voters, it was now a case of the lesser of two evils. Miriam and Jim, now known as Ma and Pa Ferguson, campaigned successfully with the slogan, "Two governors for the price of one," and Ma Ferguson became the first female governor of the State of Texas.

Immediately after Ma's inauguration on January 20, 1925, Pa Ferguson strode into the Ferguson 2 governor's office, disposed of an open Bible left by the departed Pat Neff, and proclaimed, "Sunday School is dismissed. The Governor's Office is now open for business." And for the Fergusons, it was business as usual. Notable among the activities of Ma's term in office was the large number of pardons granted to convicted felons—1,161 in two years. Ma defended these releases by claiming that most of the released prisoners could better serve society by supporting their families at home.

Although Ma Ferguson was the titular governor, Pa Ferguson was the real governor. This working relationship gave rise to a number of jokes and stories told at their expense. One such story, reported by historian David G. McComb, captures the essence of their relationship and their prolific pardons:

Ma was riding an elevator when another passenger accidentally stepped on her foot. "Oh, pardon me," he said.

Ma replied, "You'll have to see Pa."

Running for reelection in 1926, Ma Ferguson failed to win her party's nomination as she lost to Dan Moody, the State Attorney General who is credited as being a major force in destroying the Ku Klux Klan in Texas. Once seated in the Governor's Office, Moody instituted a series of long-needed reforms throughout the State. The ever-present Ferguson's made a final comeback in 1932 when Ma Ferguson managed another victory for two more years in the Governor's Office along with Pa.

References:

David G. McComb, *Texas: A Modern History* (Austin: The University of Texas Press, 1989).

Ken Anderson, "Konvicted," *Texas Alcalde,* July-August, 2000.

QUANAH BECOMES THE COUNTY SEAT OF HARDEMAN COUNTY
~ QUANAH, TX ~

BEFORE 1890 THE SMALL COMMUNITY of Margaret served as the county seat of Hardeman County, Texas. But residents of Quanah wanted to have the county seat and subsequently found a unique law that worked in their favor.

Margaret, at that time, was larger than Quanah and had more males of voting age. Thus the citizens of Margaret thought they could easily outvote the citizens of Quanah if ever the question of moving the county seat should appear on a ballot. But Quanah found a way to add to its list of voters.

The Fort Worth and Denver Railroad had just built through Quanah on its way northward, and there was a law along the railroad that if a man had his washing done in a town for six consecutive weeks, he thereby could be counted a citizen of that town. So the citizens of Quanah went into the laundry business. By the time election day came on February 10, 1890, every FW&D railroad employee between Fort Worth and Texline on the Texas-New Mexico border was a qualified citizen of Quanah and a certified voter. On election day, three Quanah saloons added incentives by keeping open house and offering free drinks to any man who voted "right" as long as he could take them standing.

The Hardeman County Commissioners Court records show that Quanah received 688 votes compared to 164 for Margaret and one for Chillicothe. Thus Quanah became, and still is, the county seat of Hardeman County, Texas.

Reference:

The Medicine Mound Gazette, printed at Quanah, Texas.

CHARACTERS

RUSSIAN BILL: A MAKE-BELIEVE BAD MAN

~ TOMBSTONE, AZ ~

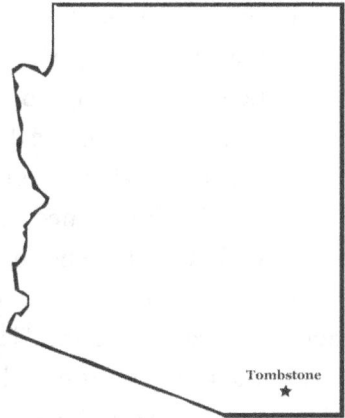
Tombstone

MENTION OF TOMBSTONE, ARIZONA usually brings to mind Wyatt Earp, Doc Holliday, and the Gunfight at the OK Corral. But Tombstone in those days had a host of other characters, one of whom was known as Russian Bill. No one knew his true identity, for he never used any other name. Whenever asked, he simply replied, "My name is Russian Bill."

Russian Bill was known as a bad man. He wore two six-shooters on his belt, and with four notches carved into one of them, he claimed to have killed four men before coming to Tombstone. Doc Holliday once referred to Bill as a "famous outlaw and desperado."

But there was something inconsistent about Russian Bill. His cowboy regalia seemed to be too new. His white, sugarloaf sombrero, high-heel boots, and jangling spurs only drew attention to himself. Still, he blended in with the citizenry, not as a person to be feared, but more as a person who needed recognition of some sort. A heavy drinker, Bill enjoyed games of poker and faro with the other men. When mellow with liquor, he frequently recited verses from poets such as Shelley and Keats. Russian Bill was also a lady's man. He was quite handsome, and his blond, shoulder length hair appealed to the ladies of the evening.

No one in Tombstone ever saw Russian Bill commit a crime. Despite his reputation as a gunslinger, Russian Bill never used his guns in Tombstone. The only trouble he ever caused there were practical jokes that he occasionally perpetrated. One night at the Bird Cage Theater, Russian Bill sat in an upper box with a few of his lady friends. On stage, the Tombstone Nightingale was entertaining the audience with operatic arias. On one of her high notes, a loud, drunken voice called out from Bill's box, "Rotten. Who ever told you you could sing?"

With astonishment, the Nightingale stopped her singing and stood flabbergasted as Billy Hutchinson, the theater manager, rushed out onto the stage. Calling up to Russian Bill, Hutchinson said he would not put up with any more disturbances.

"Interrupt this lady again and you'll get what's coming to you!"

As the singer resumed her song, the loud voice was again heard.

"Awful. Rats. Take her out."

With that, Hutchinson sent his bouncers up to Bill's box, and the audience began to chant, "Throw him out."

Sounds of a scuffle and savage yells were heard, and then shots rang out. As the audience jumped to its feet, a body tumbled from Russian Bill's box and landed on some of the audience who had not been able to get out of the way. But it wasn't a real body. It was a straw dummy made up to look like a man. Laughter roared from Bill's upper box. He and Hutchinson had pulled the "best joke of the season."

In time, Russian Bill's dissatisfaction with his pretense of being an outlaw reached a climax. He was wasting his life as a sham, and he ached for the genuine recognition he so craved. So he made up his mind. It was time to stop pretending to be an outlaw; it was time to become the real thing.

One morning, Russian Bill rode out of Tombstone and was never seen there again. Traveling eastward toward New Mexico, he met two outlaws known as Curly Bill and John Ringo. After introductions, the two outlaws agreed to let Russian Bill join their gang. Russian Bill rode with the outlaw band and socialized with them. He blended in with the gang and made himself useful in a variety of ways. On one occasion, when Curly Bill had been wounded, Russian Bill nursed him back to health. But whenever the gang was in action rustling or stealing, Bill seemed always to be in the background.

Russian Bill was with outlaws, and he was living like an outlaw. But he knew that he still wasn't really a true outlaw because he still had never done anything except make believe. To remedy that shortcoming, Russian Bill had to do something himself. So one day he went out and stole a horse. And he was immediately caught in the act. The deputy sheriff in Shakespeare, New Mexico, arrested Bill and put him in jail. Sandy King, another of Curly Bill's gang, was in the same jail for having gone on a second shooting spree in Shakespeare. A vigilante committee sentenced both men, the real outlaw and the make-believe outlaw, to be hanged. It has been written that Russian Bill, to his credit, met his death like a man.

A few months after Russian Bill's execution, Tombstone's Mayor Thomas received a letter from the United States Consul General at St. Petersburg, Russia, inquiring about a Lieutenant William Tattenbaum, formally of the Imperial White Hussars, who had disappeared from Russia after wounding one of his superior officers in a quarrel and who was last heard of somewhere in Arizona. The missing soldier's mother was the Countess Telfrin, a lady-in-waiting at the Czar's court, and she was very anxious to locate her son. A photograph accompanied the letter. Everyone to whom Mayor Thomas showed the photograph identified it as a picture of Russian Bill. In a gesture of humanity to the anxious mother, Mayor Thomas wrote back that "Lieutenant Tattenbaum, long a prosperous citizen of these parts, honored and respected by all, had recently been the victim of an accident resulting in his untimely death."

Reference:

Walter Noble Burns, *Tombstone: An Iliad of the Southwest* (New York: Grosset and Dunlap, 1929).

A MEMORABLE LESSON IN HUMILITY

- TEMPLE, TX -

HIGH SCHOOL FOOTBALL HAS ALWAYS been big in Texas, and the city of Temple was second to none in its enthusiasm for the sport. Their high school football teams were, and still are, powerhouses. Now if you have a powerful football team, you can expect to have some big, powerful players who are community heroes. But back in the early 1900s, two particular players on the Temple High School football team received a memorable lesson in humility.

Superintendent L.C. Proctor believed in order and discipline, and his enforcement of these principles rubbed against the grain of some of Temple's football players. As local hometown heroes, they felt that Superintendent Proctor should be more lenient with them and their antics. Frank and John were especially resentful of Proctor's "no nonsense" policies.

"One of these days we'll get him off by himself, and we'll beat the hell out of him," they would boast to the other players.

So when word got back to Proctor one day that two of the huskier players were vowing to "beat the hell out of him," he took up the challenge without hesitation.

Calling Frank and John into his office, Proctor invited them to have a seat. Then without another word, Proctor, who was a former wrestler as well as an educator, locked the office door from the inside, went to the window and threw the key out, pushed his desk against the wall, and then took off his shirt, exposing a thick neck, a hairy chest, and lots of muscle. He circled the room as a wrestler might do, then, crouching in front of the boys, he challenged them to make good their boasting.

"OK, guys. I understand that you two are telling people that you are going to beat the hell out of me. Which one of you wants to go first?"

Dumbfounded and chagrined, Frank and John sat there, unable to say a word.

"The door is locked, the key is gone, and we won't be interrupted. Maybe you both want to take me on at the same time," Proctor further challenged.

Needless to say, Frank and John continued in silence as they felt themselves becoming weaker and limper by the minute.

"Now, you watch that wind-blowing boastfulness that's pouring out from a bragger's mouth," Proctor admonished. He then delivered a brief but powerful lecture which the boys never forgot.

Having made his point, Superintendent Proctor then picked up the phone and asked the school principal to come open the door and take the boys back to class.

Frank and John continued as students and as football players, and they now had the utmost respect for their superintendent and his discipline. They became numbered among his staunchest supporters.

Reference:

A. Bryant Messer, *Prairie Queen and Her Choo-Choo Train* (Temple: M and M Publishing Company, 1976).

CARRY NATION ATTEMPTS TO PURIFY DENVER
- DENVER, CO -

WHEN THE "KANSAS TORNADO" BLEW into Denver on a warm August day in 1906, the citizens of Denver braced themselves for action. Carry Nation's reputation as a saloon smasher was already well established, and she had been very vocal about her intentions to clean up Denver and save its fallen women. Although most of Denver's citizens were satisfied with things as they were, they turned out in droves to witness whatever action might take place.

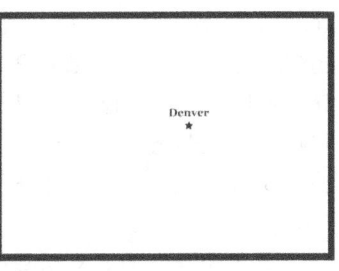

Saturday night at 11:00 was Carry's appointed hour, and Denver's Market Street was her appointed destination. Descending from her room to the lobby of the Midland Hotel, Carry accosted one of the waiting reporters.

"Young man, you have been drinking tonight. You smoke cigarettes. Don't take another drink tonight, and never smoke another cigarette. Never drink again, for surely it will ruin your life."

Then after launching into a diatribe against Theodore Roosevelt, Carry led her followers from the hotel to the Market Street cribs where she found only one girl, a French woman named Blanch Carpentier, clad in the usual abbreviated costume.

"You poor, degraded wretch," Carry proclaimed. "You are the victim of bad, bad men, rotten heredity, and a terrible environment. I am your friend, and I have come to help you."

The police arrived at that moment, and Patrolman Kaylor informed Mrs. Nation that she was under arrest. Noticing the "23" on Kaylor's badge, Carry cried out, "Number 23! Skidoo, Mr. Policeman, don't you interfere with me. I am Carry Nation. I am trying to save these girls, and I will see at least twenty-three of them tonight just to show that your number doesn't frighten me."

The police prevailed, however, and Carry's escapade for that night ended as she was taken to jail.

The following Saturday, Carry was back in Denver. After lecturing to a full house at Denver's Convention Hall, she distributed souvenir hatchets to a group of young boys and then she lectured to a large group of women at the People's Tabernacle. Reading a list of prominent Denver citizens who own property on sinful Market Street, Carry proclaimed, "These hypocrites' wives and daughters are ladies and they wear silk dresses purchased with the slimy coin of shameless sin."

That night, 100 women gathered and followed Carry to Market Street where she vowed to wreck every saloon open past midnight in violation of Colorado's Blue Law, which forbade selling liquor on Sunday. Over 7,000 people gathered to witness the action, but they were disappointed as the police again arrested Mrs. Nation before she could do any damage. Off she went again to jail shouting to the girls of the street to "wash that paint off your cheeks" and to the men for "making these women what they are." Carry spent the rest of the evening reading the Sermon on the Mount to the other prisoners in the jail and leading them in singing hymns. Although Carry didn't get to smash any bars in Denver, she nevertheless left her mark indelibly etched in the memories of the citizens.

Reference:

George U. Hubbard, *Carry Nation and Her Denver Crusade of 1906* (Colorado Springs: Leland Feitz, 1972).

INTRODUCTION

Humans don't have a monopoly on intelligence. Indeed, the phrase "horse sense" is much more than a clever pair of words.

Various types of animals and various breeds within those types may have inherent instincts that make them especially adept at performing certain tasks. Wolves are clever hunters. Sheep dogs can be better shepherds than humans. An endless number of examples could be cited.

Occasionally, within these types and breeds, an individual critter will be blessed with seemingly special intelligence and understanding, thus making that critter especially useful, or adversarial, to man. Such natural intelligence in the animal world is both mystifying and awe inspiring. It is doubtful that the Southwest could have been won without the use of animals. Horses provided rapid transportation and mobility. Mail delivery, warfare, and buffalo hunting relied on the horses. Cattle, buffalo, and sheep provided necessary clothing, shelter, and sustenance. Oxen and mules were needed to pull the wagon loads of machinery, supplies, and a host of other needed items. Camels were even considered as beasts of burden for the arid southwestern desert regions. Dogs are always useful, not only as companions, but for protection and for various kinds of helpfulness according to their natural instincts. And beaver, whose pelts were precious in the east and in Europe, brought needed revenues.

In addition to natural intelligence, male animals aspire to leadership. Every herd or flock or pack will have a natural leader who either assumed his position or attained it through battle.

Animals who are leaders with special intelligence or instincts can be worth their weight in gold. And when in action, they are marvelous to behold.

LARGE ANIMALS

OLD BLUE WAS KING OF THE LONGHORNS
- DODGE CITY, KS -

WHENEVER A GROUP OF INDIVIDUALS remain together for a period of time, leaders emerge. This is true of humans, and it is true of animals. Eventually, a supreme leader will be acknowledged. Old Blue, a longhorn steer born in South Texas, was such a leader.

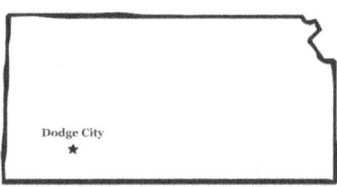

In the spring of 1877, the three-year old Blue was part of a herd of thousands bound for Charles Goodnight's ranch on the Arkansas River just west of present-day Pueblo, Colorado. Each day, Blue, with his long, steady stride, made his way to the front of the herd, and he marched between the pointers as they traveled the Goodnight Trail up the valley of the Pecos. Each day the steer's bluish head and tireless legs set the pace for the rest of the herd.

Goodnight quickly recognized that Blue was no ordinary steer, and he retained the animal when the rest of the herd moved on. "Blue, you'll work no more," Goodnight declared. "You'll be the leader of our herd."

Goodnight hung a bell on Old Blue's neck and attached him to a herd bound for Dodge City where they would be loaded into railroad cars bound for the slaughterhouses of Kansas City. The steer seemed to be proud of the clanging of the bell as he walked along with head high and tail swishing. Very quickly, the rest of the herd knew the sound of the bell and accepted it as their clarion call. At night a cowboy would stuff grass into the bell to keep it quiet, but if the grass slipped out, which it occasionally did, the sound of the bell would bring the herd instantly to its feet ready to march.

Longhorn Steers Ready for Market

For eight years, Old Blue pointed herds from Texas to Dodge City, sometimes twice a year. Whenever a herd had members who were too frisky or otherwise hard to handle, Old Blue would be sent into the middle, and soon all would be following him and the sound of his bell. In every sense, Old Blue was the leader.

Old Blue won undying fame by saving a Goodnight herd from disaster one winter on the outskirts of Dodge City. The Goodnight cowboys had camped their herd just across the Arkansas River from Dodge City. It was a cold wintery night, and about midnight a severe storm arose, scattering the other two herds that were camped nearby. At dawn, the situation looked desperate for the Goodnight herd until the trail boss called out, "Loose the bell and take the river." The men saddled up, the grass was removed from the bell's clapper, and with his bell clanging, Old Blue set out for the river. Breaking the ice at the edge of the river, Old Blue swam the stream and headed straight for the railroad corrals with two thousand cattle following. Inside the corral gate he deftly stepped aside as the others crowded in. The cowboys prodded the cattle up the chutes and into the cars, and as the train pulled out, the saddle horses and Old Blue stretched their necks and watched them go.

On occasion Old Blue did other work such as being yoked to outlaw steers who needed to be brought into line. He would drag them to where he wanted them to be, and they learned quickly to conform.

Old Blue, known as the king of the longhorns, spent his last days in retirement on Goodnight's Palo Duro ranch where he was honored and admired. When he finally died of old age, his cowboy friends chopped off his horns and reverently nailed them above the ranch house door.

References:

B. A. Botkin, *A Treasury of Western Folklore* (New York: Wings Books, 1975).

Photo *Longhorn Steers Ready for Market*, Barker Texas History Center, The University of Texas at Austin, Reproduction and Print copyright fee paid by author, number PPC CN01407 CAH-2

THE INDIANS WERE RESOURCEFUL HUNTERS OF BUFFALO
- COLORADO -

BUFFALO, THOSE NOBLE AND ONCE plentiful animals, were the heart and soul of subsistence for the Plains Indians. From the buffalo, the Indians obtained the essentials of food, clothing, and shelter. The men were the hunters, and they would drag the fallen creatures back to camp, where the women would take over. The women, with help from the men, would open the carcasses and extract and dry the meat. They would tan and soften the hides, which they used for clothing and for tent coverings. From the bones, the men made knives, utensils, and weapons of war. The hair, the horns, the entrails, all had their uses. Everything was used; nothing was wasted.

The Indians of eastern Colorado, as well as those throughout the Great Plains, had to be resourceful as well as economical. Before being introduced to horses and firearms, these Indians devised a variety of ways to trap and kill buffalo. They employed different strategies depending on the terrain and other conditions.

One hunting strategy was to cause a buffalo herd to run off of a cliff and be killed by the ensuing fall onto the rocks below. In some cases, the Indians used specialists known as "buffalo callers" who knew the habits of buffalo better than anyone else. Dressed in buffalo hides, the callers would position themselves in front of a herd, snort and roll on the ground like buffalo do, and lure the herd toward a high cliff. Other hunters coming up behind the herd would instigate a stampede by roaring mightily, stomping their feet, and whirling lighted torches over their heads. Just at the right time, the buffalo callers in front of the running herd would disappear, and over the cliff the buffalo would go. Sometimes whole herds were destroyed in this manner.

Another method used by the plains Indians was to set fire to the grass so as to create almost a circle of fire around the herd. Hunters stationed at the opening of the circle would then shoot their arrows into the escaping animals.

A third tactic involved using the women. After locating a herd of buffalo, the women were summoned to come with their travois and their dogs. The women would create a semicircular fence by setting up their travois, with the small ends up, in the earth and tying them together. Fast running men would holler and chase the buffalo toward the travois fence, and then the women and dogs would make enough noise to repulse the oncoming buffalo. Rushing in with bows and arrows, the men would then shoot the confused beasts.

With the later introduction of horses and firearms, the Indians revolutionized their hunting strategies. But before these new techniques became available, the Plains Indians were quite resourceful in trapping and killing what they needed for subsistence.

Reference:

America's Fascinating Indian Heritage (Pleasantville, New York: The Reader's Digest Association, Inc., 1990).

CLEO HUBBARD MADE THE BUFFALO BEHAVE
~ CLAUDE, TX ~

CLEO HUBBARD, AN ADOPTED SON OF cattle baron Charles Goodnight, was one of the best when it came to controlling wild and cantankerous livestock. He was especially adept at controlling buffalo, beasts that could be very mean at times. Hubbard's main weapons were common sense mixed with nerves of steel, but he  also relied on a bull whip and a six-shooter loaded with salt or something equally harmless that stings.

One day, Hubbard learned that one of Goodnight's buffalo herds were not being fed properly, and he noted that they looked under nourished.

"What's the problem?" Cleo asked the person in charge of the herd.

"There's a mean old cow out there, and every time my man goes out with feed, the cow chases him away."

"Well, I'll fix that," Hubbard replied. Out he went on his horse, and here came the buffalo cow.

"I'll get her coming and going," Hubbard shouted.

Keeping his horse just ahead of the cow, Hubbard let the cow give chase. But with his bull whip, he whipped the cow's nose at every step. When the cow got tired of the whip stings and turned to go back, Hubbard turned his horse also and gave chase to the cow, this time whipping her on her rear end at every step.

There was never any further trouble from the old cow, and regular feeding of the herd resumed.

Reference:

Display in the Moore County Museum in Claude, Texas.

THE COWBOYS CHALLENGE THE CAVALRY TO A HORSE RACE
~ DALLAS, FORT WORTH, AND SAN ANTONIO, TX ~

AMONG THE ANGLOS IN THE GREAT American West, horsemanship was the way of life of two vastly different groups: the cowboys and the soldiers of the U.S. Cavalry. The cavalry, with uniforms, formal training, and the best of equipment, were proud experts with their horses. But the cowboys, self-taught and with whatever clothing and equipment they could afford, were equally adept. Each group had a healthy respect for the abilities of the other, and their rivalries frequently gave rise to occasional contests of skill.

One such contest took place in Texas in January, 1922 when Tex Austin, a rodeo promoter and president of the Cattleman's Association in Texas, challenged the 2nd Cavalry Division to a horse race. Major Terry Allen learned of the challenge when he was summoned into Col. Philip Corbusier's office at Fort Travis.

"There is going to be a horse race between a cowboy and a cavalryman," the colonel announced.

"Who will represent the Army?" Allen asked.

"You will," Corbusier replied, adding quickly, "and we expect you to win."

The race would be a three-hundred-mile trek over a five-day period from the Dallas-Fort Worth area down to San Antonio. Allen would start from Dallas, and his opponent, a cowboy named Key Dunne, would start from Fort Worth. Dunne, who was popularly favored to win, was a one-time wagon boss and a celebrated figure on the range. The two routes would converge at Waco and go through Temple and Austin on the way to San Antonio. Each rider would use only one horse for the entire trip.

Dunne chose to ride a small Texas mustang, a breed known for its speed. Allen, acting on the recommendation of the Division's horse trainer, selected a big black horse that was a combination of a quarter horse and a thoroughbred. Quarter horses were fast for short distances, and the thoroughbred traits added needed stamina.

The race began on a Friday, and Allen took the lead by traveling 52 miles, while Dunne chose a slower pace. Cheering crowds lined the streets in each town through which the riders passed.

Stopping for breakfast Saturday morning, Allen had a little fun with the restaurant owner, who didn't recognize him.

"Major Allen don't have a chance to beat Key Dunne," the restaurant owner commented. "That cowboy will wear out the army officer. And that army horse hasn't a chance to stick it out with a mustang in a 300-mile race."

Major Allen then introduced himself and said, "I'm out in front at present and still in good condition. The joke is on you, so hurry up with the ham and eggs."

Taken back, the restaurant owner replied, "The joke is not only on me, but the ham and eggs as well. Good luck, and more power to you!"

A torrential downpour fell the next day, and both riders were cold, wet, and miserable as their horses sloshed through mud and water on roads that were mostly unpaved. At one point, Major Allen heard that Dunne was having trouble obtaining hay for his horse. In an act of good sportsmanship, Allen arranged for fodder to be sent by automobile to Dunne.

Allen reached San Antonio first, and after checking the condition of his horse, the judges declared him the winner. He beat his opponent by seven hours. In this particular contest, the army dominated the cowboys.

Reference:

Gerald Astor, *Terrible Terry Allen,* New York: Presidio Press, 2003.

OLD BILL'S HORSE STAYED WITH HIM

- ALAMOSA, CO -

IN 1849, THE UTES OF southwestern Colorado were on the warpath. They had just been soundly defeated in a war with the Arapahos, and they were taking out their frustrations against the whites who were beginning to usurp the Ute's "Shining Mountains."

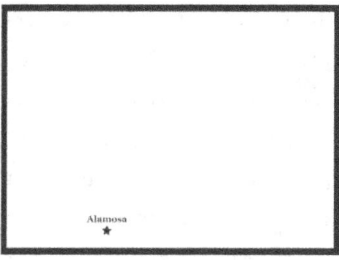

Despite these perilous circumstances, "Old Bill" Williams felt that he could still move freely among the Utes, who he had befriended on many occasions. One of the first of the mountain men, Williams was known in the 1830s and 1840s as one of the best. At various times he was a trapper, a guide, and an army scout, and he spoke the language of the Utes. But in the winter of 1849, Williams and another man known as Doctor Kern mysteriously disappeared while leading a group of Mexicans down to Taos.

For several weeks, Williams' fate remained a mystery, until one stormy afternoon when a party of mountain men were plodding through a wild and dismal canyon in the San Juan Mountains looking for a suitable place to spend the night. As the sun was about to set, they came to a place where the canyon opened into a level glade a few hundred yards in extent. This, they imagined, was a place where no man had ever been. But to their complete surprise, they discovered a horse, standing motionless, in the center of the glade.

Quoting from Stanley Vestal's book, Mountain Men, "they found it to be an old grizzled mustang with cropped ears and ragged tail, standing doubled up with cold, and at the very last gasp from extreme old age and weakness. Its bones were nearly through the stiffened skin, the legs of the animal were gathered under it; whilst it's forlorn looking head and stretched-out neck hung listlessly downwards, almost overbalancing its tottering body. The glazed and sunken eye—the protruding and froth-covered tongue—the heaving flank and quivering tail—declared its race was won."

One of the mountaineers recognized the horse as a Nez Perce steed belonging to "Old Bill." And if the horse was there, surely Williams could not be far away. Making a brief search, they found Williams' camp, and they found Williams himself, sitting with his legs crossed under him, his back to a tree. His body, half covered with snow, was frozen hard as a rock. He had been shot in the head, and a knife had penetrated his breast.

When the atrocities were ended, the Indians and the Mexicans and the animals left the scene, but Williams' horse stayed, waiting patiently and loyally for its master.

Mercifully, one of the mountaineers put a bullet into this steed who had remained faithful to the end and whose own life was far spent. It was time to free the mustang from further suffering and send it to a well-deserved reward.

References:

Stanley Vestal, *Mountain Men* (Boston: Houghton Mifflin Company, 1937).

Howard Louis Conard, *Uncle Dick Wootton* (Lincoln: University of Nebraska Press, 1980).

MULES, THOUGH ESSENTIAL BEASTS OF BURDEN, HAD MINDS OF THEIR OWN
~ SANTA FE, NM ~

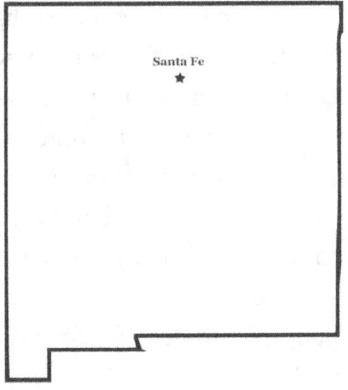

DESPITE ALL THE JOKES ABOUT MULES and their stubbornness, those venerable beasts played essential roles in America's westward expansion. A New Mexico product, mules were introduced to Missourians in 1823 by Major Stephen Cooper, who traded a caravan of goods for four hundred mules at Santa Fe. They quickly became established fixtures in the freighting business. After proving their worth as beasts of burden, mules were used throughout Texas as well as in other areas for hauling goods and people. Many Texas settlers came from the East on the backs of dependable and inexpensive mules.

According to R.L. Duffus writing in *The Santa Fe Trail*, "Cooper's four-legged booty was apparently the beginning of the now world-renowned Missouri mule. He invaded Texas, Oklahoma, and Missouri from the west, filling a need which the rush of settlement into the river country was just beginning to create."

Along with oxen, mules proved to be invaluable beasts of burden, peculiarly suited to the rigorous and arid conditions of the Southwest. The mules were especially well adapted for traveling the arid expanses of the western portion of the Santa Fe Trail. According to Josiah Gregg in Commerce of the Prairies, "This animal is in fact to the Mexican what the camel has always been to the Arab—invaluable for the transportation of freight over sandy deserts and mountainous roads, where no other means of conveyance could be used to such advantage."

Mules can travel for hundreds of miles with bulky and unwieldy loads weighing three or four hundred pounds. There was no cheaper nor more reliable transportation available.

The mules, however, were not the most cooperative of animals, and it frequently took a few hundred miles of traveling to work out their aversions to pulling wagons and carriages. It was a common occurrence for a mule to break away when being hitched, and some would run with chains and harness for a half hour or more until caught by men on horseback. Susan Shelby Magoffin, in her diary, tells of one mule that scampered off. After his pursuer finally succeeded in catching his bridle, the mule refused to turn or be led. "In defiance of all that man could do, he walked backwards all the way to camp leading his captor instead of being led."

The mules were truly useful animals, and they proved to be indispensable to the freighters. But they insisted on continuing to be mules.

Reference:

H. Gordon Frost, "The Santa Fe Trail," *Along the Early Trails of the Southwest* (Austin: The Pemberton Press, 1969).

"JEFF DAVIS' FOLLY" WAS A UNIQUE EXPERIMENT
- CAMP VERDE, TX -

An experiment in western American transportation, though conceded to have been a failure, is well worth remembering. Camels in America? Yes indeed! They were brought here to traverse the Great American Desert, but their survival was rather short lived.

Jefferson Davis, U.S. Senator from Mississippi, advocated the camels as early as 1853. A beast of burden that could navigate America's arid Southwest was needed, and that could only mean camels.

"We must have them," he drawled. "The men who are pushing through the desert and wilderness are shouting for an animal that can go without water for days and still carry a heavy pack on its back!"

When Davis later became Secretary of War under President Franklin Pierce, he got his way by convincing Congress to appropriate $30,000 for the camel experiment. Men and ships were dispatched to the Middle East to purchase 78 of the beasts and to hire some of their native keepers.

It appears that two shiploads of camels arrived in Texas in 1856: one in Indianola on Matagorda Bay, and one at Parsons Pier in Galveston. Upon touching the ground in Indianola, some of the camels broke loose and stampeded in the area, frightening horses and people, before being brought under control by their keepers. In Galveston, after being hoisted from ship to shore in slings, about 40 camels were herded into a nearby corral, where they stayed for several months. Although a curiosity for the younger generation, the camels were unwelcome guests of the city. Whenever the keepers exercised the camels by riding them through the city streets, the horses and mules in the same streets frequently were terrorized and would stampede. In addition, the camels exuded a very offensive smell, and they would occasionally spit at people. But the young boys were delighted at getting to ride the camels at exercise time.

Finally the time came for the westward trek. The first major stop was at Camp Verde just north of San Antonio. Being keeper of the camels was a dubious honor for Colonel Robert E. Lee, Camp Verde's commander at the time. In an expedition from Camp Verde to the Big Bend of the Rio Grande, the U.S. Army proved that camels could outlast mules in adverse conditions or rugged terrain. Then in a caravan, the camels were marched to California's Fort Tejon, just north of Los Angeles. But by the time they got to Fort Tejon, the Civil War had started, and interest in continuing the experiment waned. Their homesick keepers went home, and the soldiers didn't know how to handle the mangy beasts. So the government auctioned the camels to various buyers. Some went to circuses as curiosities. Some went to freight companies and construction companies as beasts of burden expected to be profitable, but they proved to be more trouble than they were worth. In 1864 Sam McLeneghan bought 31 of the beasts and placed them on his ranch in Sonoma County, California. On April 7, 1864, he promoted the "Great Camel Race" in Sacramento. River gamblers, Chinese laborers, and gaudy dance hall girls gathered to see the fun, but of the ten saddled camels who started the race, not one made it to the finish line. They were totally uncooperative. Nevertheless, the camels produced a unique excitement among the people wherever they went.

Camels grazing north of Wichita Falls, Texas

For several years people reported seeing stray camels wandering in various spots throughout the Southwest. Nevada even passed a law forbidding camels "from running at large on public highways." However, the law was rescinded in 1889 when it was realized that there weren't any wild camels left. The camels had had their day, but now it was over.

References:

Galveston Daily News, October 4, 1908.

Galveston Daily News, January 18, 1933.

Ethel Lindemood, "The Camels that Walked Miles for Uncle Sam," *Tempo Magazine,* October 31, 1968.

OLD EPHRAIM WAS A BEAR TO REMEMBER
~ CACHE NATIONAL FOREST, UT ~

OCCASIONALLY IN THE ANIMAL WORLD, one animal of a species stands out as having superior, somewhat human-like qualities. Old Ephraim, a huge grizzly bear, was such an animal. He lived in the early 1900s in the Cache National Forest east of Logan, Utah.

Measuring almost ten feet when standing, Old Ephraim weighed about 1,000 pounds. And he was smart. It took Frank Clark, part-owner of the Ward Clark Sheep Company, ten years to finally trap and destroy the huge beast.

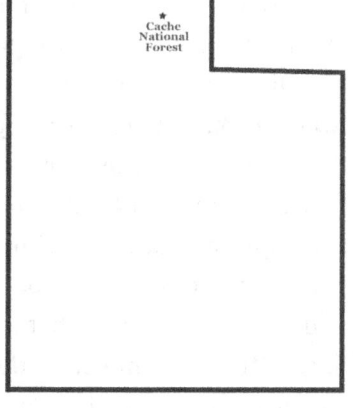

Old Ephraim roamed the woods of the Cache National Forest, and like the other bears in that area, he feasted on sheep whenever he could. The bears were not content to kill just one sheep; instead they would attack a herd and fell as many sheep as they could. Then they would start eating the ones that were down. Rolling a sheep over on its back, a bear would rip open the flesh and eat the tender parts exposed. He would then leave the sheep to die a painful death. Almost every day Frank Clark would find one or two ravaged sheep, and he would shoot them to put them out of their misery. One day he found twenty-three such sheep.

Old Ephraim was an accomplished sheep eater. People knew when he had been around by the huge tracks he left. One of his tracks showed only three toes. But a sighting of Old Ephraim was a rare thing indeed. One day, Sam Kemp, a friend of Frank Clark, suddenly found himself face to face with Old Ephraim. As the huge bear rose up to an erect position, Sam became so unnerved that he was unable to shoot his rifle. Fortunately, Sam and Ephraim parted company without incident, each going in opposite directions. On another occasion, Clark also saw Ephraim. The bear was carrying a sheep up the side of a mountain. Firing his rifle several times, Clark failed to hit the bear, but made him drop the sheep as he scampered out of sight.

Old Ephraim lived in a wallow, a large hollow in the ground that usually had water in the bottom. Old Ephraim apparently enjoyed a mud bath each morning before going out to forage for food.

On many occasions Clark would set a bear trap in Ephraim's wallow. But when returning to inspect the results, Clark would find that the trap had been moved up on the bank of the wallow without having been set off. This went on for ten years until one day when the trap sprang shut. Ephraim had not been caught, but the closed trap was again on the bank, and Ephraim had dug a new wallow below the old one. Clark knew that success was at hand. This time Clark set a larger trap and hid it in the mud. He also attached a heavy logging chain to the trap and wrapped the other end of the chain around a log about one foot in diameter and nine feet long.

Back at his camp, Clark was awakened by Old Ephraim's loud roars. The bear's right forefoot had been caught securely and painfully in the trap. The enraged bear made an attempt to run, but the log at the end of the chain quickly became caught in the trees. Then gnawing at the chain with his massive teeth, Ephraim managed to free it from the log, but only after breaking one of his huge teeth and bleeding profusely in the mouth and nose.

Ephraim knew where Clark was camped, and he headed in that

direction, roaring with pain and rage. Clark was now awake, and with his .25-35 rifle, he headed in the direction of the roaring. As the two foes came within sight of one another, Old Ephraim rose up to full height with the twenty-three pound trap still securely clamped on his uplifted right foot and the logging chain wrapped around his leg. Clark fired six steel balls into Ephraim's body, but the bear kept coming. With only one shot left, Clark thought it best to retreat and head for Logan, about twenty miles away, but he tripped and fell flat on his back. Clark's dog, Jennie, then took up the fight, and Ephraim began to swat at the dog. On his feet again, Clark took a chance, and at a distance of only six feet from the crazed bear, Clark sent his last shot into Ephraim's head. Ephraim fell, as his life came to an end.

Ephraim's body was too large for removal, and the rocky mountain side would not permit a full burial, but Clark and others buried the animal as much as possible. They then piled branches and logs on top of the still exposed parts and burned them in an attempt at partial cremation.

Several days later, Dr. George R. Hill, then a scoutmaster of Troop 5 in Logan, heard of Ephraim's death, and he reported it to the Smithsonian Institute in Washington, D.C. Scientists at the Smithsonian doubted the existence of a grizzly bear in that part of Utah, and they requested his head, with an offer of $25.00 if the animal was truly a grizzly. Hill led his scouts to Ephraim's resting place, and they removed the head and shipped it to the Smithsonian.

They got their $25.00.

Reference:

Newell J. Crookston, *The Story of Old Ephraim* (Privately printed, 1959).

SEA MONSTERS? IN UTAH?
- BEAR LAKE, UT -

ALTHOUGH LOCH NESS IN SCOTLAND has the famous sea monster, there are many other locations throughout the world also claiming to have sea monsters of one type or another. But in the desert of the American west? Why not?

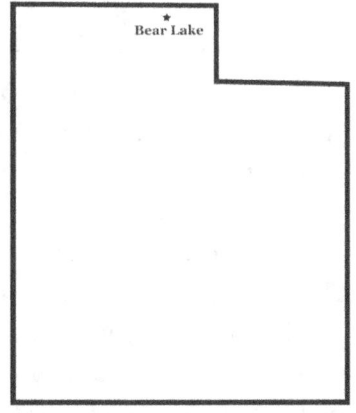

According to legends in both the Shoshone and Ute Indian tribes, Bear Lake, lying across the Utah-Idaho border, was the home of a giant snake-like monster with a mouth large enough to devour a human. Bear Lake, measuring some twenty miles in length and five miles in width, is considered to be a beautiful body of water and a prime tourist destination in the summer. It is sometimes referred to as "the Caribbean of the Rockies."

Although descriptions vary depending on who is telling about it, the monster is thought to be about ninety feet long. It has flippers, big red eyes, and is a fast swimmer. The Utes also claimed to have seen monster babies.

Tales of the monster first attracted public notice when Salt Lake's *Deseret Evening News* in 1868 published accounts of the monster written by Joseph C. Rich. Although Rich did not claim to have seen the monster himself, he nevertheless gave prominence to the concept, and stories about the monster spread across the western states and territories.

Skeptics were quick to point out that Rich owned a general store in the Bear Lake area, and increased patronage by curiosity seekers would make his cash register ring more often.

There have been many additional reports of sightings. In the summer of 1871, the *Salt Lake City Herald* reported a sighting by a local citizen who claimed to have actually captured a baby monster. It was about twenty feet long, and was propelled through the water by its tail and legs. But no one ever saw the captured creature, and no one knows what happened to it.

It is interesting to note that the reports of new sightings always seem to come at the beginning of the tourist season. "It's good for business," says Vie Tritt who, along with his wife, owns a convenience store in the area. Judy Holbrook, a local tourism director, invites people to come and see for themselves. "But plan to stay at least a week," she adds.

The most recent known sighting was reported in 2002. Brian Hirschi, who rents boats on Bear Lake, likes to take tourists out in a special boat he owned that had been designed to look like a sea monster. One evening while Hirschi was anchoring the boat for the night, he looked backward and saw two large humps racing toward his boat. About thirty seconds later, Brian felt something scrape the bottom of the boat and then lift the 80,000 pound boat about six inches out of the water. The monster then shot away leaving a large wake, and about two hundred feet away it disappeared into the middle of the lake.

It should be noted that Hirschi's account of the sighting appeared in a Salt Lake City newspaper on Memorial Day weekend, at the start of the summer tourist season. In response to skeptics, however,

Hirschi has been quoted as saying, "When you join the elite group of people who've seen it, you don't care what everybody else thinks."

Reference:

Articles about the Bear Lake monster posted on Google.

SMALL ANIMALS

THE SAGA OF BUMMER AND LAZARUS
~ SAN FRANCISCO, CA ~

NORMALLY THESE VIGNETTES FOCUS on the human element of the winning of the west. But this one is not about humans. It is about two dogs who captured the hearts of San Franciscans back in the 1860s. Bummer, half Newfoundland and half everything else, was well known on Montgomery Street. He acquired his food in the various Montgomery Street restaurants, and every owner, chef, and waiter knew him. But Bummer didn't beg; he was an aristocrat. Choosing a restaurant, Bummer would station himself at the door and eye the customers as they entered. When he sensed a customer who might have a sympathetic feeling for a hungry dog, Bummer would follow the patron in, settle underneath the patron's table, and gratefully accept any food that dropped to the floor. He was a dog of epicurean tastes. By his selection of restaurants, he dined on delicacies of frog legs, wild duck, roast pork, bear meat, or venison. He ate on the spot and never carried out any bones nor meat scraps. Although he was a bum (hence his name), he was a high-class bum. Still, had Bummer's life been nothing more than this, he would have been little more than just another dog.

Bummer's real claim to fame began in 1861 when workers uncovered a huge nest of rats while excavating for a new building near the Blue Wing Saloon. San Franciscans hated rats, which had been a bane of the city since being introduced by the sailing ships of 1849. The uncovered army of rats started scattering and were overrunning the sidewalk, when suddenly from out of nowhere came Bummer at full speed. With a growl and with teeth showing, this dog waded into the rat colony and began destroying them by the score. When the battle ended, Bummer was the clear victor. The local newspapers proclaimed his feat in headlines, and citizens began to brag of their personal friendship with this special dog. Bummer, the Montgomery Street epicurean, was now the hero of San Francisco.

Bummer added to his fame shortly thereafter when a large, ferocious dog viciously attacked a small, mangy cur near the Parrot Building where Bummer was sleeping in the shade. Realizing that the little dog was about to be killed, Bummer shot out of his resting place, leaped on the larger dog's back, and somehow drove him away. He then sat by the wounded mongrel, and a mutual bonding occurred. The next day Bummer made his usual rounds of the restaurants, but he didn't eat the dropped morsels. For the first time he carried them out in his mouth. Curious, some of the Montgomery Street citizens followed him, and he led them to some empty packing crates in a vacant lot where the injured little mongrel lay, too weak to move about. There, Bummer dropped the food, and with whines and guttural sounds, he coaxed the little dog to eat. Again, Bummer was the toast of San Francisco.

After Bummer's new friend recovered from his wounds, the two dogs were inseparable. Wherever Bummer went, the little dog tagged along, and he soon became a favorite of San Franciscans along with Bummer. "He needs a name," the people said. "Bummer brought him back from the dead, so we'll call him Lazarus."

For months Bummer and Lazarus were companions until one day

when someone shot Bummer in the leg. Instead of helping Bummer in his recovery, Lazarus disappeared, leaving Bummer all alone. The citizens were outraged by Lazarus' disloyalty. Again the newspapers headlined the situation, praising Bummer for his former courage and loyalty, and castigating Lazarus for his infidelity. Eventually, Bummer recovered, Lazarus returned, and all was forgiven.

Stray dogs, however, were overrunning San Francisco, and the city fathers passed an ordinance that any dog caught on the streets without a muzzle would be impounded and destroyed if not picked up within 24 hours by his owner. "But what about Bummer and Lazarus?" cried the people. "Make them an exception. They belong to the whole city." So the city supervisors, in executive session, issued an order under the seal of the city that Bummer and Lazarus were wards of the city and were authorized to roam the streets freely, unmuzzled and unfettered, and without the restraints being imposed on dogs of lesser distinction.

Bummer and Lazarus became even more endeared to the citizens of San Francisco when they attached themselves to Emperor Norton. With a Midas touch, Joshua Abraham Norton amassed a fortune, and then he set out to corner the rice market of the world. All went well for a while, but then the bubble burst. Norton lost not only his wealth and friends, he also lost his mind. Wearing a splendid uniform, he became a fixture in the city as he proclaimed himself emperor of the United States and Protector of Mexico. San Franciscans went along with the antics of this now harmless man. He even printed his own scrip which restaurants and theaters honored. And wherever Norton went, Bummer and Lazarus were with him. The two dogs were even allowed to sit at Norton's feet as he sat in his permanently reserved seat at the opera house.

All went well until October, 1863 when a fire truck racing to a fire ran over Lazarus and killed him. The city declared a day of mourning, and in a funeral procession, thousands of San Franciscans, led by the fire trucks, paraded down San Francisco's Market Street. But instead of being buried, Lazarus' body was stuffed by a taxidermist and preserved on display. Bummer was inconsolable. He dropped his regal bearing, abandoned his usual routine, and became a guttersnipe. His friends forgot about him until one day he was found mortally injured after being kicked by a drunken person. Then the city remembered him again. Each day the newspaper carried a report of his condition. When he finally died, the city went into mourning again. Although there was no funeral procession this time, the press printed four quatrains of elegy, and Mark Twain wrote a long eulogy for the *Enterprise*. Bummer's body was also stuffed, and with Lazarus, the citizenry placed it on display in a museum in Golden Gate Park, where they both remained until a later generation decided it was silly to save the bodies of two dirty old mongrel dogs.

Reference:

Samuel Dickson, *Tales of San Francisco* (Stanford: Stanford University Press, 1957).

SPIKE WAS BORN TO FIGHT
- CLARENDON, TX -

Spike started life as a town dog in Donley County, Texas. But this wirehaired fox terrier was born to fight. It can safely be said that every cat in town dashed to the nearest tree whenever Spike came around. On Spike's best day, his unofficial toll stood at six fights, two dead cats, and seventeen chickens. It was clear that Spike had to leave town.

Swede Larson, a government hunter, agreed to take Spike and give him a country home. Swede had a pack of lion dogs, and Spike immediately demoralized the whole pack by picking a fight with every one of them. Again, Spike had to go.

A cowboy named Hank Rowden became Spike's next owner. Hank theorized that any dog too tough for lion dogs should be excellent as a cow dog. Spike rose to the occasion. He helped herd the cattle by day, and he was always after the biggest steer in the herd. Spike also guarded the cowboy's camp by night, and it wasn't long before even the skunks stopped coming in to scavenge for food. Spike and Rowden developed a love for one another, and Spike insisted on sleeping each night at the foot of Rowden's cot next to Rowden's boots. The two spent many months together on the JA and the XIT ranches in the Texas panhandle and on the Double Circle Ranch in Arizona.

For some reason, Spike had a special aversion toward Apache Indians and their dogs. One day as he nipped an Apache's horse on the heel, the horse bucked, throwing the rider to the ground. Spike added insult to injury by grabbing the Indian by the pants and ripping them.

With Rowden standing by, the not very happy Indian muttered, "Me killum little dog. Someday me killum pooch."

Rowden replied, "You killum little dog and cowboy killum Indian."

One night a stray cow puncher rode into camp accompanied by his own dog. Spike immediately whipped the dog, although outweighed by 20 pounds. The impressed cow puncher exclaimed, "Queer looking mutt."

"Mutt nothing," Rowden rejoined. "Spike's got a pedigree. There ain't many dogs like him in this country. He's a rare breed. He's a hardware terrier."

Although a fighter, Spike didn't learn some of the lessons he should have learned. He never learned to lie flat after nipping at the heel of a horse or cow. As a result, he took several kicks, but he always came back for more. Another of his traits was to jump up and grab the tail of an animal and hang on by his teeth. But he did this one time too many. Grabbing onto a mule's tail on the Double Circle Ranch in Arizona, Spike slipped and was in just the wrong place when the mule kicked back. The blow put Spike into a sleep from which he never awoke. In a rage, Rowden took out his knife and killed the mule. In so doing, he showed his love and devotion for his fallen companion, but it cost him his job at the ranch.

Reference:

"Spike," a typescript account by Ross Santee on display at the Saints Roost Museum in Clarendon, Texas.

A DOG NAMED THORNBURG?
- MEEKER, CO -

Trouble was brewing at the White River Indian Agency near present-day Meeker, Colorado. Following the Civil War, hunters, trappers, and prospectors flooded into Colorado, pushing the Ute Indians aside and usurping their hunting lands. With Chief Ouray away on a hunting expedition in 1879, Ute Jack, Ouray's second in command, was eager to send the Utes into battle against the encroaching whites.

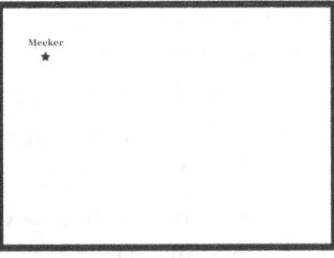

Sensing the gravity of the situation, Nathan C. Meeker, the White River Indian agent, sent out a call for help. In response, Major Thomas Thornburg, commandant at Fort Steele in Wyoming, led three companies of cavalry and one of infantry to reinforce Meeker's employees. About 20 miles northeast of the agency, a band of Utes ambushed Thornburg's force, killing Thornburg and half of his soldiers. The others made their escape back to a wagon train that had accompanied the expedition. (These events constituted the opening scenes of a later tragedy known as the Meeker Massacre, in which the Utes killed Meeker and all males at the White River Indian Agency.)

When the surviving soldiers returned to the scene of the ambush, the only living thing they found was a small, hungry, and thoroughly frightened puppy cuddled next to its dead mother. After feeding the puppy and making him more comfortable, the soldiers named him Thornburg in honor of their dead commandant. When they returned to Fort Steele, the soldiers took the puppy with them.

As Thornburg grew to maturity, there was nothing to distinguish him from the other dogs in camp except that he made it clear that he did not like Indians, and he had an almost equal disdain for civilians. As a grown dog, however, Thornburg began to distinguish himself with special acts of loyalty and bravery.

There had been a rash of thievery at Fort Steele, and on one stormy night a sentry heard loud barking and growling. Rushing to investigate, the sentry found Thornburg with bared fangs standing over a fallen civilian. When the corporal of the guard also arrived, they found a sack of stolen contents near the prostrate man. Thornburg instantly became the camp hero, and he was granted privileges not accorded to the other dogs, who were to be exterminated whenever caught on the parade grounds.

During the melee, the thief had slashed Thornburg with a knife, and thus knives were added to the list of things Thornburg hated.

For a while, Thornburg had no master. He ate at the fort's kitchen, and he allowed all the soldiers to pet him. But in time a civilian teamster known as Buck Buchanan made friends with Thornburg, and a bonding resulted. As Buck's dog, Thornburg found himself moving to Fort Bridger in southwestern Wyoming.

On one occasion in this new environment, two drunken men in a game of faro began quarreling, and when one raised his arm to stab the other with a knife, Thornburg instantly sprang and sunk his teeth into the wrist of the attacker. Even though the attacker had to go to the hospital to have his wrist repaired, he was later grateful to Thornburg for preventing a murder he did not really want to commit.

Thornburg showed his exceptional qualities in a number of other ways. No unfriendly Indians could sneak up to the fort when Thornburg was there. He always sounded alarms of such occurrences. He also saved a young boy's life by leaping into a raging torrent of water and dragging the helpless boy to its banks. As a gesture of thanks, the boy's grateful parents gave Thornburg a new collar with a silver plate engraved with the dog's name along with the words: "For most distinguished gallantry."

Thornburg also became a mule herder for Buck. The army allowed Buck to keep his own mules in the same corral with the army mules, and Thornburg knew which mules belonged to his master. Whenever Buck wanted to separate his mules from the others, Thornburg would dash into the corral and perform the task. Thornburg was good at this task, and he seemed to enjoy it. But it eventually cost him his life.

One day when Thornburg was separating out Buck's mules, some new shave-tail mules were also in the corral. Shave-tail mules were unbroken mules that were distinguished by having the hair on their tails clipped short. Most of the army mules in the corral knew Thornburg and stayed clear of him, but occasionally the dog would jump at one of them to get him out of the way. On this fateful day Thornburg jumped at a new shave-tail and received a kick that sent the dog flying. It was a kick from which Thornburg never recovered. He died on September 27, 1888.

Thornburg's Grave at Fort Bridger, Wyoming

Today Thornburg's grave is lovingly preserved at Fort Bridger. Surrounded by a white picket fence, the grave contains a headstone on which the following sentiment is engraved:

> *Man never had a better, truer, braver friend.*
> *Sleep on old fellow.*
> *We'll meet across the Range.*

Reference:

Albert Cooper Allen, *Thornburg* (Pamphlet printed by the Fort Bridger Historical Association).

THE LACEY DOGS BROUGHT IN THE HOGS
- LLANO, TX -

LLANO COUNTY IN TEXAS ABOUNDED in acorns and wild hogs. Because they lived in the wild, these hogs didn't know what an ear of corn looked like, but they relished the acorns that were free for the asking on the ground. Therefore, in years in which there was a bumper crop of acorns, there was also a bumper crop of fatted hogs to send to market. That is, if you could catch them.

Catching the hogs was one of the challenges the Lacey brothers took on after moving to Llano County from Tennessee. Riders on horseback can't corral the hogs because they run between the horses' legs, goring them with their tusks as they go. The riders can't rope them because they run with their noses close to the ground. Ordinary dogs can't handle the hogs either.

The Lacey brothers had three members of the canine family, none of which could be used for rounding up hogs. Frank Lacey had an English Shepherd dog that was good at working sheep and cattle, but not hogs. John Lacey had a female greyhound, and George Lacey had a wolf that he kept tied to a live oak tree.

One day, Frank got an idea. If they could merge the characteristics of these three animals into a three-way cross breed, they might produce an animal having the natural herding instinct of the shepherd, the speed of the greyhound, and the stamina and trailing ability of the wolf. They succeeded in accomplishing the breeding, and the result was an instant success. The Laceys now were producing "hog" dogs that became known in those parts as Lacey dogs. Comparable in size to a wire-haired terrier, the Lacey dogs were reputed to be "tough as a boot, hard as nails, and enduring as a pocket knife."

A Lacey dog brought the hogs in by leading, not chasing, them into the corrals. After finding a hog out in the open country, the Lacey dog would torment the hog and cause him to start squealing. Then, as a whole family of fifteen or twenty hogs would rush in to the rescue, the "Lacey" would circle about them at a safe distance and get them bunched together. Continuing to bark and snarl, the dog would tease the hogs until they got mad and started chasing him. Then off the Lacey would run, straight for the corral with the hogs hot on his tail. Inside the corral, the hogs would think they now had the dog cornered, but the dog merely jumped the corral fence as the men closed the gates of the corral. "The dog does it by instinct," Jake Winkel, a Llano County rancher claimed. "We don't teach him."

Lacey dogs were also useful for driving hogs to market. One local resident remembered his father buying several hundred hogs in Mason and driving them to the railroad pens at Llano. "Those hogs would string out like a bunch of steers. Out in front would be our old lead dog, Jep, with other dogs on the sides to keep them out of the brush."

Lacey dogs were prized animals. "I wouldn't take a thousand dollars for my dog if I couldn't get another," one rancher claimed. "My dog is worth the pay often men. Last year I gathered seventy head of fat hogs with my Lacey dog. So you see, that dog was worth $3,000 to me in one season."

Reference:

Sam E. Harris, "Hog Dogs!," *True West,* January-February 1956.

THE LOBOS WERE MEAN BUT NOBLE ANIMALS
- SAN MARCOS, TX -

THE LOBO WOLF, ALSO CALLED A timber wolf, is a fascinating animal. Although mean, the lobos also commanded the admiration and respect of those who knew them.

In earlier years before their ranks were decimated by ranchers and bounty hunters, lobos traveled and hunted in packs, and they used clever strategies. Predetermining the course they wanted their intended victim to travel, pack members would station themselves at intervals along the course. A couple of lobos would then go into a herd, cut out the fattest animal, and drive him to the course that had been laid out. The lobos would then nip at the hind legs of the fleeing animal, seeking to cripple it by biting through its hamstring. Working as a relay team, fresh lobos would take up the chase until the animal collapsed from exhaustion or from being injured. Now the lobos would attack in mass, first ripping open the rear flanks, and then opening the middle and disemboweling the still alive, but dying, animal.

In later years, the lobos were reduced to hunting in families or alone. Rather than subjugating themselves to a pack mentality, the lone wolves exhibited their own personalities and wiliness. Some were more successful than others, and almost every sheepherder had his own stories about certain wolves that had evaded capture for years. Old Black, in the Big Bend area, did an estimated $30,000 of damage and was alleged to have killed two Mexican herders. Old Reddy, in Hays County, did $15,000 over a ten-year period. When finally captured, he was taken to the town square in San Marcos, Texas, and publicly executed.

A good lobo could survive for six or more years and kill up to $50,000 worth of sheep. A toll of thirty sheep in one night was sometimes achieved. Sometimes the lobo killed for food; sometimes just for sport.

In the late 1800s the lobo population of Archer County, Texas grew to such proportions that county officials offered a $50.00 bounty for every lobo hide brought in. The lobos would do their marauding at night and then spend their days in a thicket too dense to be entered by man or horse. But a local Castleberry company thought they knew a way to dislodge the lobos.

Thinking to cash in on such the opportunity of the offered bounties, the Castleberry Company brought in 50 Russian staghounds from Chicago. Upon being led to the wolves' lair and set loose, the hounds charged toward the thicket, but the lobos did not run. Instead, working as a team, they placed themselves in a semicircular pattern around the openings to their lair, and awaited the charging hounds. The human bystanders heard sounds of a terrible fight. At the end of the fight, only four hounds were still alive, and they limped away with difficulty.

The great reduction of the lobo population came as the result of concerted efforts by the ranchers. Sometimes the ranchers would go out on their own forays, and sometimes they would hire professional "wolfers" to do the job. On occasion, it would take months to trap and kill a certain troublesome lobo. Each lobo had his own style of operation. "You can't catch every lobo by the same tricks," the wolfers would explain. Time was required to study the lobo's habits and learn where and when to expect his appearances. One of the tricks used by wolfers would be to capture a female lobo, spend a few months taming her, and when in heat, put her out as a lure for the killer lobo.

One significant trait of the lobos is that they rarely attacked humans. In Europe and Asia, wolves attack people, but in America they learned to stay away from the Indians arrows and spears, and they transferred that same respect to the white men. Lobos may taunt, but they generally maintained a distance from the Indians and from the white men. When putting out a trap, every human sign and smell must be removed. Even when using a rabbit for bait, human smell must not be present. Lobos are smart and wary, and a human smell will cause them to leave everything alone.

In another way, wolfers were smart too. After displaying a lobo scalp to a rancher and collecting a bounty, the wolfers would ask to keep the scalp as a souvenir. They would then take the same scalp to the next rancher and collect an additional bounty. The ranchers soon caught on to the scam, and they stopped it by marking each scalp before returning it.

When caught in a trap, a lobo was not averse to chewing off the entrapped paw and limping away on the stump of a leg. Occasionally when following the trail of a lobo, the pursuer would be following tracks consisting of three paw prints plus the print of a stump. Those animals that had escaped from traps were much more difficult to trap a second time, and their endurance frequently led to sobriquets of nicknames. Old Club Foot, Old Crip, Old Stubby, and Old Two Toes were typical names used. One such lobo, called Old Three Toes, eluded capture for so long and killed so many sheep that he attained a heroic status. When finally caught, he was stuffed and displayed in the First National Bank at Memphis, Texas.

Daring, independent, proud, and crafty, the demise of the lobo symbolizes the demise of the frontier in the Southwest. The lobos possessed a nobility that is no longer to be seen.

References:

Winifred Kupper, The Golden Hoof (New York: Alfred A. Knopf, 1945).

Jeannine Hodge, History of Holiday, Texas (Quanah & Wichita Falls: Nortex Offset Publications, Inc., 1972).

THOSE MAJESTIC ROCKY MOUNTAIN BIGHORN SHEEP
~ COLORADO ~

ROCKY MOUNTAIN BIGHORN SHEEP are majestic animals. Standing on a rocky precipice, head proudly held high with massive horns curving gracefully up and back and down, a bighorn sheep presents a magnificent sight. Designated officially as  Colorado's state animal, it is unlawful to pursue, take, hunt, wound, or kill a bighorn sheep except under prescribed circumstances.

Rocky Mountain bighorn sheep are found from the southern United States all the way up to Alaska, but only in the mountainous areas. In Colorado, which claims to have the largest population of these animals, they are found mostly at elevations above timberline. With a keen sense of balance that enables them to have stability on ledges only two inches wide, bighorn sheep do well in places inaccessible to humans.

Bighorn males are three to three and a half feet tall at the shoulder and weigh up to three hundred pounds. The females are slightly smaller. They graze on grasses and other plants, and they can go for long periods of time without water, especially in the winter. They eat during the day and sleep at night. They have excellent eyesight which makes it difficult for humans to approach unnoticed. On level ground bighorns can run at speeds up to thirty miles an hour, and they are also good swimmers. They are gregarious and like to group themselves into herds of eight to ten sheep. The rams usually segregate themselves into all-male herds

In addition to their majestic appearance, bighorn sheep have interesting fighting and mating traits. The rams don't defend territories, but they do fight for the right to mate with a particular female. Fighting among rams is done by head butting, and some fights have been observed to last over twenty-four hours. Mating is done in the fall or early winter, and lambs are born the following spring.

Another interesting characteristic of bighorn sheep is that they do not vary their migration patterns between summer and winter ranges. The young lambs, traveling with the rams and ewes, learn one route, which they follow year after year. When the lambs become independent adults, they still do not vary from the route they have learned. Thus attempts to transplant bighorn sheep from one locality to another have generally failed because the sheep cannot manage the seasonal migration in their new localities.

Coloradoans are justly proud of their official state animal.

Reference:

Colorado Division of Wildlife website, and other bighorn sheep websites.

INTRODUCTION

CONSIDERING THE HARDSHIPS AND THE INTENSE LABOR REQUIRED TO earn a livelihood on the western frontier, the people who settled that area were amazingly literate, social, and cultured. Although far removed from established civilization, social and cultural values remained important to the settlers even though the means of accommodating these values frequently carried unique aspects.

When time permitted, the people gathered together for any number of reasons: to help one another in erecting a building or harvesting a crop, to dance following a pot luck social, to engage in contests of skill or strength, to have a quilting bee, or just to relax and exchange the time of day and ease the feeling of isolation.

Traveling troupes of entertainers provided drama, music, and other types of cultural performances. As these entertainers traveled their circuits, they found no shortage of people in their audiences. Because of the distances involved and the sparse population density in many areas, weeks or even months would pass without entertainment from traveling troupes. In these situations, the locals took to the stage and created their own cultural performances.

Dances were held monthly (weekly when possible) in some central location convenient to the local populace, usually in the school or church building. Often, one building served both functions. Fiddles and harmonicas were the main music makers. When brass or reed instruments were available, that was extra special.

Education of children was important. If teachers could not be imported from the East, local ladies would rise to the occasion. The only problem of importing teachers, mostly female, was that most school districts required their teachers not to marry during the term of their contracts. In an environment where males outnumbered females by a wide margin, new teachers were always in demand.

Reading was a popular pastime, and many families prided themselves for the libraries they had in their homes. And when news from the East came in the form of newspapers or mail, everyone wanted to be updated. Local newspapers were also quite popular.

As time progressed, towns and cities came into being, and home life and city life became more as we know them today. Even so, activities in those early homes and in those new and developing towns had their share of unique social interaction, as some of these stories will attest.

When one remembers that the Native Americans in this land were replaced by people from foreign lands and that originally this nation was a melting pot of foreign cultures, the term "Ethnic Influences" seems illogical and almost irreverent. But very quickly, the ethnicities involved in conquering the harsh realities of the Southwest were swallowed up in the common cause of survival in a land that was generally very inhospitable to human encroachment.

As individuals, an amalgamation occurred. But as large groups of immigrants arrived from Asia and Europe, customs were brought that endured the pioneering times. Many of these imported customs endure to this day.

From Asia, large groups of Chinese were brought to this country, primarily as cheap labor in the gold and silver mines and as railroad builders. From Europe, large groups from many nations emigrated to this nation for a variety of economic and religious reasons.

While the stories in this section (as in other sections) deal with human interest aspects of these immigrants, it is hoped that the cultural roots of these peoples will also be evident. It is the amalgamation of all that made the American West great!

CULTURE

CULTURE? IN DEATH VALLEY?
~ DEATH VALLEY, CA ~

DEATH VALLEY, THE LOWEST POINT IN the Western Hemisphere, is arid and barren and very inhospitable to human existence. The only human activity there in the 1880s was from gold-seeking prospectors and from travelers to northern California's established gold mines. But instead of finding gold in Death Valley, the prospectors found large deposits of borax.

With the discovery of borax, an influx of people came seeking the wealth to be had. Mining towns were established with the usual collection of hotels, saloons, and social halls. Businesses came into being. Men began extracting the borax from the surface salts, and they shipped it 165 miles south, across the Mojave Desert, to Barstow under the famous "Twenty Mule Team" brand.

Along with their mining ventures, the Death Valley population wanted a degree of culture and some social activities. Almost every western mining camp had some kind of facility for plays and concerts by traveling groups of performers. The residents of Death Valley Junction built a social hall for just such a purpose. But their sojourn in Death Valley became short lived when richer deposits of borax were discovered in the Mojave Desert to the south. The people moved south, and almost everything in Death Valley was abandoned. Death Valley Junction's social hall, and almost everything else, remained an empty shell for about 80 years until discovered in 1967 by a New York City dancer named Marta Becket.

In her youth, Marta fell in love with dancing as she attended operas, concerts, and ballets with her father, a New York City newspaper reporter. She soon was on stage herself, performing in night clubs, Broadway shows, and at Radio City Music Hall. But dancing with others was not to her liking. She wanted to be on her own.

At the age of 29, Marta created her own show, arranged the music, sewed her costumes, and went on the road, performing mostly at various colleges. She also had talents as a painter, and she helped support herself by selling paintings in New York's Greenwich Village.

Marta's life changed in 1967 while on a camping trip in Death Valley with her husband, Tom. Because of a flat tire on their vehicle, they made their way to Death Valley Junction seeking a gas station where repairs could be made. It was a case of love at first sight. Marta fell in love with the abandoned Amargosa Hotel, the adobe houses that had the look of a Mexican village, and the abandoned social hall with its tiny stage. She and Tom returned to New York, gathered a few belongings, and moved to Death Valley Junction. Marta was 42 years old.

Marta and Tom rented the social hall for $45.00 a month, and after extensive repairs and renovations, they renamed it the Amargosa Opera House. She staged her first performance in 1968. The attendance was not overwhelming; only the three Mormon families living in the area attended. Each family donated $1.50 for admission.

Marta has been performing at the Amargosa ever since. "It's mystifying. I feel as if this is what I was intended to do," she once told a newspaper journalist. Marta writes the songs and dialog, paints the sets, and makes her own costumes. Her fame has spread, and she now gets audiences that sometimes fill the 114 seat theater, but in the early years there, she frequently performed to an empty house. An empty house, though, was no excuse for canceling a show. Marta danced anyway.

"I'll create my own audience," she decided in the early years. For six years, she drew and painted royalty, nobility, bullfighters, and various other characters on the walls of the theater, and she had them all cheering for her.

At last count, Marta has created a repertoire of fourteen shows, and tourists are sometimes lined up outside the opera house waiting to get in and be entertained by a 78-year-old lady who has passionately devoted her life to dancing. Death Valley Junction's social hall is alive and well.

Reference:

The *Denton (Texas) Record-Chronicle,* January 6, 2002. (Article by Angie Wagner, Associated Press Writer.)

INA COOLBRITH HELPS LAUNCH SEVERAL WESTERN WRITING CENTERS
~ SAN FRANCISCO AND OAKLAND, CA ~

IN 1915 THE CALIFORNIA Legislature bestowed the title of Poet Laureate of California on Ina Coolbrith. During her long career in Oakland and San Francisco, she produced several volumes of poetry that were appreciated not only in California, but also in the more sophisticated East and in Europe. New England's John Greenleaf Whittier once offered Ina a place in his home. In England, George Meredith referred to Ina as "one of the few lyric poets who have impressed me."

In July 1868, Ina, along with Brett Harte and Charles Warren Stoddard, produced California's first literary magazine, the *Overland Monthly*. The three were known in California literary circles as the Golden Trinity, and on almost any day they could be found sitting on the parlor floor in Ina's Russian Hill home reading poetry to one another and planning future issues of the *Monthly*. That same parlor was a gathering place for many literary visitors, including Mark Twain, who is reputed to have adored Ina.

Although a renowned poet in her own right, Ina's major contribution to Western literature may have been the encouragement and impetus she gave to others.

Working with Ina as co-editors of the *Overland Monthly*, Brett Harte, who was as yet unpublished, complained to Ina about a lady proofreader who refused to work on a story he had written for the *Monthly*. Dejected by the proofreader's vehement complaint about the story's low moral quality, Harte had decided to withdraw it. Ina read the story and liked it.

"It's a good story," she proclaimed. "Don't you dare withdraw it. We're going to publish it. "

As a result, "The Luck of Roaring Camp" saw the light of day, and Brett Harte's writing career was launched.

Cincinnatus Heine Miller once visited Ina with a volume of his poetry that had been rejected and apparently not even read by a publisher. "With a name like yours, it's no wonder he didn't read it," she surmised. "You have to have a simpler and more musical sounding name." Then thinking of the California bandit, Joaquin Murietta, Ina said, "I know. We'll call you Joaquin Miller. That has a nice sound to it." Following Ina's instructions, Miller sent the same volume of poems to the same publisher but under his new pen name, and the volume was accepted and published. Thus was the beginning of Joaquin Miller's literary career in California.

While Ina served as Oakland's first public librarian in the early 1870s, a small, dirty, young boy began coming in and asking for books to read. Taking a special interest in the young boy and his ravenous appetite for reading, Ina offered praise and encouragement along with recommendations. Years later, Jack London spoke of his love for Ina Coolbrith and acknowledged her influence during his younger years in the Oakland library. In a letter to Ina, he wrote the following:

> The old Oakland library days! Do you know you were the first one who ever complimented me on my choice

of reading matter? Nobody at home bothered their heads over what I read. I was an eager, thirsty, hungry little kid-- and one day at the library I drew out a volume on Pizarro in Peru (I was 10 years old). You got the book and stamped it for me; and as you handed it to me you praised me for reading books of that nature.

Proud! If you only knew how proud your words made me! For I thought a great deal of you. You were a goddess to me.

Ina Coolbrith was a poet of renown in California. She was also a humanitarian who touched the lives of scores of aspiring writers and artists. She gave liberally of herself for the benefit of others.

References:

Ina Coolbrith's Scrapbooks at the Oakland (California) Public Library.

Ina Coolbrith Collections at the Bancroft Library in Berkeley, California, and the Huntington Library in San Marino, California.

READING, 'RITING, AND 'RITHMETIC
- ELK SPRINGS, CO -

FRONTIER SCHOOLS WERE VERY different from today's schools. But despite the hardships and privations of those days, the school children, for the most part, received good educations.

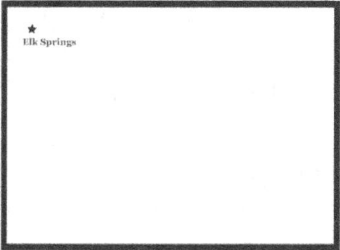

One-room school buildings were the rule, rather than the exception, on the frontier, and teachers taught several grade levels at the same time in those one-room facilities. It was an unwritten rule that a school teacher should be a woman, and it was frequently a written rule that she had to be single. The requirement of "no marriage" was usually written into their contracts. In the 1920s the school board at Elk Springs in northwestern Colorado fired a teacher for getting married, and then they reluctantly re-hired her when no other person applied for the job.

Because of the "no marriage" rule, many frontier teachers taught only one or two years. There were many more men than women on the frontier, and marriage proposals occurred frequently from the single men to the educated and cultured school teachers. In school districts that required the candidates' photograph, cowboys made it a point to get onto the school boards so they could "preview" the coming teachers.

In addition to being instructors, teachers had several specific daily responsibilities written into their contracts. Typical are the following:

Before school opens and pupils arrive

- Arrive before 7 a.m., start fire to warm school
- Fill lamps, trim wicks, clean chimneys
- Provide bucket of clean drinking water
- Carry coal for stove

At end of school day after pupils leave

- Tidy up school room, sweep floor
- Clean blackboard, dust
- Remove snakes, small animals

Other responsibilities

- Plan, supervise successful social and cultural events
- Scrub floor with sand and hot soapy water weekly
- Collect student tuition
- Treat snake, insect and small animal bites

Quality education could be expected in the frontier schools even though the physical facilities were often crude and the winter climate harsh. A case in point is the Elkhead school district in Routt County in northwestern Colorado.

In Colorado, whenever ten or more school-age children lived in close proximity, their parents could petition for an election to create a school district. Such was the case in Routt County in the early 1900s. When the railroad built into Hayden, land seekers began moving into the back country, and soon they needed a school closer to their new

SOCIAL, ACTIVITIES, AND CULTURE

holdings. Breaking away from the Hayden school district, they formed their own Elkhead district, and they built a school building. Begun in 1915, the building was ready for use in 1916. The building had a basement and a main floor that could be divided into two rooms by pulling a curtain.

The new school district advertised for teachers, and two young women, both educated at Smith College in Massachusetts, came out and taught that first year. Dorothy Woodruff taught the younger children in the first through fourth grades, and Rosamond Underwood taught the older children in the fifth through ninth grades. Both teachers roomed and boarded with a family named Harrison that lived about three miles from the school, and they traveled back and forth on horseback. Traveling through deep snow was difficult, but they loved it. Both became permanent Coloradoans.

In addition to the normal academic subjects that included reading, elocution, history, and math, Rosamond and Dorothy had story times, and they had frequent plays and dances. The older students learned shoe cobbling, but they also learned algebra and Latin and became familiar with Tennyson and other figures of great literature.

In one letter written to family members at home, Dorothy described her feelings about story time. "I wish you could see them. They make a mad scramble to pick up all their loose papers, put their desks in order, then fold their hands and sit at attention. When I stand there and look down at those eighteen eager little faces, I forget how naughty they have been, and I try to thrill and please them as I never tried before."

Life in the harsh winter weather had its challenges, but the two ladies from the east adapted quickly. In a letter to her aunt in Auburn, New York, Rosamond wrote the following:

"I have never piled the clothes on so in my life. We wear enormous German socks over our shoes and our galoshes, men's size, countless tights, bloomers, fur coats, scarves, and so forth. We can hardly heave ourselves into the saddle. But once there we sit warm as toast and the riding in the snow is most exhilarating."

Rosamond died in 1974. Her first husband, Robert Perry, had died in 1934, and some years later she married Farrington Carpenter, the man who had been instrumental in getting the Elkhead schoolhouse built and in importing Rosamond and Dorothy from the east. As a tribute to Rosamond, Carpenter invited all of her 1916-17 students who could be found to attend a memorial service for her. Many came to Hayden for the occasion, and a few took the opportunity to say a few words about the influence Rosamond had had on them.

"Slowly and steadily it began to dawn on most of us that a couple of teachers had arrived who could only be classed as something special," spoke Lewis Harrison, a fourteen-year-old student at the time, and with whom the teachers lived. "I don't believe there ever was a community that was affected more by two people, than we were by those two girls," Bobbie Robinson opined. Continuing, Anderson added, "We never missed a day of school, and that school lunch at noon was about the greatest thing in our lives."

Speaking of Rosamond, Ione Smith Ratcliff recalled: "Our new teacher was one of those rare people who loved children and young people, and was able to bring out the best in them. ... There has never been a teacher that was more loved and respected than she was."

Both Rosamond and Dorothy taught only one year, but their effect on their pupils was long lasting. Of the five students in Elkhead's first graduating class, all attended college. Two became college teachers, one became a public school teacher, and two became registered nurses. Although frontier schools are almost extinct these days, it must be acknowledged that pupils back then got good educations from caring teachers.

References:

Sharon Frickey, "Frontier Bloomers: Schoolmarms in Colorado," *Colorado Country Life,* September 2004.

SOCIAL, ACTIVITIES, AND CULTURE

Farrington Carpenter, *In Memory of Rosamond Underwood Carpenter,* Privately published.

Personal conversations between George Underwood Hubbard and Farrington Carpenter

THE CHRISTMAS STAR OF PALMER LAKE

~ PALMER LAKE, CO ~

IT STARTED IN 1935, THE BRAINCHILD of B.E. Jack, a regional manager of Mountain Utilities based in Colorado Springs. A huge lighted star erected on the east side of Sundance Mountain at the little village of Palmer Lake, Colorado, could be a seasonal gift to locals and to travelers alike.

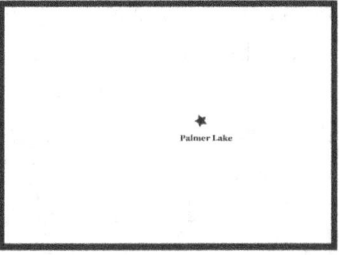

The heavily used automobile highway between Denver and Colorado Springs ran through Palmer Lake at that time. Ten trains passed through daily. And overhead, airline flights were beginning to be seen. The star could be enjoyed by a multitude of travelers.

Mr. Jack explained his idea to Bert Sloan, owner of Sloan's Cafe in Palmer Lake. If Sloan approved, it would happen; if he didn't, then forget it. Sloan approved enthusiastically.

It would be a 500-foot, five-point star. The townspeople approved of the idea, and one of the Mountain Utilities linemen drew up the wiring plans. Funds were raised, Mountain Utilities donated poles and cable, and the work began.

It was a labor intensive task. Poles were manually carried up the mountain slope. Post holes were dug with pick and shovel. Concrete for the holes was mixed below and manually carried up in buckets. Wire and light bulbs were also carried up manually.

One of the more valuable workers was not a man, but a German Shepherd dog named Dizzy. Wearing a small pack designed for the occasion, Dizzy would carry supplies from one working group to another. Dizzy transported everything from hammers to electrical wire to light bulbs. A short whistle or a call was all he needed to know where to go.

After a little over three months of labor, the star was ready. From a distance it was discovered that the 100-watt light bulbs gave off too much light, giving the star's outline a fuzzy appearance. Bulbs of 25 watts were then installed, and the star then had a sharp outline. When lighted at night, the star became a spectacular attraction for travelers between Denver and Colorado Springs. Motorists stopped in Palmer Lake, thus constituting a boon to the town's business establishments. Passing trains slowed so passengers could get a lingering view. Airplanes dipped and circled so their passengers could see without leaving their seats.

All this has now changed. Palmer Lake cannot be seen from the interstate highway that now runs between Denver and Colorado Springs. Passenger trains no longer run through Palmer Lake. The airlines are too busy trying to maintain tight schedules.

The star, however, is still there, and is lit each December and at a few other times. A yule log hunt and accompanying festivities provide an annual Christmas celebration. Palmer Lake is still making its contribution to the celebration of Christmas.

Today, although the star still shines, all its components have been replaced with new and longer lasting materials airlifted to the bright spots by helicopter. GE 4440-watt, five-filament Survivor lamps are now used. But the past has not been forgotten. In 2006 the Palmer Lake Historical Society erected a bronze sculpture of Dizzy, the dog that never seemed to get tired.

Reference:

R. Davis and H. Edwards, "Star Light, Star Bright" (L. Vaile Museum, 2005).

AMUSEMENT

NEVER UNDERESTIMATE THE POWER OF WOMEN
- TEMPLE, TX -

IN 1893, W. GOODRICH JONES HELD A stag party at his home in Temple, Texas. It was a Thanksgiving Day dinner to which he invited business men, ministers, farmers, bankers, and politicians from Temple and its surrounding communities. The party was deemed such a success that it was repeated the next year, and then it became a regular Thanksgiving Day fixture that endured for 32 years.

As the attendance grew over the years, the party was held in larger facilities such as the Harvey House and the Carnegie Library. The program was essentially the same each year. The men sang "America" and gave each other the "grand handshake" symbolizing unity. Following the invocation and the supper, there would be speeches and stories. The evening always ended with prayer following the singing of "God Be With You".

Everything went well with these stag parties except for one thing. The women were excluded except to prepare and serve the meal—and on Thanksgiving Day, of all days. Finally they decided enough was enough. They would institute their own Thanksgiving Day parties.

Organized by Mrs. Zollie Luther Jones, wife of W. Goodrich Jones, the first women's only party was held on October 30, 1916. This annual event flourished for 45 years, eclipsing the men's tenure of 32 years. On one occasion, over 400 women attended.

In 1924 the women moved their party to the Tuesday before Thanksgiving, and they began permitting men to attend. But although the event was free for the women, the men had to pay. This turn of events marked the end of the men's stag parties ,while the women continued for another 37 years. Thus the women had a measure of satisfaction and triumph over their "superior" male counterparts.

Reference:

Atcheson, Topeka, and Santa Fe Railway Museum, Temple, Texas.

E CLAMPUS VITUS
- SIERRA CITY, CA -

IN THE LATE 1850S, THE FERVOR AND excitement of California's gold rush had subsided. Men were still seeking gold, but in more organized and methodical ways as company employers and employees. Life in the gold fields had become more of a routine existence, and the men of Sierra City, California decided that renewed excitement was needed. After pooling ideas of what to do, someone said, "Let's have a lodge."

The idea gained quick support with the assumption that it would be a fun lodge. So in 1857, in a secret meeting, the men of Sierra City organized the Ancient and Honorable Order of E Clampus Vitus. A leader would be needed, so they created the office of First Noble Grand Humbug and gave the title to Sam Hartley of Sierra City.

Although they agreed not to have any formal meetings, they did adopt a few rules. One rule declared that any traveling man, drummer, or commercial salesman who came to town would be ineligible to sell anything without first becoming a Clamper. Eligibility requirements were simple; merely contribute all the gold the person carried to the Clamper's treasury. Because every merchant in town became a Clamper, the town was essentially closed to all non-Clampers.

The intermediate result of this policy was that visiting salesmen avoided Sierra City and sold their wares in neighboring towns such as Downieville, Goodyear Bar, and Moore's Flat. Then the merchants in these other towns caught the vision of what could be done, and they organized Clampus chapters of their own. The visiting merchants, therefore, had no choice. They had to join the Clampers or not do business anywhere in the area. Although the visitors learned not to carry very much gold on their persons, the Clamper treasury, nevertheless, swelled, and it became a very wealthy organization.

Word came, one time, of a family of grubstakers who were in desperate need. The father was tubercular, the mother was trying to care for a dozen children, and some of the daughters were being tempted by unsavory allurements in the mining camps. The Sierra City Clampers got together, but instead of dipping into their ample treasury, they decided to solicit contributions. The members gave generously, and they delivered effective relief to the needy family.

E Clampus Vitus then became a charitable organization, and they rose to the occasion whenever anyone worthy was in need. Using a horn (called a Hew-gag) from a ram or sheep or cow, they called their members together and solicited contributions whenever an emergency was at hand. Whenever the Grand Noble Musician blew the Hew-gag, members immediately dropped whatever they were doing and gathered to their designated meeting place to determine how best to render assistance. On one occasion after fire destroyed almost all of Sierra City, the Hew-gag horns blew in all the surrounding towns, and thousands of dollars poured into a Sierra City relief fund.

E Clampus Vitus became one of the richest charitable organizations in the country. Then, for reasons unknown, it died out and became just a tradition and a joke. The Humbug Lodge remained a memory in the minds of many former members and their descendants. Finally, about 1930, three men, Leon Whitsell, George Dane, and Carl Wheat, revived the lodge in San Francisco, and it again spread throughout northern California and even as far east as Colorado.

When Downieville was devastated and marooned by a flood in December 1937, the survivors determined that there could be no Christmas that year for the children. As a result, Hew-gag horns sounded all over that part of the state. On Christmas Eve, E Clampus Vitus rolled into Downieville with toys and funds and they saw to it that Christmas was not denied to anyone.

Reference:

Samuel Dickson, *Tales of San Francisco* (Stanford: Stanford University Press, 1957).

WHEN A DANCE IS HELD IN YOUR HONOR, YOU SHOULD ATTEND
~ NO MAN'S LAND, OK ~

PROBABLY THE MOST IMPORTANT social activity for both men and women on the frontier were the dances that were frequently held. As a partial compensation for the hard- 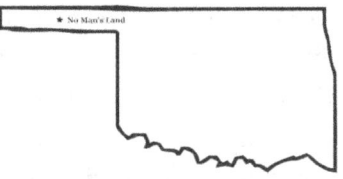 ships and privations of frontier life, some recreation was needed, and the dances were well attended. They sometimes lasted all night. In Texas and Oklahoma, these dances seemed to be especially popular. Invitations were never sent out; word just circulated, and people came from miles around.

Music was usually furnished locally with whatever instruments were available. Adhering to unwritten dress codes, the ladies wore dresses with high neck lines made of anything from silk to calico, and the men generally came in a coat with some kind of a tie and had their pants tucked into their high-top boots. Hats and guns had to be checked at the entrance to the dance hall.

Because the male population was much more numerous than the female, the male attendees were given numbers, and the floor manager would call out numbers identifying the men to participate in each dance. In this way participation was distributed equally and potential trouble was avoided. It was rare that a female sat out any of the dances, and whenever a large number of ladies were present, the dance was truly a special occasion.

On one occasion in No Man's Land (now the Oklahoma Panhandle), it became known that a family named Dale was moving in from Missouri. The thing that made this family special was that John Dale had nine daughters, and several of them were of dancing age. Excitement spread through the ranks of eligible bachelors as they anticipated the arrival of this family of nine daughters.

"We'll have a dance to celebrate their arrival," they voiced in unison. "And we'll give those daughters a real welcome." Plans were made for the welcoming, and the dance was held on the night of the Dale family's arrival.

Now, another custom with frontier dances was that explicit invitations were never sent out. News of a dance spread naturally, and everyone came who wanted to come. All were welcome who behaved themselves, and people sometimes came from as far away as thirty or fifty miles. But the Dales did not know the frontier customs, and without explicit invitations to the dance, the Dale daughters not only did not attend, they went to bed early to rest from their arduous journey.

"Where are they?" the men at the dance asked.

"Maybe they think they are too good for us," one opined.

"We need to give them a real cowboy welcome," voiced another.

The Dales were all sleeping peacefully when suddenly they were awakened by pistol shots. Looking out their window, they saw cowboys riding around the house shooting and yelling like Comanches. The girls were thoroughly frightened, and they cried to their father to make the men leave. Wisely, John Dale did nothing, thinking that the riders would go away soon, which they did.

A few days later when everyone understood what had really happened and why, the cowboys became nice and friendly, and the Dale family was made to feel truly welcome.

Reference:

Carl Coke Rister, *No Man's Land* (Norman: University of Oklahoma Press, 1948).

FROM BLOOMER GIRLS TO THE MAJOR LEAGUES
~ OURAY, CO ~

IN THE EARLY 1900S, BASEBALL WAS A very popular sport in the West, and it was played by women as well as by men. Although there was no organized league for them, there were hundreds of women's teams, and they were known as "Bloomer girls." They 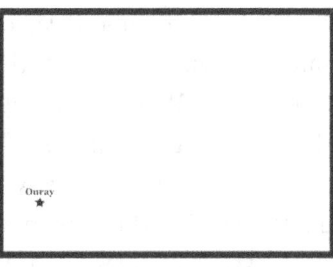 were barnstorming teams who traveled around playing against all comers—local teams, semi-pro teams, college teams, anybody.

But the odd thing about the Bloomer girls' teams was that they all seemed to have one or more men playing with them. For example, Rogers Hornsby, a major league Hall of Famer, got his start on a Bloomer girl team. Another noteworthy example is that of Howard Ellsworth Wood, who later became known as "Smoky Joe" Wood.

Although born in Kansas City, Wood grew up in Ouray, Colorado. At the age of fourteen and with a love for baseball, he served as mascot and as an occasional relief pitcher for the Ouray semi-pro team. The family was poor, and Wood and his friends would go up and down the alleys of Ouray picking up bottles, old copper, brass, rubber, and anything else that they could sell. He especially remembered a wealthy man named Thomas F. Walsh, who would toss nickels and dimes from his wagon for the kids to pick up.

From Ouray, the Wood family moved in 1906 to Ness, Kansas, and Wood became a pitcher for the Ness team. In an exhibition game against a Bloomer girl team, Wood pitched so well that the Bloomer girls offered him twenty dollars to finish the season (three weeks) with them. So at the age of sixteen, Wood became a Bloomer girl player. The following year, 1907, Wood signed a contract with the Cedar Rapids minor league team, but he was good enough to move up to the Boston Red Sox in the American League the following year. Because of his blazing fast ball, Wood quickly became known as "Smokey Joe" Wood.

"I threw so hard I thought my arm would fly right off my body," Wood once said.

When asked about Wood's fast ball, the legendary Walter Johnson said, "Listen, my friend, there's no man alive can throw harder than Smokey Joe Wood." Satchel Paige concurred, saying, "Smoky Joe could throw harder than anyone."

Wood's best season with Boston was in 1912 when he won 34 games. During the season he had 16 consecutive victories, and he won three World Series games, striking out 11 batters in one of those games. The next year, however, he slipped on wet grass fielding a bunt and hurt his arm and broke his thumb on his pitching hand. Although he continued pitching for two more years, he never regained his dominance over the batters. In 1917, Boston sold Wood to the Cleveland Indians, where he played in the outfield with occasional pitching stints. Nevertheless, when Wood retired in 1922, he had an enviable pitching record of 116 wins and 57 losses with an earned run average of 2.03.

Wood then became the head baseball coach at Yale University, a position he held for twenty years. In 1984, he received a standing ovation at an Old Timers Day in Boston's Fenway Park. It is fitting that Smoky Joe Wood has been inducted into the Red Sox Hall of Fame and also into the Colorado Sports Hall of Fame.

References:

The Official (Web) Site of "Smoky" Joe Wood.

"Smoky Joe Wood," Wikipedia Encyclopedia

Displays at the Ouray County Historical Museum.

HOME LIFE

FLOUR SACKS MAKE EXCELLENT FRONTIER UNDERWEAR
- TEXAS -

FLOUR-SACK UNDERWEAR IN TEXAS was probably just like flour-sack underwear anywhere else in the West during frontier times. The normal procedure was to bleach out the printing and then cut and sew the material to fit the body as needed. Frills such as tucks and ruffles were frequently added to give the female wearer a little more feeling of femininity.

A story from the Texas frontier shows the humor that sometimes creeps into such situations. Although the story is true, the lady's name has not been preserved, so let's just call her Jane.

Reared in Philadelphia where she had been trained for a musical career, Jane married a man named John and moved with him to Texas, where they began a life of raising sheep. It was rather a severe adjustment for this Eastern-bred lady who had hardly washed a dish or mended a stocking before making the move. She enjoyed Texas, however, and relished the frontier life.

After two years in Texas, Jane's underwear began to wear out. Her dresses, made of good strong material, were holding up nicely, but the more delicate fabrics underneath were going to have to be replaced.

"John, do you think you could get me a few yards of white material at the store the next time you go to town?" she asked.

Although wanting to oblige, John explained that they barely had enough money for maintaining the sheep and that he had already borrowed more money than he felt good about. "Could you possibly wait until the wool is sold this fall?"

Jane later claimed that she had not yet heard of flour-sack underwear, so when she decided to sew two flour sacks together to make a pair of drawers, she thought she was doing something ingenious and original. It turns out that Jane had also never heard of methods for bleaching out the printing on the sacks.

She managed to make the drawers, complete with ruffles, tucks, and featherstitching, and she was very proud of the completed item. She could hardly wait for John to come in that evening so she could show off her handiwork. Dancing in front of him and twirling around as she lifted her skirt, she asked, "How do you like it?"

Breaking out in laughter, John could hardly control himself. Taken by surprise, Jane was more than a little bit hurt as her husband's laughter continued. When finally he regained his composure, he was able to tell her what he had seen. Quite visible on the rear of his wife's anatomy were large pink letters spelling out "THE PRIDE OF TEXAS."

Needless to say, Jane quickly learned the art of bleaching.

Reference:

Winifred Kupper, *The Golden Hoof* (New York: Alfred A. Knopf, Inc., 1945).

HOME REMEDIES ON THE FRONTIER

- LEE'S FERRY, AZ -

JOHN D. LEE WAS A FRONTIERSMAN IN every respect. As an adopted son of Brigham Young and as a devoted adherent to the restored gospel of Jesus Christ, Lee spent the greater part of his life as a pioneer in various locations in southern Utah in the late 1800s. His 19 wives and 65 children attest to his dedication to the tenets of Mormonism at that time.

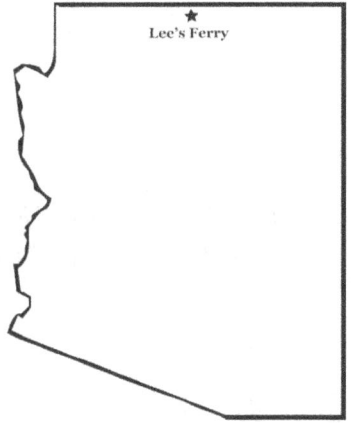

Lee was resourceful; he had to be to prosper as he did in the barren environments where he was called to settle. One example of this resourcefulness shows itself in the experiences he had in healing himself and his livestock in the absence of doctors.

On one occasion, Brigham Young had advised a person whose horse was bitten by a rattlesnake to "mix the spirits of Turpentine with Tobacco, wash the wound, and Pray for the recovery of the Beast." When one of Lee's horses was bitten by a snake under the jaw, Lee applies this same remedy "which soon counteracted the poison."

On another occasion, having been taught that tobacco is "not for the body, neither for the belly, but for all sick cattle," Lee steeped some tobacco in hot water and drenched some 10 sheep that had lain all day almost lifeless. "To my astonishment, they all recovered," he wrote in his diary.

For himself and for members of his family, Lee used such remedies as "Essences, oil, ointments, Salve, and Tinctures."

One time when one of his own illnesses went into its third week, Lee resorted to the use of "Spirits of Turpentine, coal oil, Dr. Lee's liniment, Salt Peter, wild sage & vinegar, Roast Onions & carrots, white Beans, Mountain soap, Camphor & Salt, & last of all ... a Poultice of charcoal & carrots grated. This together with the Prayer of Faith seemed to check the inflammation & gave me ease."

As a frontiersman, John D. Lee knew how to take care of himself, and he and his family and his livestock were healthy most of the time.

Reference:

Juanita Brooks, Ed., *A Mormon Chronicle: The Diaries of John D. Lee, 1848-1876* (San Marino: The Huntington Library, 1955).

CITY LIFE

TEMPLE, TEXAS GOES TO WAR AGAINST ITS RATS
- TEMPLE, TX -

Like most other frontier towns, Temple, Texas, had its share of growing pains. Mud, flash floods, and washed-out bridges were typical problems with which the early residents had to cope. But Temple, also known at various times as Mudville and Ratsville, had another problem. The town had too many rats. Besides being unsanitary carriers of diseases, the rats were simply odious, and the town fathers, urged by the town mothers, hit upon some schemes to reduce the town's rat population. For one thing, they invented the sport of "ratting."

The idea of ratting was to catch as many rats as possible and keep them alive and caged. Then on the appointed day, called Ratting Day, bring all the rats and ratting dogs to the city square. On being given the signal, the residents would release their rats and let the dogs take over. The dogs killing the most rats were the winning ratting dogs. The owners of the winning dogs received prizes, and their dogs received something better to eat.

One human participant recalled those days. "We had all kinds of rat dogs—mine were mostly fox terriers. Excitement ran high when the traps were opened and ratting began. Prizes were given to the best dogs. Sometimes a rat would get away and run under our legs, and then we did some high jumping."

Another rat eradication scheme involved competition among the town's public schools. The school claiming the most rat casualties during the school year received a $25 first prize. Second, third, fourth, and fifth prizes were also awarded. Individual boys and girls also received prizes,

These ratting schemes apparently brought forth the desired results. In 1921, for example, it was estimated that 11,000 rats were killed. The rat population may not have been eradicated by these schemes, but at least it was brought under control.

References:

Atcheson, Topeka, and Santa Fe Railway Museum, Temple, Texas.

Temple Daily Telegram, January 7, 1928.

SAINTS ROOST: UTOPIA IN THE TEXAS PANHANDLE
- CLARENDON, TX -

THERE WAS NOTHING NEW NOR unique about wanting to create a utopian community free of sin. Numerous such communities were founded during America's developmental years. But one, that of Clarendon, Texas, is still living with a part of the legacy of its past.

The Rev. Lewis Henry Carhart, a Methodist Episcopal minister in Sherman, Texas, needed a way to raise money for his rapidly growing church that wanted to build a new brick sanctuary. Hearing of the availability of land in the Texas panhandle, Carhart hit upon the plan of buying large tracts of such land, subdividing it, and selling it for handsome profits. The church bought land certificates from the State of Texas, and sent Carhart out to inspect the area and sell the land. Somewhere in the process, Carhart became inspired with the concept of staying in the panhandle and establishing a community where temperance and Christian living would be the rule. It would be a utopia free from the sins of the world.

Enlisting the aid of family and of two brothers-in-law and others in 1877, Carhart purchased 343 sections of land in what is now Donley County, and he then began using his magnetic personality to attract settlers who started coming in the spring of 1878. Carhart's dream was becoming a reality.

The original colony, located at the confluence of Carroll Creek and the Salt Fork of the Red River, became known as Clarendon, a name chosen by Carhart in honor of his wife Clara. But the cowboys of Charles Goodnight's JA Ranch to the north, who quickly found that their intemperate ways were not welcome in Clarendon, began calling the colony "Saints' Roost," (a name given as a direct antithesis of the well-known "Robbers' Roost," a hideout from the law in northwestern Colorado).

Known as Clarendon from within and Saints' Roost from without, the colony flourished for almost ten years until the Ft. Worth and Denver Railroad bypassed it in 1887. To survive, Clarendon businesses and residents began moving to the railhead six miles to the south. By September 1887, "Old Clarendon" was largely abandoned, and "New Clarendon", without temperance restrictions, had replaced it. L.H. Carhart left the following year in discouragement, never to return.

Despite the intemperate influence of the railroad workers and the cowboys, the "Saints' Roost" concept did not die when the town relocated. The Old Clarendon residents who now lived in the new community began to campaign for reforms and for a more cultural environment. The Clarendon College & University Training School opened in 1898. Music, drama, and literature flourished, and Clarendon became known as "The Athens of the Panhandle." In 1899 a newspaper, *The Agitator*, started by another Methodist minister, campaigned aggressively to make Donley County dry again.

I.W. Carhart, a brother of L.H. Carhart, was still on the scene, and the temperance movement was in his blood also. On September 24, 1901, I.W. Carhart became first mayor of the new Clarendon, and under his leadership the citizens voted the county dry on July 1, 1902, and they gave the saloons until September to close their doors.

SOCIAL, ACTIVITIES, AND CULTURE

The "Saints' Roost" concept is still alive and well in Donley County which was dry until voters changed the law in 2013.

References:

The Clarendon Enterprise, 125th Anniversary Edition, Clarendon, Texas.

The Saints' Roost Museum, Clarendon, Texas

"WATER WORKS" WILEY SAVES THE DAY FOR MUSKOGEE
- MUSKOGEE, OK -

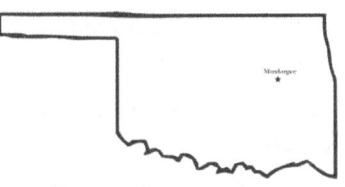

AS AMERICA MOVED WESTWARD, IF THE promoter of a proposed town site could induce a railroad to build into his town, he was assured of financial success, especially if it meant the demise of a neighboring, competing town. Muskogee and Checotah, in Indian Territory (now Oklahoma), were two such competing town sites. Both towns were vying for the Katy railroad and also for the headquarters of the Union Indian Agency. The principle characters in the drama to be played were Charlie "Water Works" Wiley and George W. Ingalls. Charlie, a man with more brains than his nondescript ways would suggest, had the monopoly of hauling water by the barrel to the stores and homes of Muskogee, and when sober, he tended the business well. Ingalls was the local Indian agent, and therefore was a man of considerable influence in the area.

The Katy railroad favored building into Muskogee, but as competition between Muskogee and Checotah mounted, Ingalls, who maintained his agency headquarters at Muskogee, worked secretly to promote Checotah's cause. This was in part a campaign of personal revenge because of some prior incidents in which Ingalls had felt snubbed by the citizens of Muskogee. But Ingalls also saw it as a lucrative business opportunity. If he could convince the Katy officials to divert their route to Checotah, he would move his Indian Agency there and thus control the business licenses issued to relocating Muskogee merchants.

Ingalls based his strategy around the expectation of being able to demonstrate the superior quality of water in the Checotah area to that of Muskogee water. After digging a well in Checotah, Ingalls would regale the Katy officials with tasty tidbits and quench their thirst with the cool, clear water from his new well.

As Ingalls' well reached its final depth, "Water Works" Wiley was savvy enough to recognize a threat to his monopoly of delivering water in Muskogee. So on the night before Ingalls' planned demonstration, a wagon loaded with salt left Muskogee for Checotah. Ingalls wore a broad smile the next day as he and the Katy officials gathered in Checotah to consider the proposed new routing of the railroad. But his smile quickly disappeared when the Katy officials sipped and then spit out the water from his well. It was as salty as the ocean. Ingalls was forced to abandon his venture, and Muskogee was saved.

No one knew for sure how the salt got into the well, but Muskogee's citizens were very forgiving that day when some of their water deliveries were missed because "Water Works" Wiley was asleep.

Reference:

Vincent Victor Masterson, *The Katy Railroad and the Last Frontier* (Norman: University of Oklahoma Press, 1952).

CULTURES

THE FREDERICKSBURG EASTER FIRES COMMEMORATE A TREATY
~ FREDERICKSBURG, TX ~

EACH YEAR, THE FREDERICKSBURG'S Easter Fires proclaim the Easter season and also serve as a poignant reminder of a treaty made with the Indians many years ago.

Between October 1845 and April 1846, the Society for the Protection of German Immigrants in Texas sponsored the arrival of over 5,000 immigrants from Germany.  From their port of entry at Galveston, the new settlers made their way to New Braunfels in Comal County and then to Gillespie County, where they organized the settlement of Fredericksburg. Disease and exposure took their toll, making the first year very difficult for the new community. The Indians constituted another problem by making raids and by shooting arrows at the settlers as they worked in their fields.

Realizing the necessity of peaceful relations, Baron Otfried Hans von Meusebach led a party of forty men to seek peace with the Indians. Riding out to the Comanche's winter encampment in the San Saba country during the Easter season of 1847, Meusebach and his party succeeded in making a treaty with the Comanche chiefs to the effect that the Indians would perpetrate no further hostilities toward the German colonists in exchange for $3,000 worth of presents. From that point in time, the German colonists had less trouble with the Indians than any other group of settlers in Texas, and in later years the Germans took well deserved pride in their friendly relations with the Indians. While the negotiations were in progress, the Indians built huge fires on the hilltops around Fredericksburg. These fires, which were first seen the night before Easter Day, would be used as smoke and fire signals in case any treachery toward the Indians became apparent. Peaceful conditions prevailed, however, and the fires were allowed to burn high—high enough that the children in one of the community's families became quite frightened. The mother soothed her children's frightened feelings by telling them that the Easter rabbit had built the fires and was cooking eggs and dyeing them with colors from the wildflowers that the little rabbits were bringing to her.

When Meusebach and his party returned from their treaty negotiations, they were so intrigued by the story that they vowed to build the fires at Easter each year that the treaty remained in force. The custom continued for many years and grew into an annual pageant, but like so many customs, it is now no more.

Reference:

Gillespie County and Fredericksburg, Texas mimeographed document from the Fredericksburg Information Bureau.

HOW DO YOU MOVE A WAGON WITHOUT A TEAM?
- NORSE, TX -

WHEN PETER HOFF AND HIS FAMILY arrived in Galveston, he knew he would need a wagon to haul his family and their belongings to the Norwegian community of Norse in Bosque County. Hoff's problem was that he had only enough money for a wagon. The team of animals needed to pull the wagon were beyond his means.

Having purchased the wagon, Hoff was forlorn and discouraged. He and his family were ready for the journey, but they had no animals. In a conversation with a kindly old gentleman on the streets of Galveston, Hoff expressed his plight. With sympathy in his heart, the gentleman came up with what may seem like a novel idea.

"I'll get my team, and we will pull you for one day. Then we will go to the nearest farm house and ask for lodging. We will explain your situation to the farmer and ask if you can use his team the next day while I return home with my team."

Actually, this proposed plan was in keeping with an old Norwegian custom of "posting stations." In the southern part of Norway, there was a network of over a thousand posting stations, each about a day's journey from those next to it. At each posting station, a traveler could expect an evening meal and overnight sleeping. Then a farmer had the compulsory duty of transporting the traveler to the next posting station on the traveler's route. With this system, travelers could make journeys without having their own means of conveyance.

Although Hoff doubted that the plan would work in his case, he had no better alternative. And besides, each day's journey would get him that much closer to his intended destination. So off they went on the first day of the journey. They met an accommodating farmer that night who agreed to furnish a team for the next day, and Hoff and his family traveled for another day. Each night, Hoff found a farmer willing to help, and he successfully got his family and their belongings to their destination at Norse. It seemed that the further into the interior of Texas Hoff traveled, the more enthusiastic the farmers became about helping. It was an example of Texas hospitality which, in general, was helpful to many of the Norwegian immigrants.

Another interesting thing about Peter Hoff is his name. "Hoff" is not a Norwegian name. From Norway, the Hoffs migrated first to La Crosse, Wisconsin, in 1866 and then to Texas a year later. Peter's name was Peter Olson. County officials at La Crosse dissuaded him from using "Olson" because Peter already had a brother there with that name. So Peter then assumed the name "Holstenhoff." Told that this was too long a name to use in America, Peter then settled on "Hoff" for his surname.

References:

William C. Pool, *A History of Bosque County, Texas* (San Marcos: San Marcos Record Press, 1954).

William C. Poole, *Bosque Territory: A History of an Agrarian Community* (Clifton: Bosque Memorial Museum, 1964).

"YOU HAD A BETTER PIG STY AT HOME"
~ LA GRANGE, TX ~

AUGUSTIN HAIDUSEK, WHO BECAME A successful newspaperman and politician, was probably the best-known and most influential of the early Czech pioneers in Texas. But his initial years in Texas were not at all glamorous. The Haidusek family endured many hardships as did so many other immigrant Czech families in those early years.

At the age of eleven, Augustin Haidusek arrived in Texas with his parents. Settling on the east bank of the Navidad River in Fayette County, along with a colony of other Czech immigrants, the Haidusek family struggled to survive. In their first year of farming, the colony produced only one bale of cotton, which they managed to sell at La Grange. Life that first year was extremely difficult. In addition to exhausting all the money they had brought with them, the colony had to cope with an epidemic caused by the hard work and contaminated water.

"But God was with us," Augustin later reminisced. "The following year crops were better and with the kind help of those of English speaking extraction, we became firmly established."

Still life was not easy, and their dwellings, for example, were extremely crude. These early Czech immigrants had neither the time nor the means for building homes comparable to those they had left behind. Devoting all their efforts toward eking out a subsistence, they had to be content for a while with living in shacks and hovels made of hastily thrown together materials.

Four years after the Haidusek's arrival, a friend newly arrived from Moravia visited the Haidusek family. Aghast at the crude shelter in which the family was living, the friend exclaimed to Valento Haidusek, Augustin's father, that "you had a better pig sty at home."

The father replied, "I had rather live in this hut as an American citizen, than to live in a palace and be under the Austro-Hungarian oppression."

With such feelings, the Czech immigrants were bound to survive despite their many hardships, and Augustin and many others eventually became leaders and prosperous citizens in their new country.

Reference:

The Czechs in Texas (San Antonio: The Institute of Texan Cultures).

IF WE CAN'T FIGHT SOMEONE ELSE, WE'LL FIGHT AMONG OURSELVES
~ SAN ANTONIO, TX ~

IN SAN ANTONIO, THE IRISH SETTLED an area just north of the Alamo that became known as Irish Flat. Bounded by Houston Street on the south, Broadway on the west, 6th Street on the north, and the Acequia Madre (about where Nacogdoches Street was located) on the east, Irish Flat was a low, damp area into which a  number of Irish families poured in the mid-1840s. It is believed that the men were primarily employed as teamsters and civilian employees working with the U.S. Army quartermaster outfit headquartered at the Alamo.

Historians are uncertain about the origin of the families in the Flat. Some think they came directly from Ireland, others say they moved southward from northern American states. It is also possible that they came from earlier Irish colonies at Refugio and San Patricio.

Regardless of their points of origin, Irish Flat was home to a happy and lively group of Irish families. These were proud families, and they took special pride that they all owned their own homes. The area contained mostly single-story homes made of creamy limestone with green shutters extending almost to the ground and porches running the length of the houses. When quarried, the limestone was soft enough that they could cut it with ordinary knives, but it hardened by exposure to the atmosphere. Pecan trees, crepe myrtles and various flowery shrubs added shade and beauty to the area.

Whenever a new house was to be built, it became a community project attended by relatives and friends throughout the flat. These were always gala occasions. Instead of waiting to celebrate after the construction, the Irish celebrated in advance with food and plenty of spirits. There were lots of jugs of whiskey, and as a result, several houses were built on uneven foundations having corners that were not exactly square. Still, the houses were well built and endured for many years even though some stood as permanent reminders of the festivities that accompanied their construction.

Fighting and dancing were favorite sports among the Irish Flat denizens. They had dances every week, usually on a Saturday night, and many of the dances lasted all night. Fiddlers played Irish reels, and an ample supply of coffee and rye whiskey kept things lively. As the whiskey took effect, there would be much singing and occasional eloquent orations. When singing their favorite song, "Brave Jimmie Folia," they became vicarious fighters as the men visualized their hero going forth to war at the head of their army.

The Irish men were physically large and powerful, and there is nothing they enjoyed more than a good scrap. Anytime strangers walked through the flat, challenges could be expected. When there were no strangers to fight, they would fight among themselves. Then afterwards they would shake hands and continue their friendships.

Fighting was not limited to the adults; the children were equally ready for such encounters. John J. Stevens, who later became postmaster, recalled that the Irish and American boys would combine to fight any other boys. And if other boys could not be found, they also fought one another.

Stealing fruit was another favorite pastime of the Irish boys. Samuel Maverick's orchards, where the St. Anthony Hotel now stands, were close enough to the Irish Flat for frequent raids by adventuresome boys. Maverick has been described as a loveable character who would invite the boys to his house to eat more fruit. "But, boy-like, we did not care a continental for any but the stolen fruit," Stevens recalled.

If the Irish were fighters, they were also a generous people. No one went hungry nor went without a friend in those days.

In later years, many of San Antonio's leading citizens were of Irish descent. The Irish voted as a bloc, and it was generally acknowledged that a person could not be elected to any public office in San Antonio without the Irish vote.

References:

'Fighting Irish' Had Their Own Colony. (Unidentified newspaper clipping in the files of the Institute of Texas Culture, San Antonio.)

Interview Given by Mr. A. T. Stevens. (Typescript in the files of the Institute of Texas Culture, San Antonio.)

ITC Alliance Ambassador Newsletter, March/April 2005.

THE CHINESE TONG WAR AT WEAVERSVILLE

~ WEAVERVILLE, CA ~

IN JULY 1850, GEORGE WEAVER picked a spot in California's Salmon Mountains just south of Mount Shasta and looked for gold. He found the precious metal, and soon others were on the scene. The town that sprang up where Weaver had built his cabin became known as Weaverville.

Three years later, hundreds of Chinese laborers arrived in Weaverville to work some of the mines in behalf of the mine owners headquartered in San Francisco and Sacramento. These Chinese laborers were there merely to work. They were not allowed to buy land nor to do their own prospecting. But in the course of a short period of time, they did manage to organize themselves into two factions, or tongs. For reasons that are still unknown, a dispute arose between the two tongs, the Cantons and the Hong Kongs, and it grew to such proportions that it became widely known that all-out war would be the only way of settling things. So the date for the battle was set—July 14, 1853.

When Weaverville's white officials learned of the planned battle, they thought it would make a great spectacle, and they made no effort to stop it. Instead, they established rules, primarily that no firearms could be used. So the Chinese kept Weaverville's blacksmiths busy making pikepoles, three-pronged spears, swords, and metal shields. Excitement and anticipation were running high.

On the day before the scheduled battle, people began gathering to Weaverville from the nearby mining camps. They positioned themselves on hilltops and other places where they would have a commanding view of the battle area, and they spent the night in their strategic locations.

The next morning, over 2,000 spectators were in place overlooking the flats of Five Cent Gulch just east of town. Cheers rang out as the Chinese began assembling in the Gulch for the battle. The Hong Kongs, wearing red turbans, lined up at one end of the Gulch. There were 300 Hong Kong fighting men armed with swords, clubs, and shields, and with red flags waving in the breeze. Led by Charlie Yung, the Hong Kongs appeared to be ready. Between 600 and 700 Canton warriors showed up wearing black turbans. Hi Long Chang, brandishing a long-handled sword, led the numerically superior Cantons, who were also well armed with forks and swords.

It appeared that the battle was ready to begin, and the excited spectators were calling to both sides to get with it. But the Chinese were not as impatient as the white spectators. The two sides marched back and forth across the flats and shouted taunts and insults at each other. But they kept their distance. This went on for the entire morning, and many of the spectators, disgusted with this lack of actual conflict, got up and went home.

Finally, in the afternoon, the warriors got close enough to one another to engage in hand-to-hand combat, and the battle began in earnest. The action was fast and furious as the battle seesawed back and forth. Soon some of the spectators were on the field adding to the noise and confusion. In a daring move, the red-turbaned Hong Kongs drove a wedge into the ranks of the black-turbaned Cantons. Seeing that their force had been split in two, the Cantons turned and ran for their lives. As the battle ended, eight Chinese lay dead and some two dozen more were wounded.

It later became known that in preparing for the battle, Charlie Yung, the Hong Kong leader, has secretly persuaded some of the white spectators to enter the fray and cover the exposed rear of his warriors. And so it was that the Hong Kongs defeated the numerically superior Cantons. Apparently, the unknown cause of the war was put to rest, for the two tongs never battled again.

Reference:

Charles Crowder, "The Weaverville War," *Air California Magazine,* May, 1980.

CHINESE COOLIE LABOR GETS THE CENTRAL PACIFIC OVER THE MOUNTAINS
- SACRAMENTO, CA -

JAMES STOCKBRIDGE WAS WORRIED. "We'll never get over these mountains in time," he complained to Charlie Crocker. Crocker, along with Leland Stanford, Mark Hopkins, and Collis Huntington, were the moving forces in building the Central Pacific railroad eastward from Sacramento, California in the 1860s. They were building what would become the nation's first transcontinental railroad after its connection with the Union Pacific Railroad, which was building westward from Omaha, Nebraska. Actual construction for the Central Pacific began in 1865.

The rugged Sierra Nevada Mountains were causing severe time delays, and Stockbridge, the construction superintendent for the Central Pacific, had run out of ideas as well as resources. Cutting a roadbed through those hard granite mountains was almost an impossible task. In addition, Stockbridge couldn't keep a steady work crew. The men would work for a short while and then drift off to the mines in hopes of more instant wealth with less effort. Reduced to using twelve-year-old boys to lead the horses hauling dump carts, Stockbridge's progress was essentially at a standstill. At the same time, the Union Pacific was moving westward at a normal rate, and it appeared that when the two companies met, the Union Pacific would own much more than half of the trackage and thus be in a commanding financial position when the transcontinental railroad began its operation. Something had to be done.

"I know what we will do," Crocker proclaimed. "We'll bring in Chinese coolies to cut out the roadbed through the mountains." There were thousands of Chinese laborers who had been brought to California to work in the mines who were now out of work.

Stockbridge thought it was a preposterous idea. Picturing the Orientals as small, slightly-built, rice-eating weaklings, he demanded to know how they were going to build a railroad over such a rugged route.

"They built the Great Wall of China, didn't they?" Crocker responded. "If they can do that, they can build this railroad."

So the plan was put into effect. Hired at $26.00 a month, fifty Chinese workers rode flat cars from Sacramento to the railhead and went to work. Arriving in the evening, they set up camp, cooked a supper of cuttlefish and rice, and then went to sleep. At dawn the next morning, they were up and at work with picks and shovels, and they were still working when the sun went down that evening. Stockbridge was amazed, but Crocker had a knowing smile on his face.

The experiment was successful, and soon over six thousand Chinese laborers were on the job. They did work no Caucasian man would do. Known as "Crocker's Pets," they picked, they chipped, and they blasted, and they did it for twelve hours a day. They would make their way up the mountain side with seventy pounds of black powder balanced at either end of a bamboo pole, and they would manually drill holes in the granite, fill them with black powder, and blast the rock away. Not infrequently, they blasted themselves away also. In places where there wasn't enough room to stand and work, they got into baskets and allowed themselves to be lowered down steep granite walls so they could do more picking, chipping, and blasting.

In the wake of Crocker's Pets, who created the roadbed with their cutting and blasting, the specialists came and laid the crossties and track and erected the telegraph lines. Construction got back on schedule. Having conquered the Sierra Nevada, the Central Pacific raced eastward across Nevada while the Union Pacific raced westward across Wyoming. "Raced" may be the wrong word, for it took four years for the two railroads to meet at Promontory Point, Utah in 1869. But they did meet, and the rest is history.

Fifteen thousand Chinese coolies had been used in the endeavor, and theirs is one of the great success stories in America's expansion into the great southwest.

Reference:

Irving Stone, *Men to Match My Mountains* (Garden City, New York: Doubleday & Company, Inc., 1956).

OTHER BOOKS BY GEORGE U.
HUBBARD

Marauders, Misfits, and Mormons: True Stories of Early Utah

Fight On! World War II and Cold War Experiences of Lt. Commander. John R. "Jack" Hubbard, USNR

When the Saints Came Marching In

Images of America Krum

The Last Man to Die by Creek Law

Which End of A Buffalo Gets Up First?

The Humor and Drama of Early Texas

www.ingramcontent.com/pod-product-compliance
Lightning Source LLC
Chambersburg PA
CBHW072140100526
44589CB00015B/2014